THE LAST IRJ

THE LAST IRISH PLAGUE

The Great Flu Epidemic in Ireland 1918–19

Caitriona Foley
University College Dublin

IRISH ACADEMIC PRESS
DUBLIN • PORTLAND, OR

First published in 2011 by Irish Academic Press

2 Brookside,
Dundrum Road,
Dublin 14, Ireland

920 NE 58th Avenue, Suite 300
Portland, Oregon,
97213-3786, USA

www.iap.ie

British Library Cataloguing in Publication Data

Foley, Caitriona.
The last Irish plague : the Great 'Flu Epidemic in Ireland.
1. Influenza Epidemic, 1918-1919—Ireland. 2. Influenza
Epidemic, 1918-1919—Personal narratives.
I. Title
614.5'18'09415'09041-dc22

ISBN 978 0 7165 3115 9 (cloth)
ISBN 978 0 7165 3116 6 (paper)

Library of Congress Cataloging-in-Publication Data
An entry can be found on request

Printed by Good News Digital Books, Ongar, Essex

Contents

Foreword

The Great Flu pandemic 1918–19 that swept the world in the dying days of the Great War further devastated a beleaguered Europe and in mortality terms massively eclipsed the international conflict. In a matter of months, the pandemic claimed five times more victims than the First World War. Ireland did not escape the suffering. Yet, internationally, historians were slow to afford the pandemic the depth of analysis such a catastrophic event demanded. In the Irish case the dearth of scholarship was compounded by the predominant focus of Irish scholars on political history, which resulted in an almost total exclusion of this significant event from the Irish historical record, thereby distorting and diminishing that record. The pandemic hit Ireland during a particularly turbulent period in the country's political history and it is these events that have attracted the attention of scholars. However, the Great Flu permeated all aspects of Irish life between 1918 and 1919, paralysing political groups, schools, and communities alike. The Sinn Féin 1918 election campaign was seriously hampered by the flu, the German Plot internees were finally released as a result of the death of two prisoners from flu, and those destined for a political future were taken in a matter of hours by flu.

This book is the first in-depth analysis of the Irish experience of the pandemic. Caitriona Foley's study not only accords the 'Spanish flu' its place in the Irish story, it also reveals how problematic the traditional historical boundaries of political, social, and cultural history are. Foley clearly reveals in her comprehensive study how the history of the flu pandemic in Ireland had consequences for the political, social, and cultural landscape, and in doing so she documents the history of lived experiences. The children orphaned, the Sinn Féin volunteers incapacitated, the doctors exhausted, the government caught off-guard, and the mental asylums ground to a halt are all intertwined and interconnected in this subtle and complex telling of the history of the Great Flu in Ireland.

While Ireland may have been excluded from international scholarship on the flu, Foley has left no stone unturned in her research of international studies. While she has drawn on these studies, she has clearly mapped the ways in which Ireland both fitted into the European experience and the ways it differed and why. Foley's study draws on many disciplines beyond history and the result is an imaginative, thought-provoking and riveting study of illness, death, fear, and survival. In Ireland 20,000 people were killed by the flu of 1918–19, and four times that amount were laid low by the disease, many suffering lasting health effects and probably premature death. This book, based on extensive primary research of Irish and English language sources, captures the pace of the disease, the feel of it, even the smell of it, offering the reader insights into how society grappled with the challenges it presented. Foley handles with ease the local and the global impact and meaning of the disease. She skilfully interweaves her extensive primary and secondary research with poignant personal narratives.

The Great Flu confounded many comfortable expectations as the benign flu became a killing stalker, its chief victims the young and resilient of society. The various names ascribed to it ('plague', 'black flu', 'Khaki Flu', 'mysterious malady', 'an tinneas nua') hinted at the confusion and the difficulty in ascribing meaning to it, the inability to contain it and disarm it. Apart from political connotations ('Khaki Flu' pointed the finger at the British war) the flu also had moral significance for contemporaries, many believing it to be punishment for the war; this sense was heightened as it appeared to target young men, who had also been the chief fodder of that conflict.

Irish society responded in many ways: schools, businesses, and theatres were closed. Dances and Gaelic matches were cancelled. Sufferers sought relief in scientific medicine but some also resorted to alcohol, others to garlic, to ward off the threat of contagion. People drew on science and/or faith to understand and console. Communities searched their collective conscience when families were discovered dead, alone, and unaided, as a result of the flu. Contributing to the growing field of the history of emotions, Foley's study looks at the role of fear, and the fear of fear itself, in the Irish flu experience. In the communal and medical response to the disease Foley examines how society understood and perceived the body, contagion, and illness. While providing the reader with the important statistics, maps, and graphs of the disease and its impact on Ireland, she places the patient narrative at the heart of this telling. She explores how people recorded the trauma around them, how they conceptualised what was happening, and how they dealt with its aftermath. In this final aspect Foley addresses the issue of 'remembering the past' and concludes that the flu was not forgotten, but rather it was remembered in silence by the generation that survived it. It was historians that failed to pick up the trail and carry the thread through the historical narrative. That is until this book.

This study is in places beautiful and throughout meticulous. The great power of this book lies in its author's ability to draw the reader in to the complex and multifaceted impact of the Spanish Flu epidemic in Ireland, without ever reducing the past to clinical snapshots or distant happenings. This book brings the past to life with scholarly precision and poetic grace.

Lindsey Earner-Byrne, Lecturer in Modern Irish History, Centre for the History of Medicine in Ireland, UCD

Catherine Cox, Director, Centre for the History of Medicine in Ireland and Lecturer in Modern Irish and Medical History, UCD

List of Illustrations, Graphs and Maps

Acknowledgements

Thanks are first due to my supervisors at University College Dublin who guided me as I wrote the thesis on which this book is based. Lindsey Earner-Byrne and Catherine Cox went above and beyond throughout, and were always so giving of their time, help and encouragement; I can't thank them enough for their generosity. Lindsey was kind enough to read a draft of the book, and her help has made all the difference (needless to say, any remaining errors are entirely my responsibility). I am also extremely grateful to Lisa Hyde at Irish Academic Press for taking a chance on publishing the following pages.

I owe a debt of gratitude to the archivists in Wicklow County Archives, Galway County Council Archives, Donegal County Archives, and Cork City and County Archives who sought out countless dust-laden books and obscure documents for a Dublin blow-in. The collected staffs of the National Library of Ireland, the Royal College of Physicians, University College Dublin, Trinity College Early Printed Books, and the National Archives of Ireland were also immensely helpful and accommodating. I am especially thankful to Brian Donnelly at the National Archives who answered my many tedious queries on medical sources, and provided much-needed and much- appreciated assistance in navigating source material.

My sincerest thanks go to William Murphy and to Eve Morrison who were good enough to share some of their own research findings with me, and to point me in the direction of incredibly useful sources. I would also like to thank Conor Mulhern for lending his whiz-kid abilities to create the maps which are reproduced in Chapter one.

I owe huge thanks to Irene Whelan for invaluable encouragement and counsel along the way, and to John Scally who brought history to life for a bunch of unruly 15-year-olds. As a postgraduate student, I was fortunate to receive funding from the Irish Research Council for the Humanities and Social Sciences, for which I am very grateful.

The last debts outweigh all others. My dad and sister have been wonderful throughout and did so much to enable the pages that follow. And finally, I owe an inexpressible amount to my mum. We miss her every day, and it is to her memory that the book is dedicated.

Glossary

Board of Guardians: elected by the rate-payers, these boards managed each Poor Law Union and under the Medical Charities Act of 1851, were also responsible for operation of the union's dispensary

Chief Secretary: usually a member of the British Cabinet, the Chief Secretary was the political head of the Irish administration and also President of the Local Government Board

Cumann na mBan: translates as 'women's league'; Irish republican women's paramilitary organisation established in April 1914, functioning as an auxiliary to the Irish Volunteers

Defence of the Realm Act (DORA): passed in August 1914, this legislation gave emergency powers to prescribed authorities while the war was on, including the rights to imprison without trial and to impose censorship measures

Dispensary System: a medical system based on the Poor Law and established under the Medical Charities (Ireland) Act, 1851 which permitted Boards of Guardians to divide Unions into dispensary districts which would each maintain a dispensary to provide free medical treatment to the poor

Epidemic: occurs when the number of people in a city, region or country who become infected by a disease greatly exceeds the numbers expected. When the infection spreads across international borders or takes place in several countries at the same time, it becomes a pandemic

Gaelic League: founded in 1893 by Douglas Hyde, this organisation was part of the cultural revival in Ireland, focussing on promotion of the Irish language. Clubs were formed around the country and by the turn of the century, the Gaelic League had a wide network of branches, although its popularity was greater in urban areas

Gaelic Athletic Association: founded in 1884 to promote Irish games, including hurling, camogie and Gaelic football, with clubs set up in parishes around the country

'German Plot': used as a short-hand for the arrest of separatist activists, including a substantial number of the Sinn Féin leadership, by British authorities in May 1918 on suspicion of conspiring with Germany to overthrow British government in Ireland

Guardians: elected officials who administered the workhouse of each union

Internment: the act of confining people in prison without trial, often for political reasons; can be distinguished from imprisonment, which signifies close confinement usually as punishment for a crime

Irish Parliamentary Party: dominant political party in Ireland in the late nineteenth and early twentieth centuries pursuing Home Rule for Ireland (self-government within the British Empire)

Jubilee Nurses: in celebration of Queen Victoria's Jubilee, money raised in Ireland was used to set up an institute of nursing with the purpose of training women to nurse the sick poor at home. Known as 'Jubilee Nurses', these women were employed in communities who raised money locally to supply their salaries

Local Government Board: the central authority responsible for all forms of local government in Ireland, presiding over the poor law and dispensary systems; it was the central body to whom the boards of guardians were responsible. Although the Chief Secretary was its President, routine administration was left in the hands of the Vice President. From 1898 to 1920, Sir Henry Robinson held the office of VP of the Board

Medical Officer (MO): each dispensary and workhouse employed a doctor or medical officer to treat patients; responsible to the Guardians of the Union, the same doctor often fulfilled both roles

Miasma: a noxious vapour, believed to emanate from decomposing organic matter or swamp areas, and thought capable of causing sickness. Based on the idea that certain diseases were due to impure or poisonous air, the miasmatic theory of diseases was still current in the nineteenth and early twentieth centuries

Pandemic: an outbreak of disease that has reached international or global proportions, occurring when a new virus emerges among humans and spreads easily from person to person

Petty Sessions: equivalent to the modern District Court, these were the lowest level of courts in Ireland in the nineteenth and early twentieth centuries

Poor Law (System): providing social services in Ireland, this was a system of relief for the poor, established in Ireland under the Poor Law Act of 1838. The Poor Law system was abolished in the Irish Free State in 1925, with boards of guardians replaced by county boards of health. In Northern Ireland, the Poor Law was replaced by the National Health Service in 1946

Poor Rate (often abbreviated to 'rates'): this was a system of local taxation introduced by the 1838 Act, which levied taxes on the owners and occupiers of holdings in the union

Relieving Officer (RO): one of the officials of the Poor Law Union; among his duties were the tasks of assessing the eligibility of candidates for admission to the workhouse or for outside relief and arranging for this relief

Rural (and Urban) District Councils (RDCs/UDCs): rural and urban district councils were created in Ireland under the Local Government (Ireland) Act, 1898 for administration purposes; the councils had authority over matters such as local planning and sanitation. Under the Local Government Act, membership of the councils often overlapped with that of the area's boards of guardians. A 'rural district' corresponded to a Poor Law Union with its urban districts subtracted

Sinn Féin (SF): political organisation founded in 1905 by journalist Arthur Griffith. The name is taken from the Irish 'we ourselves', reflecting the party's promotion of the idea of Irish self-sufficiency. By 1918, Sinn Féin was the leading political party in Ireland, and had come to encompass a spectrum of nationalism, from moderate nationalists to advanced republicans. At the SF Ard-Fheis (conference) of 1917, the party committed itself to establishing an Irish Republic

(Poor Law) Union: under the Irish Poor Law Act of 1838, Ireland was divided into 130 administrative units known as 'unions'. Each union was made up of a group of electoral divisions which in turn were constituted by a number of townlands; each union had its own workhouse

(Irish) Volunteers: set up in response to the establishment of the Ulster Volunteer Force in 1913; disagreement over whether to enter the First World War split the organisation into the National Volunteers, under the Irish Parliamentary Party's John Redmond, and the Irish Volunteers, under Eoin MacNeill. By 1918, militarised nationalists were being referred to as 'Volunteers', and over the course of 1919 the organisation began to be known as the Irish Republican Army (IRA)

Workhouse: locus in the union from which relief was administered

'The story of a new disease' [1]

For it was truly a plague, a Black Death or what you will, but not influenza as we know it today...only the young and active were destroyed...terrible fear...was everywhere...Those who saw that terrible affliction as I saw it must always feel that nothing in or of this world could have halted it. (Dr D. W. Macnamara, 'Memories of 1918 and "the 'Flu'", *Journal of the Irish Medical Association*, 35, 208 (1954))

This document deals with one of the great historic scourges of our time, a pestilence which affected the well-being of millions of men and women and destroyed more human lives in a few months than did the European war in five years. (Ministry of Health, *Report on the Pandemic of Influenza 1918–19* (London, 1920))

On the last Saturday evening in February 1919, John Maguire, caretaker of the Corporation Buildings in inner city Dublin, grasped a hammer and chisel and broke open the door of the room occupied by the young Phelan family. None of the Phelans had been seen for several days, and the neighbours had grown concerned, eventually prevailing upon Maguire to check on his tenants. Inside the dilapidated room, he found four bodies in a single bed. Twenty-seven-year-old Frances Phelan, a domestic servant, was already dead, the autopsy later revealing that a bout of influenza had been quickly followed by pneumonia, leaving her lungs in an 'advanced stage of congestion'. Lying beside her were her husband Peter and their only child Nicholas, a baby of fourteen months, still with his comforter in his mouth. Draped across the foot of the bed lay Peter's sister. The latter three were unconscious but alive.

Maguire did his best to rouse Peter, and helped him to dress. Peter's sister was partly clothed already, and Maguire wrapped her in a coat and put her sitting on a chair before contacting the police and arranging to have the Phelans transported to the South Dublin Union Infirmary. Hours later, all three died of influenza or pneumonia following influenza. At the inquest, the Coroner 'referred to the case as a tragedy, and said it was a sad thing to think that in a crowded neighbourhood like this a poor family should be lying dying, and the neighbours... unable to render assistance'.[2]

The tragedy of the Phelans is a microcosm of the often brutal reality of the Great Flu pandemic of 1918/19, which claimed an estimated fifty million lives in just under a year, many times the toll taken by the First World War. But while the war has generated scholarship that fills countless libraries and is considered a defining event of the twentieth century, the history of the flu outbreak has been almost overlooked by comparison.

Described as 'the largest outbreak of any infectious disease known to medical science' with a reach that extended worldwide, there is an abundance of dramatic illustrations of the sickness and death that attended the Great Flu. Rivers in India became clogged with bodies, as firewood supplies ran short due to the sheer number of cremations made necessary by the disease. In the Punjab, streets were littered with corpses, and at railway stations, the trains had to be periodically cleared of dead and dying passengers. Steam shovels needed to be used in New York in order to dig trenches large enough to temporarily inter bodies of flu victims. In parts of Africa, flu outbreaks were reputed to have caused people to die from fright, while in Newfoundland, dogs prowled around flu-stricken households, picking over the bodies of the dead.[3]

In Ireland, journalist David Hogan would later recall his impression of how 'there were few who had not lost a relative'. Travelling the country on a publicity tour for Sinn Féin in the run-up to the General Election of 1918, Hogan's view from the train windows was of 'funerals everywhere'. Gravediggers 'could not work hard enough to keep up with the flow of coffins', with bodies left 'to wait on the unopened sward'. A writer in the *Farmer's Gazette* marvelled at the way in which 'a strong healthy man suddenly becomes unwell, goes to bed, gets rapidly worse and is dead in two days', and in places as far apart as Athlone and Philadelphia, coffin supplies were exhausted by this influenza which was 'unlike any known before'.[4]

Summing up the pandemic, historian Alfred Crosby has commented that 'nothing else has ever killed so many in as short a period', while John Barry has described the tale of the Great Flu as one of 'havoc, death and desolation'. The term 'plague' featured repeatedly in contemporary discourse on the outbreak around the world, and was employed both as a literary device – to denote the vast scale of morbidity and mortality – and in a literal sense: many victims of the flu exhibited symptoms which bore a close clinical resemblance to pneumonic plague. D.W. Macnamara, a junior doctor in the Mater when the flu broke out, was firmly convinced that the disease he saw was a form of plague rather than influenza and in Ireland, the epidemic would later be described as the 'last Irish plague', with one folklorist writing that the flu elicited as much panic and fear as any visitation of epidemic disease in ancient times.[5]

Erupting in the closing stages of the First World War, the pandemic is generally portrayed as having struck in three waves. The first of these began in spring 1918 and lasted roughly until July. Though it spread easily, this introduction to the flu brought relatively low mortality. Its successor was characterised by a virulence that shocked and frightened those who saw its worst effects first hand. First emerging in early September 1918, this cycle of infection lasted for about 6–8 weeks with fatality rates shooting up due to the sharp increase in pneumonic complications in flu victims. In the early spring of 1919, a third wave of flu materialised, distinguished by lower mortality rates than the second, but still marked by more widespread sickness and death than the first wave.

Over the course of this year of influenza, the virus seemed to reach 'nearly every quarter of the globe', causing extensive social disruption, and leaving in its wake a bequest of grief, loss, and physical debilitation. The 'source of the epidemic' was initially traced to Spain, leading to the sobriquet 'Spanish influenza', although the British Ministry of Health would later admit that 'it is beyond doubt that at the same time outbreaks were occurring in other European countries, including France and Germany and in Russian war zones'.[6]

Any narrative of the Great Flu is inevitably steeped in irony as the epidemic exposed a troubling incongruity between expectation and reality. Influenza was usually seen as a 'homey, familiar kind of illness' but was suddenly inflicting damage on an almost unprecedented scale, causing 'a havoc to which the Black Death of 1348–49 alone affords a parallel'. In comparison to outbreaks of influenza in the past, the Great Flu of 1918/19 was deemed by officials to have 'far surpassed anything previously experienced'.[7]

Doctors at the time considered that the virus responsible for the pandemic demonstrated a remarkable degree of clinical uniformity, and the 'Irish influenza' did not present 'any uniform variation' from the type which circulated in England and Wales, where it took over 200,000 lives. In the majority of cases, those who fell ill from this new strain of influenza were ill for a few days or weeks, but eventually recovered, although many faced a lengthy recuperation period. However, in the most serious cases, 'homey, familiar' flu became a disease with a violent and unsettling symptomology.[8]

The conspicuousness of blood was striking; doctors recorded the occurrence of projectile nosebleeds and cases where patients lost over twelve ounces of blood 'at one bleeding', or coughed up 'almost pure blood'. Some patients bled from their ears, and autopsies revealed blood-sodden lungs, sometimes laden with pus, which reminded physicians of the effects of exposure to poison gas. The most ominous sign though was when the patients' skin began to turn 'a dusky blue', as their blood stopped circulating sufficient oxygen. This symptom led to one of the disease's many nicknames – the 'Black Flu'.[9]

Autopsies showed the startling degree of internal damage that the disease could wreak: kidneys that oozed blood, livers that were swollen and enlarged. In one group of cases observed by an English medic, the disease had left the colon 'in a state of extensive and acute ulcerative colitis', destroying the mucosa – the innermost layer of the colon – in a similar way to dysentery. In others, the disease had caused their thyroid gland to swell, sometimes to 'three times the average size'. S. W. Patterson, an Australian doctor who had served in France during the pandemic, saw cases in which damage to the respiratory tract extended all the way up to the vocal chords, where 'standing erosion and ulceration had occurred'. Among Patterson's concluding observations was that 'the whole picture was...thought to resemble pneumonic plague anatomically'.[10]

It was not uncommon for patients to exhibit signs of insanity; in Ireland and abroad, there were accounts of flu victims killing themselves and others. Doctors also noted the peculiar smells emitted by the bodies of flu sufferers, which they found difficult to describe and to trace. The 'dramatic suddenness' with which death could come was yet another cause for concern, and in the pages of the medical journal *The Lancet,* doctors wondered if the epidemic was 'one of influenza' or 'something new?'[11]

The strain of influenza which caused the pandemic of 1918/19 was distinguished by an 'unprecedented lethality', and comparisons of the 1918 flu with modern strains have provided arresting illustrations of its potency. A day after infection with the 1918 virus, human lung cells released fifty times as many virus particles as they did after exposure to a contemporary strain. Scientific research now suggests that the virus responsible for the pandemic may have been composed of a unique combination of genes, the effect of which was an extraordinary virulence. US virologist Jeffery Taubenberger has stressed that 'no single change or gene is the answer. It's a combination effect.'[12]

The infection responsible for the Great Flu was unusual not only in terms of its virulence, but also with regard to the age profile of its victims. Usually it is the youngest and oldest in society who are the most vulnerable to the flu virus. In 1918/19, however, 'the toll taken at the young adult ages of life' was one of the most extraordinary aspects of the outbreak. The report issued by the British Ministry of Health commented explicitly on this sudden change in age incidence, noting that 'it was a striking feature of the epidemic that strong, healthy adults, especially those between 20 and 40, and more particularly between 25 and 35 years of age, were those most likely to succumb'. This meant that the flu of 1918/19 'appeared to be entirely different to epidemics of the past in which, as a rule, the deaths have been largely among the elderly or the very young'.[13]

This aspect of the Great Flu elicited many melancholy remarks, both at the time and subsequently. A local politician in Cork was struck by how 'it seemed to claim for its victims the young, the beautiful and the strong'. A Meath Volunteer would later recall that 'a great many young people' died during the epidemic, and doctors too were conscious of the flu's preference for the 'very strongest' adults. This was one of the 'peculiar' features of the epidemic – its ability to destroy youth 'in its full bloom'.[14]

Scientists now attribute this ability of the virus to strike hardest at young adults to the 'dysregulation' effect it had on the body's immune system. Infections of all kinds typically stimulate the host's immune system to resist the pathogens. However, excessive or unchecked stimulation of the body's immune response can be harmful, working to intensify the virulence of the infection. Breakthroughs in influenza research now indicate that this is what may have led to the high levels of young adult fatalities in 1918/19, as the virus was characterised by 'a genetic composition and rapid replication kinetics' which prompted an 'excessively vigorous innate immune and inflammatory response'. The 1918 virus was able to turn the defence mechanism of the body on itself, with the irony that those with the strongest immune systems – the young adult population – witnessed the highest mortality rates.[15]

The pandemic is also marked by the irony that despite the magnitude of sickness and death it wreaked, the history of the Great Flu is not widely known, and until recently, rarely featured in narratives of the twentieth century. Scholar Robert Brown, whose research has focussed on the effects of the flu on the Great War, describes it as the 'forgotten

pandemic', and *New York Times* journalist Gina Kolata has written that
the Great Flu is a 'story that no one knows and few remember'.
Historians Howard Phillips and David Killingray similarly comment
that 'given the extent of the death rate from influenza in 1918–19, it is
surprising that the history of the outbreak is not better known'.[16]

Although it was 'the greatest pandemic in the world's history – at
least in regard to its toll, speed and extent', and though it caused many
more deaths than the First World War, the flu pandemic of 1918/19
has failed to inspire the same levels of historical interest as those generated by the war. It was only in the mid-1970s that historical study of
the topic 'effectively took off', with Alfred Crosby's 1976 examination
of the outbreak in the US constituting one of the first major works on
the pandemic. Academic interest in the subject gained momentum in
the decades that followed Crosby's work, but in-depth analyses of the
effects of the pandemic on individual countries are still relatively scarce,
with those completed by Crosby and John Barry (America), Howard
Phillips (South Africa), Geoffrey Rice (New Zealand), and Niall Johnson (Britain) among the exceptions.[17]

This irony of neglect is magnified by the fact that the pandemic is inextricable from the First World War, as the two formed a 'symbiotic and
destructive partnership'. The origins of the Great Flu, for instance, have
been traced to French and British army camps in 1916 and 1917, with
Professor John Oxford positing that the disease may have been seeded
several years before the 1918 outbreak, transforming the 'Spanish Lady'
of 1918 into the 'French Lady' or 'English Lady' of 1916 or 1917. This
theory corresponds with genetic analyses of the virus, which place its
emergence around 1915.[18]

A study of mortality patterns for New York City also suggests that
seeding of the disease took place prior to 1918, as the age distribution
of flu deaths in New York in the 1917/18 season shifted, skewing
towards the younger demographic of the Great Flu. Here, a distinct
increase in young adult deaths was accompanied by a 'lack of impact
among older age groups', providing persuasive evidence of an early
phase or herald wave of the 1918 pandemic, and further indicating that
the disease may have originated in Europe before 1918, arriving
subsequently in the city on ships during the First World War – New
York was the chief embarkation port for American troops sailing to the
European battlefields.[19]

Also showing the close links between the war and the flu, the movements of troops accelerated the spread and facilitated the pervasiveness
of the disease. American historian Harry Rudin has noted how the flu

compounded the trials of war for the various sides involved. Erich Ludendorff, one of Germany's leading generals, grew tired of hearing daily reports from his Chiefs of Staff detailing the number of men incapacitated or weakened by the infection, while the spread of flu on the German domestic front was one of the factors contributing to low morale at home. At the end of October 1918, Prince Max of Germany contracted this new influenza, his illness coming at a critical time for the head of Government to be out of direct touch with developments that seemed like 'the prelude to "Finis Germaniae"'.

In England, the flu epidemic, along with lack of replacements for the army, the increasing coal shortage, and 'the perennial Irish question', were among the factors which prompted Lloyd George's desire to bring the war to an end. It has also been suggested that during the Paris Peace Conference, President Woodrow Wilson was severely weakened by a bout of flu, compromising his performance at a crucial point in the peace negotiations. The Great Flu was intricately linked with the First World War, impacting on a key moment in political history.[20]

The unfolding of the Great Flu in Ireland also reveals the influence of social history on the political narrative, demonstrating that these are overlapping stories rather than divided aspects of existence. The epidemic arrived in Ireland just after the 'German Plot' arrests were being carried out, the first and second waves coinciding with the months leading up to the general election of 1918. Unrest simmered in the country as illegal drillings and arms raids took place. On 21 January 1919, Dáil Éireann held its inaugural session, the same day on which the Soloheadbeg ambush in Tipperary took place – these incidents have been described as marking the beginning of the War of Independence.[21]

In the same period as these momentous events of the Irish 'revolution' were unfolding, the Great Flu raged around the country. 'Wanted men' were laid up with the flu, with papers such as the *Roscommon Herald* criticising the RIC for pulling them from their sickbeds. Members of the Irish Volunteers remembered carrying their sick comrades from safe house to safe house in their attempts to evade police capture. In October 1918, Joseph Devlin, leader of the Irish Parliamentary Party, was prevented from attending Nationalist demonstrations as he himself had fallen ill with flu. When finally released from his period of internment in Belfast Prison, Michael Brennan, one of the leaders of the Volunteers in east Clare, was unable to go home straight away, still too weak after his bout of the new influenza. A fall from his bike a few weeks later due to 'some sort of weak fit' was a sharp reminder that his body was not yet over the disease, and though the tumble put him 'out of action for a while', he admitted that 'it also probably gave me a much needed chance to pull up after the 'flu'.[22]

The virus struck down many of those who had been interned on the pretext of the 'German Plot' and political activism, scuppering jail-breaks and transforming prison cells into hospital rooms as inmates did their best to nurse each other. It was ultimately the death of two of these men from the disease which prompted the British authorities to release the remaining internees. Ruth Barrington has noted the promi-nence usually given to political and military events in histories of this period; by its investigation of the effects and ramifications of the Great Flu in Ireland, this book addresses an event which affected not only the social but also the political history of the years 1918/19.[23]

In Ireland, the Great Flu claimed more than 20,000 lives in a few months, infecting as many as 600–800,000 people, yet the full extent of its effects has never been explored. A report compiled by the British Ministry of Health in 1920 announced that it would deal 'with influenza in Great Britain and Ireland', but devoted fewer than three pages of the 500-plus page tome to the Irish experience. In analyses covering the years 1918/19, Irish historiography has maintained a largely political focus, and although the epidemic coincided with the revolutionary period, nar-ratives covering this era rarely mention the Great Flu. Referring to this neglect, Diarmaid Ferriter observes: 'Distracted by the enormity of the political change, and the impending intensification of revolution, Irish historians have done little to assess its impact, and an analysis of it is long overdue.' The purpose of the following chapters is to explore the Irish experience of this outbreak of influenza which wreaked a degree of havoc in the country not witnessed since the Great Famine.[24]

As the Great Flu unfolded within a relatively short space of time – less than twelve months – chapters focus on themes rather than chronology in order to illustrate the full extent of its impact. A central aim is to tell the story of the Great Flu 'from below', from the per-spective of 'ordinary people', in order to portray what it felt like to live through this devastating outbreak of infectious disease. In this way, the book engages with Roy Porter's call to 'restore to the history of medi-cine its human face'. A comparative perspective is incorporated in order to place the Irish experience of flu in context, illuminating the high degree of universality which characterised the pandemic, but also demonstrating how each country, if not each city, community, and village, had their own distinctive epidemic experience.[25]

The first three chapters focus principally on the impact of the epidemic: its geographic spread and dimensions, the profile of flu sufferers, and its social effects. Dealing with the movement of the disease, the first chapter examines the patterns and mechanisms of spread of this new strain of flu. As was the case in places such as Canada, Britain, Spain, and New Zealand, troop movements and the railway system proved crucial in allowing the disease to advance around the country. However, the Irish experience of the epidemic deviates somewhat from international trends when it comes to the timing of the second and third waves. Although historians of the pandemic generally describe these later waves as temporally distinct (placing them in October–November 1918 and February–March 1919 respectively), in Ireland the two waves were more difficult to separate, with a gradual transition period from the second to the third wave taking place between December 1918 and January 1919.

A major trend in the historiography of the Great Flu has been the demography of its victims, with academics detecting patterns in age, gender, and class. Age incidence was uniform worldwide: among the billion people who fell ill, it was young adults who proved to be the most susceptible to the disease. Countries involved in the war saw higher female than male mortality rates from the flu, whereas in neutral countries, young men typically outnumbered female flu casualties.

When it comes to the role of class, there is much less agreement, with some scholars dismissing the Great Flu as an 'ecumenical disaster' that was 'egalitarian' when it came to its victims, while others have argued that social differences played an important role, especially when it came to a person's chances of surviving the disease. The second chapter of this book teases out these issues in the context of Ireland's experience of the flu, exploring which sectors of Irish society were worst hit by the disease.[26]

Despite the significant upheaval to society caused by the Great Flu, its social history has failed to arouse commensurate levels of interest among historians of the pandemic, leading some to observe that in comparison with other aspects of the Great Flu, 'less attention has been paid to the ways that families, households, and towns were disrupted and even destroyed by the epidemic'. This is particularly ironic in view of the fact that it was on countless families that the pandemic left its deepest, most grating marks, altering millions of lives through the deaths of loved ones and leaving many invalided for lengthy periods of time. The third chapter addresses the effect of the outbreak on community and family life, detailing some of the myriad ways in which the flu disrupted, unsettled, and irrevocably changed life for thousands of families around Ireland.[27]

The next three chapters look at how different sectors of society responded to the outbreak. Looking at popular, medical, and official reactions, they illustrate variously the fears elicited by the infection, the way in which doctors and nurses attempted to cope with the overwhelming numbers of patients, and how central and local government officials struggled to assuage the suffering.

Fear of this new form of flu runs through many accounts of the epidemic as uncertainty over the nature of the disease, and awareness of medicine's inability to stem its effects, fed anxieties. Over the past two decades, history has increasingly recognised the relevance of emotions in the study of the past, and this chapter uncovers how people felt about the Great Flu, exploring the manifestations of fear over the course of the epidemic. In the nineteenth century, outbreaks of infectious disease, and sometimes simply the threat of an outbreak, had the ability to cause widespread waves of fear and to prompt violence and panic. Did the 1918 flu have effects of the same intensity and magnitude? Did it really inspire a level of fear comparable to that brought forth by the 'ancient pestilences', as folklorist Kevin Danaher would later claim?[28]

It was perhaps one of the most profound ironies of the Great Flu that it came at a time when the medical profession was growing in confidence following recent successes in the fight against epidemic disease. The medical aspect of the outbreak has been a prominent theme in historical writing on the pandemic, with academics enquiring into what the Great Flu reveals about the health professions and medical thought at this time. Chapter five evaluates how Irish doctors and nurses fared in the Great Flu, describing the nature of the epidemic experience for them, revealing that for the vast majority of medical practitioners, the epidemic was a deeply trying period, which left them not only physically exhausted but also emotionally drained.

Few governments were able to offer a coherent, effective response to a pandemic that frustrated virtually all attempts to control it or to mitigate its effects. Official responses all around the world were routinely hampered by lack of preparation and thinly stretched resources, with the result that grassroots activism often played a crucial role when it came to relief work. In Ireland, the epidemic provided insight into how Irish men and women felt about the role of government in community life and their expectations about who should and who would provide support in times of difficulty. Some local authorities bypassed the Local Government Board completely, deciding to enlist local voluntary organisations to help flu sufferers. Although local government proved more responsive than central powers like the Local Government Board, in the main, it was civil society and the medical community which provided the fundamentals of aid during the flu visitation.[29]

Chapters seven and eight turn to the cultural history of the epidemic, exploring how it was understood and remembered. The various ways in which the Great Flu was interpreted and explained are among the 'novel angles' in its historiography, and it has been pointed out that 'no cultural history of the pandemic has been written to date'. Observing the critical need to engage with how the flu was remembered, Guy Beiner emphasises that 'the fundamental question of memory and forgetting discloses the cardinal lacuna in the historical study of the Great Flu'.[30]

Chapter seven portrays the ways in which people sought to clarify and understand this sudden and widespread appearance of sickness. The languages of science and faith featured frequently in popular attempts to locate the origins of the disease and in efforts to find a meaning for the losses sustained. Another impulse was to search the recent past for any comparable events in order to try to give the epidemic some kind of context and to diminish its unsettling character – the unprecedented nature of the experience enhanced its power to generate uncertainty and fear.

The pandemic was also commonly interpreted as an inevitable consequence of the First World War, its damages seen as a necessary atonement for the unparalleled numbers of casualties churned out by what was at the time 'the greatest of all human contentions'. In this way, the Great Flu provides insight not just into how sickness and the body were understood at this time, but also into how people felt about the war itself, especially its moral meanings. Tracing the flu to the war transformed the outbreak into a catastrophe that could have been avoided, framing it as a product of human agency rather than nature. Many saw the flu of 1918/19 as a reminder that the levels of killing perpetrated in the course of the conflict had disrupted the balance with the natural world: the Great Flu was the price of war.[31]

Memory of the pandemic is one of the most thought-provoking issues in any study of the flu. In contrast to the 'forgetting' that many historians see as having taken place abroad, for many of the generation that witnessed it first-hand in Ireland, the flu was remembered with a remarkable degree of vividness. Memories of the epidemic were overwhelmingly negative, with images of sickness and death arising frequently in people's recollections. The result was a lack of will to speak about or receded. Rather than forgetting the epidemic though, survivors put their memories away, keeping them to themselves, or within their family or locality. In the aftermath of the epidemic, it was more like a silence fell among survivors, rather than they had forgotten what took place.

The absence of the Great Flu from historical narratives for much of the twentieth century was another important factor, as this further shortened the shelf-life of the event in popular memory. The upshot was that any awareness of the epidemic which stretched beyond those directly affected by the outbreak faded more easily as its generation of witnesses aged and passed away. For many decades, the flu lacked 'remembrancers', which further diminished the chances that it would achieve a place in collective or popular memory. Looking at how an event such as the Great Flu was remembered contrasts with previous studies of memory in twentieth-century Ireland, which have focussed primarily on commemoration and memory in political rather than social contexts.[32]

The aim of chapter nine is to assess the consequences of the Great Flu in Ireland, inquiring into its aftermath and its long- and short-term ramifications. Was it a turning point, or perhaps a 'significant, symbolic moment', as other outbreaks of epidemic disease had been in the past? And on what aspects of social life did the Great Flu leave its deepest marks?[33]

Much of the research done on the pandemic reduces the Great Flu to a series of figures and maps, quantifying the damage caused in terms of lives lost, and defining the outbreak by its physical contours and travel routes. An abundance of graphs, charts and statistics document what was one of the most violent outbreaks of disease witnessed in modern history. Researchers have sketched 'city-specific per-capita excess mortality', and used devices like 'least squares regression models' and 'seasonal regression' approaches to 'extrapolate baseline mortality'. In Ireland, the report of the Registrar-General measures the effects of the epidemic in terms of the thousands of deaths, the damage caused by the epidemic compressed into neatly ordered columns and tables. However, these are unable to show the ways in which families were united in grief, how shutters went down and walls went up as anxiety spread, how blame was assigned and social space was temporarily redrawn, and how lives were changed by the outbreak. They do not show the fear caused by the rapid accumulation of bodies or the disorientation and anger brought to families suffering sudden loss.[34]

This book is not just about attempting to measure the epidemic and analysing its effects. It explores the lived experience of epidemic disease, the material reality of a fearsome virus that was vastly different from the influenzas of the past. As readers of the *Farmer's Gazette* were warned, 'the present outbreak cannot, by any stretch of the imagination, be looked upon as simple or ordinary influenza'. The remaining pages are about the impact this outbreak had on people's lives, and how 'one of the worst plagues of human history' was felt, feared, explained, understood, and remembered.[35]

CHAPTER ONE

'The country is thoroughly infected': The Geography of the New Influenza [1]

In the decades preceding the Great Flu, technology had transformed the ways in which people experienced space and time. By the beginning of the twentieth century, there was a 'new sense of world unity' as railroad networks advanced and the spread of the telephone brought people into closer proximity than ever before. In 1901, these changes allowed H.G. Wells to observe that 'the world grows smaller and smaller'. The spread of the Great Flu was aided by this greatly increased pace of human movement and annihilation of distance, as the virus moved with speed and thoroughness to affect virtually every inhabited corner of the planet.[2]

Almost a century on, the precise geographic origins of the 1918 flu continue to provoke debate. Some historians trace it to American military camps in the mid-west, where outbreaks were evident from spring 1918, but it seems increasingly likely that the disease was simmering even two years before that. Eruptions of an infection which doctors described as 'purulent bronchitis' took place in French and British military camps at Brest and Aldershot in 1916 and 1917 respectively, and may have been earlier strains of the 1918 virus.

Historian Stephen Kern has noted that the late nineteenth and early twentieth century were characterised by an increasing simultaneity in how people experienced daily life. The '"homeless" technologies' – railroads, steamships, and telephones – stretched everyone's horizons and made it possible to 'be everywhere at once'. The Great Flu was similarly distinguished by synchronicity, as far flung places experienced their first incursions of flu in June 1918 – including Ireland, Germany, Scandinavia, Australia, and New Zealand – and the majority of countries reached mortality peaks in October and November 1918.[3]

The pandemic is generally depicted as unfolding in a three-wave structure, with some of the highest death rates endured in parts of Asia and on the islands of the South Pacific. By early summer 1918, the first wave of the disease had become widespread over Europe, with civilian populations as well as soldiers at the front suffering its effects. Within a few weeks though, the disease appeared to have subsided, only to be followed in late August by the spread of a far more potent and aggressive second wave of infection. Now flu began to appear in distant parts of the world – Brest, France, the landing port for American troops; the harbour of Freetown, Sierra Leone, in west Africa; and the city of Boston, Massachusetts. By the time people gathered to celebrate the ending of the Great War, it seemed that sickness was everywhere. In December 1918, however, the flu appeared to have ebbed away, only to resurface once more in early spring 1919, flaring for several weeks before respite was finally felt by early summer. Some places, such as Scandinavia, endured a fourth wave in 1920, but in most countries, the third wave was the last appearance of the Great Flu.[4]

Influenza was an almost constant presence in Ireland from June 1918 to May 1919. The first wave hit in the early weeks of summer in 1918, abating from most towns and villages by early August. As well as being much more virulent, the second wave was much more pervasive in its spread and gruelling in its length. Its emergence was apparent from late September, but this visitation ground on until the final weeks of 1918 in parts of the west and north, leaving unfortunate families in such places with the tragic task of having to bury loved ones at Christmas time. As Beatriz Echeverri has signalled in the case of Spain, the temporal boundaries of the third influenza invasion are difficult to pinpoint, with the second wave seeping into this final visitation in spring 1919, as pockets of epidemic influenza began to spring up as January came to an end. This feature distinguishes the Great Flu in Ireland from the temporal pattern usually associated with the pandemic. In less than twelve months, influenza had coursed through almost the entire country, travelling hundreds of miles from its points of introduction in the east and north, and insinuating itself into some of the most remote corners of the island, until it finally faded away in late spring of 1919, leaving a burden of grief and disorder in its wake.[5]

THE FIRST WAVE

The least virulent, shortest and most geographically confined of the three waves of the Great Flu, the first wave, would seem to have originated in

Belfast in early June 1918. The 'extremely widespread epidemic of what is called "influenza"' was traced to the military barracks in the city, with the disease diffusing quickly, spreading to 'munition works, mills, &c., and thence all over the city and surrounding areas'. The virus was most likely introduced to Ireland by military personnel home on leave from the Western Front, echoing the experience of countries as far apart as Britain, Canada, and Iran, where troops also served as the primary vectors of disease in the early stages of the pandemic. The next reports of the flu came from Ballinasloe in Galway, where people were reportedly thrown into a panic by this illness which struck its victims initially with 'complete collapse and swooning'. Again, the role of the military was important, with reports of a minor outbreak among soldiers stationed at Garbally taking place virtually at the same time as the Ballinasloe visitation. Flare-ups of the disease in Dublin and Cork followed within days, allowing the flu to subsequently spread from several independent centres of infection.[6]

In terms of its pattern of spread, this first wave was marked by a dominant hierarchical component: urban centres were the first to show signs of epidemic. The disease seemed to jump from town to town, cascading down through the urban hierarchy, springing up initially in the most urbanised areas in each region – north, south, east, and west – and moving then to towns of lesser importance. However, its transmission process lacked a comparably strong contagious component – it was not yet readily transmissible from person to person – and it failed to infiltrate the hinterlands and more rural parts of the country. This first wave was thus composed of a series of local diffusion cells centred around urban areas such as Belfast, Dublin, Ballinasloe, and Cork, and as was the case in Spain, the infection first appeared in towns that were joined by the railway.[7]

THE SECOND WAVE

Combining elements of hierarchical and contagious diffusion, the second wave was much more penetrating in its reach and more damaging in its effects than its summer predecessor. Following a relatively quiescent August, there were signs that epidemic influenza was beginning to break out once more towards the end of September 1918. Howth in north County Dublin was identified as the locus of infection, with several hundred sick by the end of the first week in October.[8] Influenza and pneumonia deaths in Dublin peaked in the week ending 2 November – just seven days after the epidemic had reached its height in major cities such as Paris, Berlin, Hamburg, and New York. This considerable degree of 'chronological simultaneity' offers support for the hypothesis that the influenza virus may have undergone on-site mutation, having already been seeded by the first wave.[9]

It was in early and mid-October that influenza really began to erupt around Ireland, moving with a much greater velocity compared to the more gradual and easily perceptible development of the first wave. This corresponds with the finding of Andrew Cliff, Matthew Smallman-Raynor, and Niall Johnson regarding the epidemic in Britain, and their assertion that epidemic transmission proceeded at such a rapid rate that purely hierarchical effects played a relatively minor role in diffusing the disease.[10]

The geographical path of this second wave was difficult to pinpoint as it coursed through the transport network at a fervent pace, springing up at the same time in distant parts of the country. By the beginning of November 1918, it had touched practically every county in Leinster, Munster, and Connacht, and much of Ulster, moving in a gradual westward drift. The east coast and north Munster were among the earliest parts affected, with the western outposts of Connacht and the north-western parts of Donegal witnessing the effects of the second wave late in December.[11]

While transport networks – in particular the railway – as well as the movements of troops and labourers, were important in circulating the disease at a national level, when it came to local diffusion, social behaviours and customs were among the main mechanisms of spread. Events such as concerts and dances, wakes, Petty Sessions, ploughing matches, and even General Election activities (one Volunteer remembered that 'as a result of my work in the 1918 Election I contracted a severe cold which later developed into 'Flu and left me indisposed until March 1919') all facilitated the advance of the disease.[12]

The primacy of the railway is suggested by a variety of examples, and is in keeping with global trends in the pandemic's pathways of spread. Thurles in Tipperary was located at a point of intersection of a number of different railway lines in the south, and was one of the earliest towns to feel the effects of this second wave of the so-called 'plague'. It is also noteworthy that out of the 156 towns listed in the annual report of the Registrar-General for 1918, the only two which registered no flu deaths for 1918 were Ballyvaughan and Killadysert (County Clare), neither of which was located on the railway line. Distance from primary travel routes predictably served to delay the arrival of the epidemic, with outbreaks in remote areas only occurring when the disease was already well established elsewhere in the country. For instance, it did not arrive in towns such as Dromore West, in Sligo, until the very last week of 1918, and outbreaks at Greencastle, at the very tip of Inishowen in Donegal, and at Moyne and Kiltigan, County Wicklow, also took place in the later stages of the second wave (late November–late December 1918). All of these towns were located some distance from the main lines of travel.[13]

Once it had arrived in an area's main town, the contagious pattern of spread – person to person transmission – took over, as the flu was passed between neighbours and families. This ensured that the flu radiated out into the surrounding villages, generating a pattern whereby each of these local centres served in effect as the initial point of infection for a distinct regional cell. This tendency for the disease to unfurl outwards from town to neighbouring village and outlying districts was frequently noted at the time, and it was this ability of the second wave to combine a hierarchical component with ease of transmission between people which allowed it to achieve a lethal efficiency in its spread, distinguishing it from the first wave which had been characterised by a dominant hierarchical component.[14]

The contrast between the first and second waves becomes clearly evident through examination of the local experiences of individual counties during the epidemic. In the case of Galway, for instance, although the first wave would seem to have only reached Galway city, Gort, and Ballinasloe (also touching Garbally), the second wave was much more invasive, striking a number of large towns and small villages in the east such as Athenry, Loughrea, Portumna, Mountbellew, and Glenamaddy, and also sweeping through settlements on the west coast in a line from Spiddal to Rossaveal, Oughterard, and Roundstone, and stretching as far as Clifden and Leenane.[15]

This pattern of spread could also be seen in Sligo, where hierarchical and spatial diffusion processes combined to spread the disease through the county. By the beginning of November 1918, there were indications that the flu had arrived in Sligo town, with 'some cases locally' of 'bad colds'. A week later, there were over a hundred cases of flu in the municipality with 'a few persons' suffering in the areas around nearby Ballaghaderreen, Roscommon. The disease had by now also reached the area around the town of Ballymote, in southeast Sligo. In the following weeks, the epidemic enveloped much of the southern half of the county, and by the end of November, Ballymote counted 240 cases, with a number of the villages just outside it such as Keash and Culfadda also affected. To the west in Tubbercurry, the doctor was requesting extra help to attend to the numerous flu patients, with the flu by now also 'prevalent' in the village of Ballinacarrow. In December, it reached into the countryside in the northwest of Sligo, hitting the area around Skreen, where it wrought 'havoc', also bringing sickness to Dromore West workhouse. Whereas the only evidence of the first wave had been an outbreak of influenza among the inhabitants of Sligo and Leitrim Asylum in August 1918, the second wave spread with greater ease and thoroughness, moving from primary towns to the smaller villages, and consequently permeating the countryside to a far greater extent than its predecessor.[14]

THE THIRD WAVE

With the second wave continuing to affect some communities in the west and north even as the New Year approached, the precise beginnings of the third wave are difficult to pinpoint with certainty. Signs of another outbreak came primarily from the south, with several minor eruptions in Munster during January 1919. Flare-ups of the disease were also evident in the west in mid-January and in Fermanagh and south Leinster at the end of the month. Its subsequent development was sporadic in nature, with cases springing up in Celbridge, south Dublin, and Wicklow, as well as Meath in early February. In general, this wave was more gradual in its spread and less instantaneous in its movements than the autumn–winter outbreak of 1918, echoing Beatriz Echeverri's analysis that 'from an epidemiological point of view, this wave was less explosive than the two that preceded it'. Another feature of the flu outbreak in 1919 was its ability to extend even further into the countryside and to reach places which had not been affected by the second wave. What took place was a highly localised, contagious spread process, which is illustrated by the cases of Wexford, and of Galway once more.[17]

In Wexford, the second wave initially arrived via the towns of Gorey and Enniscorthy, stops along the main road from Dublin, but limited its effects primarily to the more urbanised areas of Wexford town, Rosslare and its environs, and New Ross (although it did reach the country districts on both sides of the Barrow on the western border with Kilkenny). The third wave, however, cropped up in parts of the county which had largely escaped the earlier visits, striking villages in the eastern half such as The Harrow, Kilcotty, and Glenbrien. In the western half of the county, meanwhile, several other villages which had eluded the second wave were also hit by this third visitation (including Kilmyshal and Clonroche), while in the south, the town of Killinick – located a few miles outside of Wexford – was also stricken.[18]

In Galway in 1919, the disease reached even more deeply into the rural heartland than it had done the previous year. The third wave struck once more at Galway city, Ballinasloe, and Gort, but also hit many parts of the northeast such as Kilkerrin, Milltown, Williamstown and Dunmore, which had gone largely untouched by the first two visitations. This final outbreak also inflicted extensive damage on the Aran Islands, Inishbofin, and Lettermullen and Gorumna Island – where 'practically all of the islanders became afflicted' – stretching inland as well along the main road from Maam Cross to Recess and Derrylea.[19]

Such instances suggest that among the areas most distressed by the third wave were those with low population density, little urbanisation, and undeveloped transportation networks. Moreover, five of the ten counties with the highest casualty rates in 1919 were considered Congested Districts – Mayo, Donegal, Galway, Sligo, Roscommon – where population density could be as little as 89 persons per square mile, a much lower figure than the Irish average of 134. Ireland's case thus contrasts with research on the epidemic elsewhere which found that 'urban areas, coastal areas, and areas well served by mass communication and transport links suffered higher mortality than rural, inland, and isolated areas'. The widespread and acute nature of the second and third waves of the epidemic in counties such as Mayo and Galway corresponds with the experience of the more isolated hamlets in parts of Japan, which also suffered badly at the hands of the later flu waves.[20]

From their research on the geography of the disease in Japan, historians Geoffrey Rice and Edwina Palmer have suggested that the severity of the flu in an area was partly determined by whether it had witnessed the 'mild' first wave, with exposure to the summer visitation conferring a degree of immunity against the later waves. A sample of towns and cities from around Ireland also points to the importance of exposure to the first wave as a key factor when it came to influenza mortality. For instance, the town of New Ross, Wexford, escaped the first wave, but was badly hit by the second, with the result that in 1918, almost one in six deaths in the town were due to flu. By contrast, the city of Lurgan, in Armagh, which had suffered during the first wave, was less affected by the second. Kilkenny town registered the third highest proportion of flu deaths of any town in Ireland in 1918 (almost one in four deaths in the town were due to flu), but had been almost completely untouched by the first wave, suggesting that the second wave was responsible for the devastation evident in the Registrar-General's statistics. Conversely, a number of places which the first wave did hit, such as Kells, Mullingar, Athlone, and Clonmel, all witnessed influenza mortality rates well below those of New Ross and Kilkenny.[21]

Contemporary observations also stressed the role of immunity in dictating the seriousness of the flu's effects. A Mullingar doctor attending soldiers was firmly convinced that immunity was given by an initial attack:

> ...undoubtedly an attack of influenza carries with it immunity for a certain time...the immunity lasts for six months at least...During the last three waves of the epidemic I have had to deal with the sick of 2000 (two thousand) troops, and during this time we treated in hospital over 400 cases. No cases admitted in June, July, or August were readmitted in October, November, or December, and no cases admitted in either of these two periods were readmitted in February of this year...Again, in private practice I have had no recurrence.[22]

David Patterson and Gerald Pyle also found that regions which were attacked in spring 1918 suffered less severely in fall: 'despite obvious differences between the viral strains, exposure provided some protection against the more virulent fall virus'. Further evidence of the importance of immunity comes from Scandinavia which witnessed a widespread morbidity wave in summer 1918, followed by an autumn wave which brought low mortality relative to other countries.[23]

Factors like poverty levels and community action and relief efforts – the 'geographies of care' – also had an impact on mortality rates. Social response is a crucial element in determining an epidemic's course, and recent studies of the pandemic have shown that the quality and promptness of local reaction were often more critical than ratios of doctors to population, or levels of income per household. The significance of local response is signalled by the experience of several parts of Ireland during the epidemic. Kilkenny was among the worst hit towns in 1918, and primary sources demonstrate that there was little attempt to launch coordinated community-based aid efforts, as had been done elsewhere. The *Kilkenny People* printed a plea for action in this regard at the time:

> ...in numerous cases entire families are lying stricken in their own wretched homes, sometimes three and four inmates occupying a single, small, ill-ventilated room. It is

surely a time when some public and concerted effort
should be made to mitigate the plight of these sorely
harassed people...money should be forthcoming, and will
be forthcoming if the necessary steps are taken to raise it in
Kilkenny, as has been done in Clonmel and other places
whose plight is not worse than Kilkenny's.[24]

A link between relief efforts and mortality levels is also suggested by the
case of Wexford town, where influenza accounted for almost one in
five deaths in 1918. Here, the corporation was criticised for 'not organising a fund for the poor and not trying to make a plentiful supply
of milk (available) for them'.[25]

In contrast, Longford town recorded comparable instances of misery
owing to the outbreak, yet its influenza mortality rate was much below
that of the badly stricken Kilkenny, suggesting that the relief work
carried out there may have done much to alleviate suffering and to
prevent deaths at the hands of the epidemic. Relief efforts were also
organised in towns including Limerick, Thurles, and Clonmel (which
was deemed to be 'the most severely hit of the provincial centres'), all
of which returned mortality rates below those of the worst afflicted
places such as Inishowen, Newry, and Kilkenny, where influenza was
responsible for the highest proportion of deaths in 1918, and which
lacked well organised relief work.[26]

When it came to national impact, the geography of the epidemic
differed considerably between 1918 and 1919. The counties least
affected by the flu in 1918 were located mainly along the west and
southwest coastlines, with a cluster of counties in the midlands region
including Westmeath, Longford, and Roscommon also escaping relatively
unscathed during the first two waves. Broadly speaking, mortality rates
decreased from east to west, with the epidemic exacting its highest
death tolls on parts of east Leinster and Ulster, in a broken arc that
stretched from Wexford to Donegal. The pattern was almost directly
reversed in 1919, with Connacht and southwest Munster registering
the highest concentrations of influenza deaths, while the lowest rates
came primarily from Leinster and northeast Ulster.[27] The contrasting
geographic imprints left by the flu in 1918 and 1919 may be reflective
of the influence of settlement patterns on the geography of the disease.

The high impact of flu on the north and eastern half of the country
in 1918, followed by high mortality in the west in 1919, is perhaps best
explained by a comment made by the British Registrar-General: 'it is
not that the towns suffered excessively, for the rates for all classes of

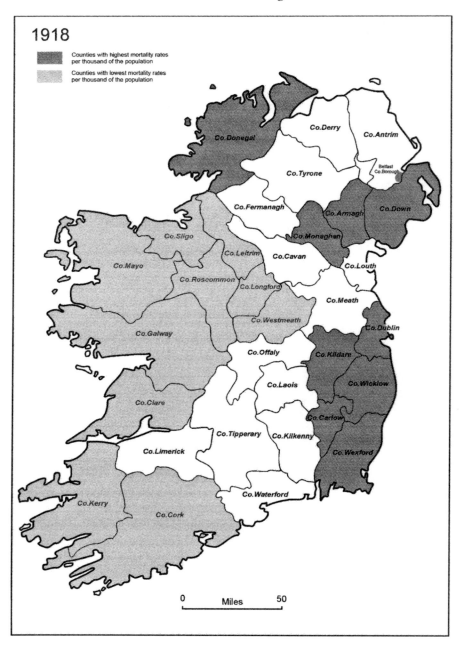

1918 map based on information provided in the Fifty-fifth Detailed Annual Report of the Registrar-General for Ireland [Cmd. 450], H.C. 1919, x, British Parliamentary Papers.

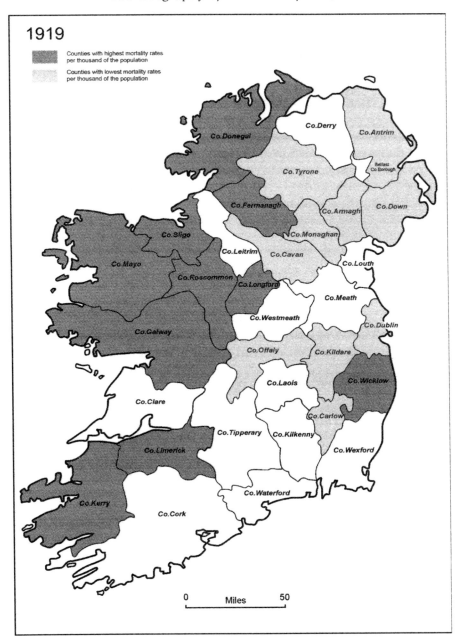

1919 map based on information provided in the Fifty-sixth Detailed Annual Report of the Registrar-General for Ireland [Cmd. 997], H.C. 1920, xi, British Parliamentary Papers.

area throughout the whole epidemic were much the same, but the towns suffered first', leading to high mortality rates in 1918 in the more urbanised counties.[28]

The timing of the flu's introduction to an area was closely linked to military presence – as soldiers brought the infection home from war, towns and counties with high recruitment rates were among those first hit by the epidemic. This thesis is supported by the way in which many of the worst-hit areas in 1918 were among those which had returned high enlistment figures. Ulster, Dublin, Wicklow, Carlow, and Kildare raised the highest numbers of recruits for the war effort, and while the northern province endured the highest number of flu casualties during 1918, all of the latter counties were among those worst hit by the first two waves of the Great Flu, with Dublin county borough and Kildare heading the list. Out of all the rural towns, Naas suffered the most, with influenza accounting for just under 25 per cent of all deaths in 1918, while in Athy, just over one in five deaths were due to flu. Further corroborating the role of the military in the initial stages of the epidemic is the fact that few recruits originated from the Atlantic seaboard, with Mayo and Kerry recording especially low enlistment ratios.[29]

Through 1918 and 1919, there was a strong association between soldiers and the disease, both in Ireland and abroad. In France, Dr Legroux of the Pasteur Institute postulated that 'it began at the front early in May', and it was noted that

> areas of heaviest infection were the base ports, the depot divisions and such training areas as had received recent reinforcements from home, including men who had been exposed to the infection that had prevailed on the transports and in the crowded troop trains.[30]

In the US, the popular belief that soldiers harboured the disease transformed the 'nation's protectors' into objects of fear for many civilians. Similarly, the Spanish press and medical observers continuously depicted military personnel as instrumental in spreading the infection. As writer Richard Collier would later put it, in 1918 'the sight of a soldier in uniform was a signal to step into the nearest tree-lot until he had passed'. In Dublin, Dr Kathleen Lynn had no doubt that returning soldiers should be monitored closely for signs that they might be carrying the flu: 'In her opinion, men returning from the front should be quarantined until they were certified all right before being allowed to mix with the population, or, at the very least, their clothes should be sterilized, because very often infection was carried in clothes.'[31]

In the third wave the link became even more explicit, with the observation that 'the disease has claimed many victims in different centres, especially those in which large detachments of troops are quartered'. The soldier's body came to be seen as a vector of contagion, as the men 'returning home from all the theatres of war' were suspected of carrying 'the latent germs of disease with them'. The annual report of the Dublin hospitals later singled out the military (as well as the Dublin Metropolitan Police) for their high instances of admission to Cork Street Fever Hospital: 'The Hospital appears to have been exceptionally full during the past year owing to an outbreak of Measles and Influenza, when the Governors admitted, in addition to Policemen, a large number of soldiers as well as their wives and children.'[32]

That the soldier should become a 'social scapegoat' for the epidemic is also reflective of the marked change in public attitudes towards the military that took place in Ireland over the course of the First World War. The Secretary of the City of Dublin War Pensions Committee, W.G. Fallon, recalled how the recruits leaving for war in 1914 departed to a fanfare of well wishes, 'applause and God-speeds', only to be received on their return with hostility and resentment. As Joanna Bourke put it, Irish ex-servicemen had become 'fugitives in their own country'.[33]

The role of the military in facilitating the epidemic is an area currently under research, but it would seem that in Ireland, as in England, the US, Spain, and Canada, troops played a notable role in introducing and disseminating influenza in 1918: Patterson and Pyle have commented that 'transmission in many places was greatly facilitated by wartime disruption and troop movements'. This aspect of the Irish geographical experience of the pandemic is consistent with what historian Robert Brown describes as the 'compelling causal links' between the First World War and the pandemic. As the flu spread, war and disease 'fused symbiotically into a dangerous partnership'.[34]

The geography of the epidemic in Ireland thus fitted in to a large extent with the experiences of other countries in terms of patterns of diffusion and spread mechanisms. As in Spain, Japan, and Britain, the first outbreaks of the summer wave took place in urban centres, with the eruption in Belfast followed by rapid spread to other regional centres such as Dublin, Cork, and Ballinasloe. In Ireland, this early wave was mostly confined to denser, more urbanised areas, as it lacked a potent spatial contagion component which in turn restricted its penetration into the fabric of the countryside. This corresponds with the thesis that connectivity, and place, in the social and national hierarchy, are key influences on influenza activity.[35]

Also consistent with experiences overseas, the second wave in Ireland was defined by its 'geographical ubiquity', spreading to every corner of the island; as Niall Johnson notes, 'it was not to spare any part of the British Isles'. An appearance in Dublin at the end of September 1918 was followed by rapid movement of the disease, with studies of individual counties revealing that the disease tended to arrive initially in one of the main towns in an area, spreading subsequently to satellite villages. This pattern of diffusion mixed elements of hierarchical and contagious spread patterns to brutal effect, with the result that the second wave flooded the landscape much more extensively than the summer outbreak. This echoes the findings of Cliff and Smallman-Raynor regarding the spatial patterns of flu epidemics in Iceland, and of Niall Johnson in relation to the geography of the Great Flu in Britain: the spread of flu was at its most efficient and damaging when it combined hierarchical and contagious patterns of diffusion. The third wave sprang up in an uneven and seemingly disconnected fashion, emerging at points in the south, west, east, and north within a matter of days in mid- and late January 1919.[36]

At the same time, however, there were important points of difference, especially when it came to the temporal structure of the outbreak. In historical portrayals, the Great Flu tends to be sketched as a three-wave onslaught, consisting of wave 1 in April–June 1918, wave 2 in August–November 1918, and wave 3 in February–April 1919. The distinct natures of the three waves, and the marked potency of the second, are largely taken for granted in discussions of the pandemic's general characteristics. Applying this template to Ireland proves problematic, however, as the second and third waves overlapped considerably, making it difficult to distinguish clear temporal patterns in the epidemic.

At a local level, the flu offensive was a picture of hits and abatements – a six to eight week period of sickness, followed by temporary respite before the next onslaught. Nationally, the picture was slightly different, as epidemic disease was an inescapable presence in the country from June 1918 to May 1919. Not all parts of Ireland witnessed the waves at the same time, with possible time lags of up to several weeks between the arrival of the flu in different areas. For the country as a whole though, it was practically a full year of sickness, as in almost every month from June 1918 to May 1919 a flare-up of the disease was occurring in some corner of the country.

Among the factors underpinning the rate of diffusion and geographical development of the flu were the relative development of the transport infrastructure – primarily the railway network – in an area;

social behaviours such as the holding and attendance of dances and wakes; and troop concentration, with centres of infection often correlating with military presence. Factors such as the character and effectiveness of local response, as well as immunity, were also important. While large towns and cities such as Dublin, Cork, and Belfast suffered all three visitations, the pattern for smaller towns and villages was that an outbreak in 1918 was unlikely to be followed by one in 1919. If sickness had been escaped in 1918, however, this heightened the chances of witnessing the third wave. This is consistent with findings regarding the Great Flu elsewhere, with data showing that the final visitation 'flared up to attack those members of a weakened population that still lacked immunity'.[37]

One of the basic determinants of regional differences on a national scale in 1918 and 1919, meanwhile, was the timing of the epidemic's arrival and spread in a county. Although not all counties appear to have been exposed to the first wave, the second and third waves touched all thirty-two, with the general pattern that the east and north recorded high influenza mortality rates in 1918, with low rates in 1919, while the west returned low flu mortality rates in 1918, with high rates in 1919. This was most likely due to the late arrival of the second wave in the west compared to the east, with the 1919 figures for the worst-hit counties in the west, southwest, and northwest thereby incorporating an overlay of influenza deaths from the second wave, as well as total influenza deaths from the third wave.[38]

*   *   *   *

Although academic research on the pandemic has tended towards the view that urban areas and places enjoying well-developed communication networks were apt to suffer the most violent effects of the flu, primary source material is replete with instances of the blanket morbidity and high death rates witnessed in areas of low density populations. In April 1920, the *British Medical Journal* printed an account by A.H. Macklin, Surgeon of the Imperial Trans-Atlantic Expedition, of his experience of the flu amongst the Lapps in North Russia. The disease reached settlements in Lapland in December 1918, with one officer describing it as a 'terrible sickness' which carried 'death wherever it went'. Macklin found that the chief complication was broncho-pneumonia, from which he gathered 'there were practically no recoveries'. From local information, he estimated that about 50 per cent of all cases died.[39]

Meanwhile, in Hebron, the most northern of the Labrador villages in eastern Canada, only 70 out of 220 of the inhabitants survived the flu's onslaught; similarly in Okak, 50 miles south of Hebron, only 59 were left out of 266 villagers. Disposal of the dead here became a serious problem, 'the few survivors left behind being too feeble to dig graves in the frozen ground'. In the end, 'holes were made in the ice and the dead bodies thrown in'. The disease was no less destructive in warm climates, and the island of Western Samoa lost 22 per cent of its people to flu, including 10 per cent of its children.[40]

In Ireland, the report of the Registrar-General for 1918 showed that of all the towns and villages around the country, the flu inflicted the worst damage on Inishowen, a sparsely populated rural region at the tip of northeast Donegal. In the first year of the flu, more than one in four deaths here was attributable to the disease, a higher rate than was recorded in any of the urban areas. At the same time though, Dublin County Borough recorded the highest flu mortality of any county or county borough. These statistics reflect how the most acute effects of the flu were felt in areas which were at either end of the urban–rural continuum: dense, overcrowded cities, and thinly populated, spread out settlements. The Great Flu could inflict as much damage on small villages as on built-up, well populated urbanised regions, highlighting the specificity of local experience and warning of how seemingly universal trends in the pandemic's movement and effects could break down at a local level.[41]

CHAPTER TWO

'An tinneas mór': The Demography of the Epidemic [1]

As the Great War entered its final stages, Irish society found itself confronted with a sudden and overwhelming number of sick bodies and 'untimely deaths', as influenza broke out all over the country. A glance at the arithmetic of this potent strain of flu goes some way to explaining how the epidemic earned the name 'the Great Flu'. Government files recorded 3,000 cases in Newry, with 'close on 200 persons affected in Gorey town'. At a meeting of the Westport Board of Guardians, attention was called 'to the necessity for a doctor at Ballycroy, where they had over a thousand cases of influenza, and the nurse found it very hard to attend to them all'. In Irish towns around the country, hundreds fell ill, with widespread reports of high mortality and overloaded medical staff. The *Church of Ireland Gazette* told of 'many sad cases of families being almost wiped out' as the epidemic claimed as many as 20,958 lives in Ireland, placing it just above the European average.[2]

Historians have frequently described the 1918/19 flu in terms of its democracy, portraying a relatively uniform social distribution, which caused problems when attempting to correlate the flu's geography with socio-economic variables. A description used in Ireland at the time suggested this apparent lack of discrimination: 'an tinneas mór' – the great sickness – expressing the popular sense that the epidemic's defining characteristics were its scale and pervasiveness. This chapter investigates the social demography of the epidemic in order to ascertain whether the flu really was indiscriminate in its reach across Ireland, or whether there were groups, professions, or classes in society which were more likely than others to suffer its effects.[3]

The story of the Great Flu in Ireland as elsewhere is inscribed with the irony that the infection struck hardest at young adults rather than

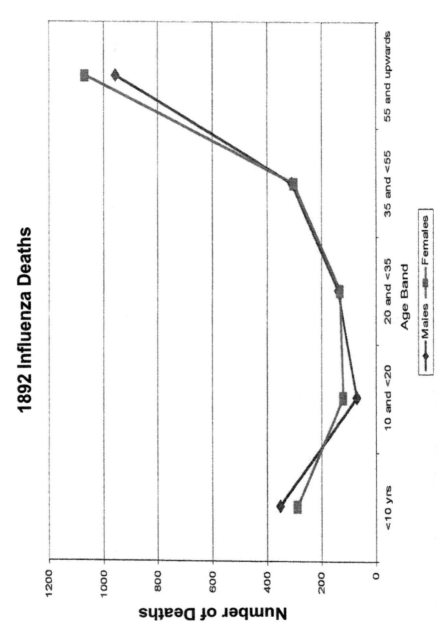

Graph 1: 1892 Influenza Deaths *(Twenty-ninth Annual Report of the Registrar-General (Ireland)* [C. 7255], H.C. 1893–4, xxi).

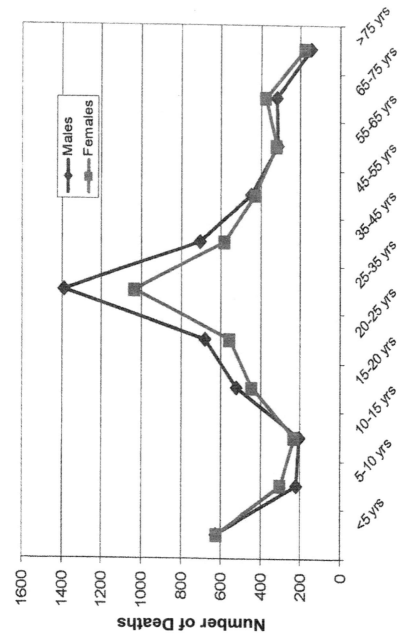

Graph 2: 1918 Influenza Deaths (*Fifty-fifth Detailed Annual Report of the Registrar-General for Ireland* [Cmd. 450], H.C. 1919, x).

older age groups or children, as had been the case in previous flu out-breaks. For instance, the year 1892 saw an 'exceptional prevalence of influenza' in the country with 54 per cent of the mortalities among those aged fifty-five and upwards, with deaths among children under 10 years of age accounting for a further 17 per cent.[4] These figures gave the epidemic the characteristic U-shaped graph, as the virus carried away many of the most physically vulnerable in society.

In 1918 though, the Local Government Board documented that 'the infant class and the aged were least affected' by the disease, corresponding with the findings of the Registrar-General, Sir William J. Thompson, whose figures revealed that the age groups worst hit were those between 25 and 35, and 15 and 25 respectively. The new profile of the disease prompted Thompson to remark on the 'markedly low percentage of deaths of persons 45 years and upwards, especially the proportion of persons 55 and upwards'. The change in the flu's social patterning also elicited the comment from Dr Rowlette of the Royal Academy of Medicine in Ireland that 'the most remarkable thing was the large number of young adults attacked in the epidemic of 1918 as compared with other epidemics'.[5]

In its report on the pandemic, the British Ministry of Health drew attention to this swift and startling change in age incidence which it considered to be one of the most 'striking' features of the epidemic, as those between 20 and 40, and 'more particularly between 25 and 35 years of age, were the most liable to succumb to the dreaded pneumonic type of the infection'. In fact, 'the chances of a man of 55 pulling through seemed better than the chances of a man of 25 or 30', which made the flu outbreak 'entirely different to the epidemics of the past in which, as a rule, the deaths have been largely among the elderly or the very young'. This altered age-patterning gave rise to the W-shaped graph commonly associated with the pandemic, as flu deaths spiked sharply among young adults.[6]

This feature of the epidemic caused disbelief at the time, as it became apparent that it was not necessarily the most vulnerable in society who were most at risk. The Protestant Orphan Society was able to report that only three orphans in its care had died, which it considered to be a 'small number in a year of such serious epidemic'. Surprise at the ability of the flu to largely bypass children, the group usually thought to be the most susceptible to disease, was also conveyed in the Local Government Board's commentary on the annual mortality statistics, which observed that in 1918 'the increase of infant deaths' was actually 'appreciably below the average excess'.[7]

Instead, it was the 'breadwinners' of families, newlyweds, brides-to-be, soldiers home on leave, young parents and honeymooners, who constituted the majority lost to the flu, as the brunt of the epidemic was 'borne by the young adult population'. The Chairman of Skibbereen Rural Council noted that 'it was the strong, healthy and vigorous that seemed to be cut down' by the virus. Bill Burgess, whose brother died from flu while away at school, was shocked by his death, as he considered Vivian to have been 'as hardy a young fellow as you'd meet'.[8]

Children were spared while their parents died, and with no definitive cure, doctors could only express their sense of helplessness at what was happening. Older parents meanwhile had to endure the trauma of seeing their grown children pass away before them, as 'old age alone' appeared to 'confer some degree of safety'. The *Connacht Tribune* reported that 'the dread epidemic that has followed the war has been peculiar in that it has not particularly affected life amongst the young or the very old, or the weakly, but has attacked and laid low the strong and robust'. In the capital, 'two-thirds of those that died' had been 'in the prime of life, the wage-earning age', and in Lurgan, it was remarked that children were not 'so much affected as adults'. In Ireland, as elsewhere around the world, the flu 'attacked youth'.[9]

Although research into the reasons why the flu virus of 1918/19 was so especially lethal among young people is still ongoing, recent findings indicate that it is linked to the response the virus provoked in the body itself. Scientists have discovered that the particular strain of influenza at work in the Great Flu managed to derail the body's usual reaction to viral infection. The result was that rather than defend the body, the immune system of flu victims often stimulated an attack on the lungs, causing them to fill with fluids, effectively drowning the victims.[10]

In addition to age, gender was another indicator of susceptibility to the flu, with Ireland sharing in the global trend for male over female mortality from the virus – male influenza deaths outnumbered those of females in 1918 by more than 10 per cent. Once more, this differentiated the Great Flu from previous patterns in the demography of influenza. In the influenza outbreak of 1892 for example, female flu deaths outnumbered male flu fatalities, and again in 1917, female deaths from flu were more common than those among males.[11]

The gendered pattern of mortality in 1918 drew much notice at the time. In Macroom, newspaper reports lamented that 'young men in the vigour of early manhood' were 'stricken down', shrouding 'many a homestead' in 'darkness and desolation'. In the area around Tuam, it was similarly observed that a 'sad feature' of the epidemic was that the majority of victims were 'young men'. This surplus of male deaths contrasted with influenza mortality patterns in the capitals of those countries caught up in the war such as London and Paris, where the virus struck harder at women than men, reflecting the imbalance of sexes within urban populations during wartime. It has also been suggested that the heavier male mortality overall may have reflected a greater 'biological susceptibility' to the specific viral strain responsible for the epidemic.[12]

A further gender-related trend was the high flu mortality among mothers-to-be. In her review of the effects of the flu in the wartime cities of Paris, Berlin and London, Catherine Rollet notes that 'pregnant women were particularly vulnerable' to this new flu. At the Paris Maternity Hospital, mortality among pregnant women reached 46 per cent, causing *The Lancet* to comment that '"woe unto them that are with child" might have been written of this influenza epidemic'. In Ireland, flu had been among the lowest causes of death among pregnant women in 1917, accounting for 0.42 per cent, or less than 1 in 200 deaths of women bearing children. In 1918, this shot up to 1 in 20, climbing again in 1919 to account for just over 10 per cent of all deaths among pregnant women.[13]

The heightened vulnerability of pregnant women may have been due to some of the changes in the body caused by pregnancy. These include altered blood circulation, reduced functional capacity of the lungs, and the immunosuppression necessary to prevent rejection of the foetus – sometimes described as 'pregnancy associated immunodeficiency syndrome' (PAIDS) – which leaves women more susceptible to infection.[14]

The precipitate and unsparing effects which this influenza was capable of exerting on the pregnant body were depicted in the diary and Bureau of Military History witness statement of Dr Kathleen Lynn, who treated the pregnant wife of Cathal Brugha (Chief of Staff of the Irish Republican Army) in Dublin in November 1918. At the makeshift hospital which she helped establish at 37 Charlemont Street with the goal of helping 'patients suffering from 'flu', the case of Caitlín Brugha stood out for Lynn. She recalled 'we had some patients that were very bad, among them Mrs Cathal Brugha who, at the time, was expecting a baby'.[15]

In her diary, she recorded how Brugha's wife first appeared to be getting better from the flu, before she was quickly gripped by pneumonia. On 24 November 1918, Lynn noted 'Mrs Bruagh (*sic*) better', but just two days later her pithy entry depicted a rapid diminishment in health: 'Mrs C Bruagh bad, definite pneum. Dr Crofton saw her, we moved her to 37, seems better tonight.' However, the patient soon took a turn for the worse again, arousing deep concern: 'terribly anxious day with Mrs C Bruagh, stayed in hosp. till 7 am. Dr Crofton hurrying up with vaccine.' By 28 November though, Caitlín finally seemed to be convalescing, and by 30 November, she was 'much better', going home just over two weeks later. That both mother and child recovered from the illness was evident in a comment made by Lynn in her diary on 30 May 1919 – 'Baby Brugha and mother doing well.'[16]

Through 1918 and 1919, influenza was particularly prevalent among those consigned to the 'civilising' institutions introduced to Irish society in the nineteenth century, including workhouses, mental hospitals and national schools.[17] Examination of the county archives in Wicklow, Cork, Galway and Donegal reveals the extensive spread of the disease within the workhouse system, with virtually all the workhouses in these counties suffering flu visitations at some point in 1918 or 1919.

In the pages of the minute books of the South Dublin Union workhouse, the phrase 'sick and unable for duty' appears continually during the epidemic, while other workhouses and fever hospitals dotted across the country also witnessed influenza outbreaks and consequent staff shortages. Particularly during the second wave, resources were considerably strained by increased admissions as people sought help for their ailing bodies. Meath Fever Hospital was 'filled to its limit', extra cases having to be sent to the infirmary. At the Kells Union Fever Hospital, the epidemic put an end to the period of dereliction which the establishment had been witnessing for several months past. At Derry Union, on learning of the large number of patients in the hospital, the Medical Officer 'suggested that an apothecary be appointed to visit the institution daily to mix and prepare the necessary medicines for the sick'.[18]

In other unions, there were difficulties with rent collection as a consequence of sickness among the tenants. The collector for Shillelagh District Council wrote to the officials explaining that he had been 'laid up with influenza during the end of the year, and was therefore unable to complete my collection for '18'. He also drew the board's attention to the fact that he had been 'seriously handicapped owing to several of your tenants being affected with the 'flu three months back, and being unable to pay up'. The other rent collector for the district witnessed similar problems.[19]

Many workhouses temporarily banned visitors, trying to seal up any potential entry points against the virus, minimising interaction between inmates and their families as a precautionary measure. Exclusion of the outside world was a necessary form of risk management, and barriers between inmates and the public were crucial if the disease was to be prevented from making its way in. To this end, the infirmaries and hospitals in Cork made 'stringent rules' that no visitors would be permitted 'except in connection with very serious cases'. Similarly, the master of Shillelagh Workhouse, Wicklow, notified the Guardians that, due to the 'prevalence of influenza in the district', he was 'not allowing any visitors to the House or Infirmary'. In Fermanagh, the Lisnaskea Guardians inverted the logic, deciding the threat was contained in the patients themselves rather than their acquaintances outside, and ordering the nurses to 'prevent patients recovering from influenza visiting the town'.[20]

The Boyle Board of Guardians in Roscommon was the most inventive, erecting physical boundaries in order to separate patients and hospital attendants from the military stationed in the main building. The issue was evidently a matter of grave concern to the officials, as they gave the Master of the workhouse instructions 'to have a wooden fence erected on the south and north sides of the front lodge of the house', with the barrier to be fortified with barbed wire.[21]

The epidemic also spread extensively through the asylum system in Ireland, with outbreaks in the Mullingar, Limerick, Sligo, and Leitrim Asylums. In the Richmond and Portrane District Asylums in Dublin, influenza accounted for almost one in five female deaths and just over one in ten male deaths in 1918, in a reversal of external mortality patterns. Dr Patrick, Regional Medical Superintendent (RMS) at the Tyrone and Fermanagh Asylum, reported to the Committee of Management that flu patients 'admitted to the institution were exceedingly bad', requiring the care of two attendants each. The RMS at Mayo Asylum observed in his monthly report for November 1918 that over a hundred patients and three quarters of the entire staff 'were stricken down with so-called influenza' in less than four weeks. Noting the epidemic had 'extended in an alarming manner', he explained that 'the whole working' of the Asylum had been 'completely disorganised' as a result.[22]

While mortality from the 1918 flu strain was between 2 and 3 per cent internationally, in Ireland's mental health institutions the proportion of deaths could be several times higher. In 1918, influenza was responsible for almost 10 per cent of deaths in the district and auxiliary asylums (243 out of 2,243 deaths) – an eight-fold increase on the number of deaths caused by the virus in 1917 – while pneumonia claimed a similar proportion, with the result that one in five deaths in Irish asylums in 1918 were due to these respiratory infections. Influenza was also identified as a 'principal or contributory' cause or 'associated factor' in the cases of sixty-two men and seventy-three women admitted to district and auxiliary asylums. And for a further forty-six men and fifty-six women, it was the 'principal' grounds for admission, and as such was among the leading causes of female insanity in 1918. This amounted to a total of 237 cases in which influenza was a significant factor in admission, an increase of more than eight times on that of 1917, when a total of only 27 were admitted to district and auxiliary asylums on the basis of influenza as a cause or factor. The ability of the virus to lead to mental instability was also evident abroad. In the Gold Coast, some patients exhibited 'queer and strange' behaviour even after the epidemic had subsided. David Killingray has asked what may have possessed the minds of the sixty people admitted to the Kingston Lunatic Asylum in Jamaica 'whose exciting cause was attributed to influenza'. In Paris, the number of suicides tripled as 'all over the world, the sick were committing suicide'.[23]

The increased flu admissions in 1918/19 reflected the startling 'frequency and severity of post-influenzal delirium and mania', and of the 'onset of maniacal symptoms' which could occur as a result of the infection. Nellie O'Toole's mother told of how the flu drove her son to beat 'his head against the wall with it'. In Dennaleagh, near Bally-jamesduff, a farmer's unexpected suicide was ascribed to his recent bout of the virus: 'he had shown no signs whatever of mental affliction up to the time of his death. Deceased had recently recovered from a severe attack of influenza, and it is believed that this may have caused some mental derangement, which led to the tragic occurrence.' Such instances further heightened the contrast between the 1918/19 epidemic and previous experiences of influenza outbreaks in Ireland, when 'late depressive and melancholic signs' as opposed to severe mental disturbance were primary features of the disease.[24]

Another institution hit hard by the epidemic was the Industrial Schools. The epidemic accounted for the deaths of one in four boys, and just over one in four girls in the detention system in 1918. This emphasised the vulnerability of those consigned to state care during outbreaks of disease – living arrangements which placed large numbers of people in close proximity to one another provided optimum conditions for an infectious virus like influenza to spread. For instance, at St Conleth's Reformatory School, Philipstown, more than 140 boys went 'down with the 'flu' during the third wave, while in Glencree Reformatory School, 200 boys fell ill.[25]

The susceptibility of those in state care was further illustrated by the way in which influenza coursed through the prison system during the second and third waves, felling both inmates and staff alike. Belfast Prison witnessed the most acute effects of the virulent second wave, and by the end of October 1918, 110 of the Irish political prisoners were suffering from the virus. Among the few who were still healthy, John Fleming described the grim reality of the outbreak:

> all the cats are up now they got off very light but for the others we have some very bad ones something about eleven removed to the City Hospital and I fear it shall be a hard task to save some of their lives...One fellow from Dublin was removed today he was in the cell opposite me and it brought back old times to me when I saw the priest with him late last night the moans were terrible and the same fellows used to make tea for me and Keating while able.[26]

Although sickness was rife, no deaths occurred and by December 1918, the prison authorities were attempting (with much resistance from the inmates) to restore the old prison regulations which had been relaxed during the outbreak.

Mountjoy Prison in Dublin suffered some of the most severe effects of the third wave that followed in the New Year. The flu spread initially from a warder who went down with 'acute capillary Bronchitis with cardiac weakness' and ultimately died from cardiac failure following influenza. It then crept into the ladies' section of the jail, moving swiftly into the male quarters. Here the hospital became 'so full of patients suffering from Influenza' that an extra warder had to be drafted in to help the staff as five officers were already out sick with another three on sick leave (two due to sickness in their own families). The epidemic caused anxiety among the inmates, pervading the atmosphere of the prison and leaving the men somewhat subdued – when they were refused permission to exercise near the hospital, their response was unusually compliant, which the Governor put down to their 'fear of influenza'.[27]

That the third wave lingered for several months after its initial appearance in January 1919 was evidenced by cases such as that of the warder at Maryboro Prison, who took ill from the flu at the beginning of April 1919, and was only able to contemplate returning to duty five weeks later. Meanwhile, Warder Fenton in the Clonmel borstal went down with influenza as late as 12 May. Almost four weeks later, although Fenton was finally convalescent and taking outdoor exercise, the prison Medical Officer was still watchful of his patient, and recommended that Fenton be given his annual holidays early, highlighting doctors' own uncertainties over the infection and their consequent unwillingness to take chances with the new disease.[28]

In terms of professions, those whose jobs necessitated frequent contact with members of the public and involved living in close quarters ran an especially high risk of contracting the virus. In Dublin, for instance, it was the 'army, police, postal delivery and prison services' which proved to be one of the most vulnerable social groups, as pneumonia mortality doubled from 1917 to 1918. This reflected how 'the great power of diffusion of the infection was most marked in circumstances where persons assembled together, as in barracks, theatres, postal and telegraph offices, factories and workshops'.[29]

Priests from both Protestant and Catholic denominations were common victims of the virus, as were doctors and nurses. It was also 'prevalent amongst policemen and tramway motor men' in Dublin, with the high incidence among the latter deeply puzzling to the 'fresh air exponents', as those workers got 'so much fresh air', and presenting a contrast with the experience of influenza in Bombay, where the epidemic was mainly prevalent among those working indoors. In Navan, the second wave of the 'flue' had 'dire effects amongst the Railway staff' at the station, with practically all porters and checkers on the passenger platform stricken. These would appear to have been among the first casualties to go down to the second wave in the area, further highlighting the role of the railway network in spreading the disease.[30]

Workers whose occupations placed them nearby to one another were likely to contract the virus once it entered the place of work. For instance, 'almost the entire staff of the *Leinster Leader* was affected, necessitating production and printing of the paper in Dublin for several weeks'. 'Virtually all members of the staff of the *Kilkenny Journal* went down to it', making a reduction in size of the paper obligatory, while the printing staff of the *King's County Chronicle* was also sidelined for a time by the infection. In Dublin Corporation too, 'many hands' were 'attacked, and in various departments, business had to be carried on with limited help'. 'The staffs of large commercial concerns and public offices' in Cork were 'much affected', while in Tuam, bank officials were 'amongst those laid up'.[31]

If newspaper reports were to be believed, post office staffs were hit especially badly. In the telegraph and sorting offices of the General Post Office, sickness was so rife that all annual leave had to be suspended. The Postmaster General did his best to obtain substitutes for the postmen in rural Ireland 'who are victims of influenza', although 'in many cases temporary suspension of delivery' was simply 'unavoidable'.[32]

The high morbidity among post office workers was reflective of the social dimension of the role of postman in rural Ireland. For one Cappaghglass postal worker, this was one of the aspects of his job which he sorely missed after retirement: 'there was all that neighbourhood and meeting people'. The social nature of the postman's work elevated the chances of contracting the virus and spreading it in turn to other postal workers upon return to the post office. The high sickness levels among postal workers also hint at the strain placed by the epidemic on the communications infrastructure at the time, as written correspondence was inevitably disrupted by the sudden reduction in healthy postal employees. At Carrigaline, County Cork, for example, 'no letters were delivered owing to the local postman being confined to his room with the disease'.[33]

The Irish soldiers fighting in the Great War also felt the effects of the flu. Rudyard Kipling recorded how the disease tainted the early weeks of summer for the Second Battalion of the Irish Guards, who were by this time located at a camp in the grounds of Bavincourt Chateau: 'But for the spread of the "Spanish influenza" June was a delightful month, pleasantly balanced between digging and Divisional and Brigade sports, for they were all among their own people again.'[34]

The flu had more adverse consequences though for the First Battalion. It reached the soldiers in early June, sending twenty-two men 'down sick', and when the Duke of Connaught visited Divisional Headquarters at Bavincourt Chateau on 30 June, there 'were seventy officers and men down with the pest, out of less than 900'. By early July, when the battalion travelled to Hendecourt to relieve the 15th Highland Light Infantry, 'they were a sick people', with diaries and letters revealing that

> all Battalion Headquarters except the Commanding Officer, and all the Officers of No. 2 Company, besides officers of other companies, were down with 'Spanish fever' on going into the line. A third of the men were also sick at one time, and apparently the enemy too, for they hardly troubled to shell by day and let the night-reliefs go without attention. The only drawbacks were furious summer thunder-storms which, from time to time, flooded the trenches and woke up more fever. The front line held here by the Guards was badly knocked about and battered, and instructions ran that, in event of serious attack, it would not be contested.[35]

The men seem to have recovered though, as there is no further mention of the outbreak until after the Armistice, when the November wave of sickness obliged the troops to forsake any rest-stops on their long march home from combat: they 'dared not halt at Sorinne-la-Longue...as the place was infected with influenza ("Spanish fever"), so pushed on to Lesves, and on the 26th November to Sorée'.[36]

The Labour movement was also depleted by the epidemic. A meeting of the Irish National Trade and Labour Insurance Society revealed the huge jump in members receiving benefit due to the epidemic – 'from a normal of 120 to 600 weekly' – with the weekly rate springing 'from £56 for the week ending 30th November to £268 per week'. The secretary reported that 'every effort was made to ensure full and prompt payment' of the benefit claims arising from 'the widespread nature of the epidemic'. The flu also laid 'a heavy hand upon the provincial workers'. Among the locally prominent figures to be lost to influenza was John Mahony, secretary to the Irish Trade and General Workers' Union in Longford, 'who had not passed out of his twenties', and had given 'promise of excellent work in the movement'. The impact of the epidemic at a regional level was also illustrated at a meeting of the Executive Council of the County Wexford Trade and Labour Union in 1919, at which the council disclosed the 'severe strain' imposed by the second wave of the epidemic on its funds.[37]

Wealth provided no definite barrier to infection in 1918, with flu infiltrating the ranks of professionals, including eminent business men, politicians, solicitors, and barristers. The *Irish Catholic* proclaimed that 'the complaint attacks all sorts and conditions' of men, while a 'medical gentleman' in Dublin stated that the outbreak numbered 'its victims among poor and rich'. The Ennis Tradesmen, in their call on the government to make larger quantities of spirits available to the public, described how the disease had 'claimed so many victims amongst our people of all classes'. The Mayor of Kilkenny noted that 'rich and poor alike' had been affected by the 'awful outbreak of influenza in the city', with the *Sligo Champion* deciding that the malady was 'no respecter of persons'. Obituaries meanwhile made it clear that there were many flu deaths among the 'old and respected' families around the country, reflecting the importance of 'oldness' and respectability as social assets at this time and illuminating some of the ways in which social status was embodied and constructed in early twentieth-century Ireland.[38]

However, even if the flu was indiscriminate in terms of who it infected, the lived experience of sickness across classes was certainly very different, as the Great Flu illuminated the wide gap between wealth and privation in early twentieth-century Ireland. In Dublin, the 'wealthy persons stricken by the malady' were able to offer 'large fees' for the services of nurses, and the better-off country families could afford to pay for 'the constant care and skill of doctor and nurse'. Although doctors were in short supply during the epidemic, the middle and upper classes nonetheless had the resources to pay for 'immediate care and attention with the best medical skill', with chances of recovery maximised through 'medical skill and devoted care'.[39]

For the subsistence farmer or for those from the working classes, resting up during illness was often a luxury that couldn't be afforded. The routine obligations for the sick person continued irrespective of sickness, and the wage-earner had to stay working for as long as physically possible. Jack Pole, a vet from Tipperary, remembered that although the whole household was down with influenza, his father 'carried on anyway. The farm had to go on. Cows had to be milked.' In Ballyshannon, Donegal, cattle or horses 'had to be attended to so that people too often got out of their sick beds before they had thrown off the flu completely…no work, no money'. Persevering through illness was a necessity, with rest simply not possible for many. As one doctor in the Royal Academy of Medicine in Ireland noted, the working classes 'continued working when the disease had a firm hold of them'.[40] Class background had a significant influence on illness behaviour.

The importance of class was clearly evident in the healthcare system at this time. Hospitals were still places of refuge for the poor whose housing or family circumstances did not allow for a minimum standard of nursing care, while those with sufficient means generally opted for treatment at home. Medical care was also closely linked with the Poor Law system and unlike in England and Wales, Irish workhouses were built with an infirmary for male and female patients. Under the Irish dispensary service established in 1851, the country was divided into 723 dispensary districts, each with one or more paid Medical Officers whose first priority was supposed to be treatment of the poor. Tickets were allocated by a Poor Law guardian for each episode of sickness, and were of two kinds: black tickets entitled the holder to attendance by the doctor at the dispensary, while a red ticket – a 'scarlet runner' – denoted the necessity for attendance at home. By 1900, voluntary hospitals and county infirmaries were seeing the increased readiness of those who were able to pay the fees to seek admittance to 'pay beds' or private accommodation affiliated with the hospitals.[41]

In places in the west, socio-economic status and geographic marginality combined to result in a particularly harsh experience of the epidemic, which ultimately led the Lord Mayor of Dublin and members of Dáil Éireann to appeal for help for these areas where 'whole families' were 'attacked simultaneously'. The survivors were 'quite unable to work', in need of both 'food and fuel' as the fishing industry was 'practically at a standstill'. The Royal Irish Constabulary (RIC) in Enniskillen also reported the damage meted out by the flu in the more rural areas: 'the country districts were hit pretty hard by the influenza epidemic and there were numerous deaths'. For those who lived beyond Ballyturin in Gort Union, Galway, attendance by a priest or doctor was not always possible due to the 'shocking state' of the roads. The people had to come to meet the priest or doctor with 'a slow conveyance travelling at a snail's pace...poor patients were left unattended and probably to die before the priest or doctor could reach them'. In the northwest, the 'dreadful disease' left Arranmore 'in a bad way', with near famine conditions reportedly resulting in parts of Donegal.[42]

Areas of towns and cities which were already distinguished by their grinding poverty also suffered significantly during the flu outbreak, and around the country, local press reports continuously referred to the way in which the epidemic had increased the distress of the poor. In the south Mayo Union of Ballinrobe, the Board of Guardians were told that in the Cappaduff district, 'whole families were prostrated with influenza', and of four deaths which had recently occurred, two were considered to have been due 'to want of nursing'. That the poor were badly affected was further evidenced by the increase of over 30 per cent of deaths in the workhouses during 1918, attributed by the Local Government Board 'mainly' to the 'epidemics of influenza'. This was in stark contrast to the rise in the number of deaths across all classes in 1918, which was only 7.9 per cent above the average for the previous four years, highlighting the severity of the disease among the poor.[43]

The role of class in flu mortality was distinctly evident in Dublin, where a St Vincent de Paul member shuddered at the thought of how the poor were coping in the face of the epidemic: 'God only knows how the poor exist and what they suffer now during the present distress and illness.' Influenza married disastrously with poverty resulting in deaths from starvation in the city, with coal and milk shortages that winter further compounding the hardship.[44]

The profile of mortality in Dublin during 1918 illustrated plainly the way in which class counted when it came to health. In the year of the epidemic, it was the general service class which suffered the highest increase in deaths, as mortality rose by almost a third. Death rates decreased in accordance with rise in social class. Among artisans and petty shopkeepers, deaths increased by just over a quarter, whereas in the middle classes, the number of deaths rose by a little over 20 per cent. Within the professional and independent classes though, the total number of deaths increased by only 5 per cent. The group which included 'persons of rank and property' meanwhile was the sole class which witnessed a decline in pneumonia deaths from 1917 to 1918, falling by 10 per cent. In contrast, pneumonia deaths among the general service class soared by almost 30 per cent.[45]

The significance of the class variable is consistent with Svenn-Erik Mamelund's findings regarding the flu epidemic in Kristiania, Norway. Mamelund's research showed that rather than being class-neutral, the Great Flu inflicted distinctly higher mortality levels on the impoverished quarters of the city than on the wealthier districts. These results also correspond with studies which have found that mortality from flu and pneumonia in annual epidemics demonstrate 'some of the largest socioeconomic differences of all causes of death'. They also signal the need to differentiate clearly between morbidity and mortality in discussions of the flu's demographic trends. While sickness spread to all classes, levels of suffering differed substantially, with one's chances of survival increasing in accordance with wealth.[46]

*   *   *   *

Although few sectors of society were left completely untouched, the influenza epidemic in Ireland was far from democratic, carving out patterns across society to build a profile that differentiated victims in terms of age, gender, standards of living, and even occupation. The vulnerability of the thousands of men, women, and children who had been placed under the guardianship of the state was highlighted, as their chances of catching the disease were high once it entered one of these 'houses of confinement'. The prevalence of flu in workhouses, asylums, prisons, and hospitals in Ireland was consistent with trends abroad, as institutions and professions which brought considerable numbers of people into close contact with each other were often hard hit.[47]

The flu presented a powerful picture of social inequality when it came to sickness and death, and class differences were an unmistakable factor in mortality trends. Although the flu spread among rich and poor alike, the living conditions of the upper classes meant that those from the middle or higher social strata stood a much greater chance of recovery, particularly since, in the absence of a cure for flu, nursing was vital in determining whether the patient would recuperate. Simple things such as the care and feeding of the sick could mean the difference between life and death. As one local official observed, 'in small poisoned rooms, the chance of recovery without complications was very limited', as the flu singled out not just the young, but also the poor, as its main victims.[48]

The role of class in the epidemic is further highlighted by the fact that many flu deaths were brought about not by the disease itself, but by the inability of families to nourish and warm themselves adequately during the epidemic. In Limavady, where the 'epidemic was rife', 'many poor people when stricken with the infection were utterly unable to provide the usual necessaries of life'. At a meeting of Strabane Urban District Council, the Chairman told of how 'he knew of a house where there was not a fire, and the sick in it had not a person from morning till night to give them a drink'. During the first wave in Belfast, it was thought that there had been 'no actual deaths from the influenza epidemic', but 'about one hundred deaths from its complications chiefly due to lack of care', while later in Wicklow, a number of people were thought to have died 'for want of proper care'.[49]

Although the acute suffering of the lower classes was frequently noted, the epidemic did not stimulate reflections on the depth of poverty and its connection to health and disease, and despite the numerous expressions of pity and sympathy for the hardships of the lower classes – the 'unfortunate poor were in a very bad way owing to the epidemic'; 'the poor are dying'; 'the plight of the poor is pitiable' – there was no attempt to examine how such suffering might be prevented in the future. This contrasted with responses to the flu in South Africa and New Zealand, for instance, where the incredible surge in deaths brought by the epidemic led to the establishment of commissions of inquiry. These in turn laid the ground for far-reaching changes in the structure of public health which saw sizeable expansions in the remit, personnel, and resources of the health systems.[50]

At the same time, the flu epidemic in Ireland was notable for the absence of any scapegoating of the poor, a conventional response to epidemics in the nineteenth century, when the spread of disease was often expected to follow a clear trajectory from poor to rich. The path taken by infection had usually functioned as a 'legitimisation of the social order', with sickness traditionally seen as originating among the lower classes, and then travelling to contaminate the higher social strata.[51]

In 1918, however, there was little evidence of the 'fever nest' idea so prevalent in the previous century, or of the casting of the poor, the working classes, or vagrants, as agents of disease. In fact, a frequent observation made in 1918 was that the flu did not seem to be confined to a specific class, nor did it seem to follow any familiar paths of transmission. Although the lower classes suffered more severely, they were not blamed for the flu outbreak. A member of the Society of St Vincent de Paul described how visits to aid recipients actually had to be curtailed, owing to the fact that many members of the society had been attacked. There was a real danger that they could end up 'carrying infection into the houses of the poor', demonstrating another way in which the flu of 1918/19 unsettled popular preconceptions of epidemic disease. Not only did this disease carry away the strongest of society, but it could move freely among rich and poor, inverting established understandings and expectations of how disease moved and who it affected.[52]

CHAPTER THREE

An 'influential presence': The Social Impact of the Great Flu[1]

Deadly Epidemic – The people of this district will long remember the events of the past fortnight. Schools closed, mails undelivered, doctors ill, death a frequent visitor, more than half the entire population of the town prostrate...such was the condition of things for ten days...The very few, who up to the present have so far recovered as to be able to make their appearance in public, bear ample traces of the ravages made by the scourge. (*Wicklow People*, 16 November 1918)

With its depiction of the chaos precipitated by the second wave of the flu epidemic in Hacketstown, County Carlow, the *Wicklow People*'s report summed up the severe social effects of the Great Flu. Reflecting on the impact of the pandemic, historian Niall Johnson writes of the 'recurring images of massive disruption of normal life', which applied to both 'belligerent and neutral nations, Western and non-Western' through 1918 and early 1919. Fred van Hartesveldt describes the difficulty in even trying to estimate the scale of economic losses attributable to the pandemic: 'the disruption of services, loss of work days and closed establishments were universal. The loss of productivity arising from the more than 20,000,000 deaths just in the Western World is hard even to imagine.' Universally, the picture was of disorder, fear, and social dislocation, as the flu temporarily shut down the ordinary workings of everyday life.[2]

In the worst hit places in Ireland, the influenza epidemic had a marked effect on society: businesses closed, local government was disrupted, police fell ill, dances and Gaelic matches were cancelled, and households had to double as hospitals with entire families going down to the epidemic. In November 1918, the town of Loughrea, Galway, was 'practically in darkness' for several nights 'owing to the men in charge of the electric power station being laid up'. The Clerk of Claremorris Union had to tell the Board of Guardians that 'there was a great delay in telegraphing' due to the epidemic – 'a wire sent from here to Tuam was delayed for four hours as there was only one man in Tuam to receive the messages'.[3]

For those involved in tending the sick such as Dr Kathleen Lynn in Dublin, there was 'no news but 'flu', as hundreds lay awaiting burial in the city, while elsewhere in the country there were stories of the sick dying unattended. In various towns, people also experienced difficulty in obtaining hearses, with interments in some graveyards doubling or reaching new records. The *Freeman's Journal* observed simply: 'bhí daoine ag fáil bháis go ró-fluirseach' – people were dying too abundantly.[4] This chapter focuses on the social dimension of the influenza epidemic, exploring how the epidemic affected daily life, and illustrating the material reality of epidemic disease in early twentieth-century Ireland.

That the epidemic resulted in substantial disruption to Irish society in 1918 and 1919 is revealed by the terms in which it was subsequently depicted in government documents. Sociologist Pierre Bourdieu has described how such sources are expressive of the 'official point of view' and are set up as inherently legitimate. The writers of these reports – as representatives of the state – are cast as 'the repository of common sense', trusted to present an authoritative account of the matter in question. In the reports concerning the various institutions and public bodies in Ireland for 1918, the flu outbreak was consistently framed in earnest and expansive terms in order to capture its extensive effects on society.[5]

The report of the General Prisons Board described how the epidemic had been 'serious everywhere, entailing considerable mortality'. The annual report of the Local Government Board was also grim in its summation, noting that the near doubling of patients attended at their homes in 1918 was indicative of 'the virulence of the outbreaks of influenza that occurred in various parts of Ireland'. The Education Commissioners drew attention to the 'ravages of influenza', and the 'severe visitation of the influenza epidemic in the autumn and winter of 1918–19'. The Registrar-General used the same phrase in his report on the epidemic, referring to the 'ravages of influenza in 1918'. The most dramatic language was employed by the inspectors of the reformatory and industrial schools, who commented on 'the widespread and virulent outbreak of Influenza which raged throughout the entire world and exacted such a heavy toll among the populations of every country', inflicting a 'high rate of mortality' everywhere. That such weighty phrases featured in official discourse on the epidemic reflects the depth of its impact on Irish society over the course of 1918 and 1919.[6]

Predictably, the health sector witnessed some of the most acute effects of the flu outbreak, as the extent of infection in society placed the public health infrastructure under considerable duress. Dublin county borough witnessed the highest county influenza death rate in 1918 (406 deaths per 100,000 of the population), with police reports relating that 'deaths have been many', and medical resources 'much strained'.[7] Problems of insufficient resources and over-crowded wards were compounded by sickness among hospital workers. In October 1918 at Dublin's Meath Hospital, there was only half the usual number of nurses available to run the institution, while members of the nursing staff at Galway County Hospital were also 'among the victims to the epidemic'. Nurses who served in the community saw a sudden surge in demand for their services: in October alone, Jubilee Nurses attended 340 cases of influenza and pneumonia on the north side of the capital.[8]

In the streets of Cork city, the corporation ambulance was a frequent sight during the first wave, 'almost continually conveying influenza patients to the various hospitals', with reports that Cork District Hospital was 'unable to cope with the demands made on it'. The Fever Hospital in Meath Union became 'filled to its limit', with extra patients having to be sent to the Infirmary. The Master of Clonmel workhouse had to impart the bad news to the Board of Guardians that the infirmary was congested with 120 influenza cases, and they needed so many coffins that he had had to employ an extra carpenter. During the third wave in Galway, the influenza raged 'seriously', resulting in crowding at all the hospitals. Glenamaddy hospital accommodation was 'taxed to its limit', with problems exacerbated by a shortage of nurses which presented a 'serious difficulty'. The Downpatrick Poor Law Guardians agreed that during the epidemic 'no man had more to do than Dr Browne of Ballynahinch, or Dr Sproule, of Killyleagh', while nurses of the Downpatrick Nursing Society found themselves attending up to 200 cases a day at the height of the third wave. Particularly during the second wave, hospitals around the country were variously described as 'overcrowded', 'full to excess', 'full to overflowing', and 'packed with sufferers'. Others neared their capacity and had to turn away patients due to lack of funds.[9]

In Dublin, doctors and nurses found their 'hands full' as 'this formidable epidemic of influenza carried off 2,418', resulting in the 'highest death-rates on record since registration began'. Although the annual report of the Board of Superintendence of the Dublin Hospitals for the year 1918/19 makes no reference to the epidemic, conceding only that 'all the hospitals are greatly in debt and that a great deal of suffering goes unrelieved', the statistics in the appendix provide some sense of the dimensions of the epidemic in the city's inner city hospitals. Cork Street Hospital especially was inundated with flu and pneumonia sufferers, enduring the highest influenza mortality rate of those hospitals surveyed in the report, as here the effects of the 'horrible epidemic' eclipsed the damage exacted by all other diseases. Influenza admissions multiplied almost a hundred-fold in the year of the Great Flu, soaring from an innocuous eight cases in 1917/18 (all of whom recovered), to a staggering 768 cases in 1918/19, a period which did not even include all of the third wave. Some 173 of these men and women proved nable to overcome the infection, which meant that in Cork Street, almost one in four of those with flu died, reflecting the way in which, for many people, the hospital was a last resort.[10]

The pneumonia figures from Cork Street, however, tell a more complex story. The twelve months from April 1917 to March 1918 saw 172 people treated for the infection, with seventeen deaths, whereas in the year of the Great Flu, the hospital actually saw a decrease in pneumonia admissions, with 143 being treated for the infection, and only twenty-four deaths. Although the proportion of fatalities did rise, the marginal decrease in admissions is indicative of the endemic nature of pneumonia in Dublin's inner city.

With such pressure suddenly placed on the health system, other public health activity was inevitably sidelined. The 'progress of vacci-nation' for 1918 was interrupted by the outbreak, resulting in an 'abnormal reduction in the volume of primary vaccinations', as these dropped by almost a quarter from the previous year. The flu outbreak also highlighted the lack of contingency plans for public health emer-gencies such as epidemic disease. In Tipperary, for instance, when the local hospital became full, there was no available alternative, resulting in calls for the town hall and local schools to be opened up to accommodate patients. In Bray and Wicklow, the RIC attributed the 'large number of fatal cases' to the inadequate 'hospital care and attendance' available, and the epidemic provided the local authorities with further proof of the need for better healthcare provision in the area.[11]

Another sector of society which witnessed some of the most serious effects of the epidemic was that of education. Much to the delight of pupils – there were whoops of glee to be heard from children in Kerry and Dublin, with similar joy reported in Offaly – schools almost everywhere shut their doors, allowing for an impromptu 'healthy and useful holiday at home'. Those that failed to close saw their attendance figures plummet as parents were apt to keep their children home even before influenza reached the area. Universities also closed for a period of several weeks as a precautionary measure to stem the tide of the outbreak.[12]

The Commissioners of National Education admitted that because of the influenza outbreaks in 1918 and 1919, school attendance had been 'unduly low', dwindling to 'the lowest figure for several years'. By December 1918, an education inspector was informing one principal in Sligo that his school was 'the only one in the province of Connacht he had to visit', all others having closed due to the epidemic. Some thought this widespread closing of schools was 'encouraging malingering and irregularity', and a member of staff in St Gabriel's Boys' School, Dublin, was appalled to hear one morning 'a group of boys who should have been in school cheering for Sir Charles Cameron', the city's Superintendent Medical Officer of Health, who had recommended the closures. Over the course of the Great Flu, thousands of children around Ireland joined the 200,000 who were already 'absent from school every day of the year'.[13]

Both the closures and the virus had implications for those sitting exams at the end of the academic year. Among the schools receiving a share of the Ulster Royal School Endowment, the epidemic was considered to have been a factor in the 'slight reduction' in the percentage of passes among pupils sitting their intermediate examinations in 1919. A letter to the editor of the *Freeman's Journal* appealed for leniency for exam candidates who had suffered flu attacks, noting that 'many students have been badly hit by the epidemic'. Some had been unable to 'study for a period of three months or more', underscoring the particularly debilitating effects of this strain of influenza. University students encountered similar difficulties, some having to simply write off the year.[14]

As they watched attendance fall and their schools shut their doors, teachers worried about the implications of the epidemic for their wages. At this time, salary was dependent on pupil attendance, and concern prompted teachers' associations to contact the Chief-Secretary, appealing that the high absentee rates caused by the epidemic should not affect their wage rate. The issue eventually reached the House of Commons, with the result that attendance figures for 1917 were substituted for those during the Great Flu, setting a legislative precedent for how the effects of epidemic disease on education were to be dealt with in the future.[15]

While there was near universal agreement on the wisdom of school closures, religious services were another matter. Closing churches was dismissed as one of the more 'extreme measures' enforced in other countries at this time. The most substantial concession made by the Archbishop of Dublin to the epidemic was to advise the clergy that 'as long as the present danger of infection continues, the solemn service of the Church should not be prolonged by the chanting of the Office of the Dead'. In most communities, the main dispensation made by the Catholic Church was simply to suspend fasting and abstinence practices for a time during the epidemic. In Spain too, churches remained open throughout the epidemic, with religious ceremonies celebrated and processions continuing to take place. This was in contrast to other public health responses abroad with churches shutting completely in Philadelphia, Winnipeg, Budapest, Dunedin NZ, and Australia.[16]

Nonetheless, around the country, religious rituals and practices were subject to the disruptive arrival of epidemic influenza. In Derry and elsewhere in the North, Sunday schools were closed 'in consequence of the prevalence of the malady', and several other parishes witnessed difficulties in 'maintaining the Services' as a result of the outbreak. In Thurles, the annual retreat for the men's Holy Family Confraternity showed a 'great thinning of the ranks in the sections' which was attributed to 'the scourge'. In Virginia, County Cavan, a mission had to be postponed 'owing to the influenza scourge', and also in Keash, County Sligo, another was abandoned 'owing to the epidemic making its appearance'.[17]

Despite these interruptions, the church played a material role during the epidemic, providing leadership and authority in many communities as the disease raged. On the beleaguered Achill Island, it was Father Colleran who established a special sanitary committee to combat the epidemic. Worried at the flu's arrival in Castlebar, County Mayo, Canon Fallon wrote to the Urban Council, asking for them 'to take steps to alleviate the distress amongst the poorer classes as a result of the influenza epidemic'. In Fermoy, the priests used the morning mass to inform the people 'that there was no necessity for a scare as there was no serious case so far in the town', whereas in Bray, they advised their congregations to 'take special precautions and to follow the advice of their doctors'.[18]

Like medics all over the country, many members of the clergy too were stretched to their limits by the outbreak as they strove to help their parishioners. In the rural area of Gleann Columbcille, at the eastern tip of Donegal, Father Phil Boyle found himself with a relentlessly hectic schedule during the flu. In the morning, he would set out for

Malainn Bheag on bicycle to anoint the dying, returning at midday, 'bathed in sweat', in order to change his clothes. After having eaten a quick dinner, he would then hasten to another corner of the parish to attend more flu and pneumonia sufferers. A district councillor in Cork spoke at a meeting of how not just doctors but priests too 'were kept busily engaged the whole day long' during the flu visitation, and had 'hardly time to take their meals'. He met a priest one night 'who had had eleven sick calls' that evening alone. At a meeting of the Castlebar Board of Guardians, Mr Collins pointed out that 'since the epidemic broke out…the Castlebar priests paid as many as a dozen visits a day to the workhouse infirmary and hospital, they were often called at the dead hours of the night to attend to poor creatures and prepare them for eternity'. In Tipperary district, clergymen worked alongside doctors and nurses 'with untiring energy and zeal', while in Westport, they provided spiritual, and 'where necessary, material help and consolation to all those stricken down'.[19]

The commercial realm suffered considerably at the hands of the epidemic as widespread suspension of trade, and to a lesser extent agricultural practices, took place. In Belfast, there were stories of men 'going to business…taken ill on the way and…compelled to return home'. Some large business establishments had 'fully half of their employees laid up'. In Cork city, the numerous National Health Insurance societies were 'kept very busy' during the first wave, dealing with sick benefits to registered members who had been 'stricken down'. Commenting on the effects of the second wave on Dublin, a police inspector noted that 'general work' had been 'much and materially retarded' as a result of the outbreak. In Clonmel, 'the most severely hit' of the provincial centres, business was 'practically paralysed', and in Youghal, sickness claims on the Cork County Land and Labour Insurance Society flew up 700 per cent above normal. Small-town rural Ireland was struck badly, with most villages seeing their local shops, restaurants and hotels close down temporarily due to sickness among staff. Even in cases where businesses or factories were able to remain open, many suffered periods of high absenteeism.[20]

Reports of impeded farming work were common. In Limerick, farming operations in 1919 were considered by the RIC to be 'rather backwards', partly as a result of the epidemic, while hay bailing in Saintfield, County Down was interrupted by sickness among the farm workers. In some of the rural districts around New Ross, the threshing of the corn could not be done 'owing to the prevalence of the disease'. One of the most harrowing reports came from the *Connacht Tribune*, which vividly illustrated the consequences of the epidemic for the islanders of Lettermullen and Gorumna in west Galway:

> practically all on the islands became infected with the influenza. Poorly fed, many succumbed. No spring work has been done, and a correspondent asks who is to sow the potatoes, who is to pay the rent or to feed the people for the coming year (in these)...plague spots.

Widespread prostration on the islands meant that the principles of reciprocity – helping out neighbours and friends in times of difficulty – which underpinned rural communities, could not operate in these places which folklorists romanticised as the 'wild western coasts of Ireland'. In this way, the epidemic exposed an unforgiving reality of rural life far removed from the somewhat stylised pictures conveyed by antiquaries at this time.[21]

When it came to law and politics, the epidemic resulted largely in widespread disruption, though not long-term damage. Petty Sessions in various parts of the country were postponed due to its effects: in many cases, witnesses were unable to attend, complainants or litigants had been 'attacked by influenza', or the solicitors or police witnesses were ill. Or, as was the case at Tinahely Petty Sessions, the summons server himself was laid up, resulting in the non-appearance of any of the accused, and the necessary adjournment of all cases. In Kerry, his concern at the possibility that the court system would help diffuse the disease led the Earl of Kenmare to write to the Castle to advocate suspension of the Petty Sessions in the area: 'people come to the courts fresh from houses infected with Influenza. There is a danger of this spreading the disease – I shall be glad if you will let me know if it is possible to arrange to suspend the Petty Sessions throughout this county until the end of the year.' During the third wave, further court absences prompted the judge presiding over Wicklow Assizes to comment wryly that 'the assizes influenza was the most dangerous of all'.[22]

As disease spread, police in some counties noticed an increase in alcohol consumption, and found that the epidemic had led to an up-surge in illicit distillation in the northwest. In Leitrim, the RIC observed that general levels of drunkenness rose in February 1919 – 'owing it is supposed to the outbreak of influenza as some doctors recommend alcohol as a preventative' – with these heightened levels continuing into March and April. In flu-ravaged Inishowen, the local constabulary considered the 'scarcity of whiskey especially at the time of the influenza epidemic' to have been a factor in causing poitín-making to break out again. With wartime restrictions limiting the availability of spirits, which were widely seen as being among the best treatments for the virus, people were willing to resort to their own methods to try to stave off the flu.[23]

Although the Great Flu coincided with the period leading up to the War of Independence, the outbreak is usually omitted from revolutionary histories. Nonetheless, the epidemic exerted an influence on political life in Ireland through 1918 and 1919 in several ways, demonstrating the inextricability of social and political history at this time.

In the run up to the General Election of December 1918, the spread of influenza disturbed rallies and demonstrations, and affected turnout for election activities. A recruiting demonstration fixed for Roscommon in November 1918 'fell through, all the speakers being confined to bed', while an East Cavan Executive United Irish League convention was postponed 'owing to the number of deaths in the district and the prevailing malady in the constituency'. A meeting at Carrickmacross, County Monaghan, at which Joseph Devlin was to have spoken, was postponed 'ostensibly on account of the influenza epidemic', although the RIC Inspector General suspected that 'the real reason of the postponement' was the reluctance to apply for a permit in the belief that permits would soon be 'dispensed with in the case of election meetings'. It was feared that prevalence of the disease would result in a low election turnout in Erris, County Mayo, and election activity in parts of Down had to be curtailed due to the prevailing illness, as the outbreak diminished 'attendances everywhere'.[24]

The flu also affected those who had been interned for their involvement in the alleged 'German Plot', and for flouting Defence of the Realm Regulations. The flu coursed through the prison system in Ireland, and by December 1918, over a hundred of the internees in Belfast Jail had come 'down with "flu"'. A portion of the prison occupied by the men had to be turned into a hospital, the Governor forced to admit that there were 'a number of very sick men among these prisoners'. Dan Domigan, interned in Belfast at this time, reported that the 'influenza epidemic is chronic. There are about 170 prisoners in all, and there are 90 of them down with the disease...All the commandants are down except Blythe, and all the lieutenants and captains are down, without exception. The hospital is full, and they have made one of the wards into an hospital. It is almost full.'[25]

Winifred Carney, President of Cumann na mBan, offered the services of the Belfast branch 'at a moment's notice to attend the Irish political prisoners now suffering from influenza in Belfast Prison'. Carney was sure that the sick men, 'numbering over a hundred' at one point, were suffering neglect, 'lying in cells and receiving no attendance but the visits daily of a medical man and the attention of fellow prisoners who have themselves recovered sufficiently to enable them to minister to the wants of their hapless comrades'. Stressing the vital importance of nursing in order to prevent the 'pneumonia setting in which results so frequently in death', she was appalled at how the men were suffering from the 'mysterious malady which threatens this fatal complaint', and yet were 'without that attendance which would be humanly accorded the least one of us no matter what the circumstances'. Her appeal was dismissed with a clipped response from the Governor of the prison: 'there is really no need for such outside aid'.[26]

That the condition of the prisoners had become critical, however, was evident when the Assistant Chaplain at the prison, James Clenaghan, wrote to the prison authorities trying to impress on them the gravity of the situation and the poor conditions of the prison – he had already felt it his 'duty to administer the last Sacraments to several of the men'. Prisoners wrote home about what they felt to be the neglectful attitude of the prison authorities. From Belfast Jail, one internee told of the turnaround in authorities' attitudes as disregard eventually transformed into attentiveness: 'some men don't get any medicine on some days unless our own fellows find that he has not got it. The lads very much neglected in the early stages of the flu. There is a day and night nurse here for the last few days, they are trying to kill us with kindness now.' John Fleming was of the view that 'as to the papers saying everything was been (sic) done for the sick you can give that the lie for there is no such thing as that...all depends upon a few prisoners who were not sick to see to us...it is the old game some one must die or some harm done before a change comes'.[27]

Although there were no casualties in Belfast, in December 1918, the first death of an Irish prisoner occurred in one of the British jails. Richard Coleman, a well-liked Volunteer from Swords, County Dublin, had been among those sent to Usk Prison in Wales as part of the 'German Plot' roundups. When the flu struck the prison in late November 1918, Coleman fell ill, eventually dying from pneumonia on 7 December 1918.

In the weeks following Coleman's death, his fellow inmate Tadhg Barry described how 'sickness and death...have scattered our little group'. As Coleman's condition had worsened, it caused anger and a quiet fear to spread among his companions. One wrote of how he wished he could vent his feelings as to happenings here – suffice to say that Dick Coleman has been anointed today and…we are waiting our chance in the same atmosphere and conditions. Coleman's people have been sent for. God grant he may get over it for the poor fellow has gone through so much and is such a gentle going character that it is awful to anticipate his dying like his old Commander. Two of those down are candidates. What are spared of us are worked off our legs. Thank God, I am safe so far.[28]

Pierce McCann, a Volunteer leader in his native county of Tipperary, was among those interned in Gloucester Prison at the time. McCann himself would later contract the flu, succumbing to its effects in spring 1919, lending a moving irony to his response to Coleman's death:

> I know Dick Coleman who died in Usk. He was an excep-
> tionally nice fellow. Only twenty-seven years of age, he was
> full of life and love, being only a short time engaged when
> arrested…I know his death brought the brutality of the
> whole thing very forcibly before me.[29]

Nationalist supporters were outraged, and framed Coleman's death in the same terms of martyrdom as that of Thomas Ashe, who had died while on hunger strike in Mountjoy Jail in 1917: 'All Ireland mourns him today…He was murdered just as they murdered Thos Ashe only in a different manner.' Some felt that 'although the authorities say his death was caused by the flu, that is not taking the responsibility off them. T. Ashe was murdered and forcibly fed – poor Coleman was left to die in the want of proper treatment in those filthy cells…Oh the savages…But however, he died for a good cause, for the love of his country.' In Lincoln Prison, Éamon de Valera also assimilated Coleman's death to the national struggle, writing to his wife of how

> Poor Dick Coleman has I see gone to join his comrades on
> the other side. They are going one by one but I know no
> greater consolation they could have than that they are
> being granted – their deaths are fresh embers to the flames
> which they lovingly tended during life. Fingal has
> contributed more than its share…May God grant Ireland
> no end of sons like brave gentle Dick.[30]

At Coleman's funeral in Dublin, over 15,000 people were thought to have followed in a public procession to the graveyard.

Despite the consequent increase in public pressure to release the internees, the British government held firm. By February 1919 though, the third wave of flu had struck. In Gloucester Prison, Pierce McCann, a farmer in his late thirties, and an MP for Tipperary East since the General Election of December 1918, was among those who fell ill, eventually passing away in March 1919. His death too was cast in terms of martyrdom, with Cathal Brugha, Minister for Defence, speaking about McCann at the First Dáil on 10 April 1919:

> Before I formally move the motion, as I have mentioned the name of Pierce McCan, I would ask the Members of the Dáil to stand up as a mark of our respect to the first man of our body to die for Ireland, and of our sympathy with his relatives. We are sure that their sorrow is lightened by the fact that his death was for the cause for which he would have lived, and that his memory will ever be cherished in the hearts of the comrades who knew him, and will be honoured by succeeding generations of his countrymen with that of the other martyrs of our holy cause.

Shortly after the death of McCann, the British Government announced that the first group of 'German Plotters' would be released, with Arthur Griffith among those who escorted home McCann's remains. Back in Dublin, Harry Boland and Michael Collins acted as pallbearers, as a cortege of some 10,000 people, among them a recently escaped de Valera, followed the coffin as it moved through the city centre to Kingsbridge station to make the journey back to Tipperary.[31]

The epidemic became a tool for portraying British neglect and mistreatment, and Volunteers' recollections of that period were often inflected with discourses of blame and victimisation. Art O'Donnell, who fell ill while in Belfast Jail, told of how the first doctor to see him 'would just stand at the door and command you to put out your tongue', only to then 'hastily retreat'. When another doctor finally took his place – this time 'a Catholic and conscientious man' – O'Donnell received a 'thorough examination'. He was then 'dispatched immediately to the prison hospital', having been found to be suffering from pneumonia. James Halpin, who also had the flu while in Belfast Jail, told of a perceptible change in attitude among the staff upon seeing the sick men, their fears of the potential political repercussions in evidence: 'the staff got very civil to us then because they thought we were going to die'. British 'meanness' was described as reaching 'a new low when they held the sick prisoners in prison hospitals that were inadequately staffed while the great 'flu was raging'.[32] Although suffering flu in prison presented its own problems, what the prisoners could not realise was that hospitals everywhere were short on both staff and resources while trying to cope with an inundation of flu and pneumonia patients.

The epidemic also played a part in some of the prison escapes that took place in 1918 and 1919, hindering some and assisting others. In February 1919, some twenty internees at Usk Prison had been scheduled to break out, but with the arrival of the flu, plans had to be changed and in the end only four men were physically able to tackle the jailbreak, two of them having barely recovered from bouts of flu. On Tuesday, 21 January 1919, as the other prisoners filed back in from the yard that evening, Frank Shouldice, George Geraghty, Joe McGrath, and Barney Mellows

> hid themselves and after a short wait, sneaked across the yard to the wall. It took but a moment to fix the rope-ladder to the coping, and with Shouldice, the fittest of the four, acting as ballast, Geraghty shinned up to the top. Next went Barney Mellows, still so weak that he felt the wall was shaking under him. Then McGrath climbed. When Shouldice climbed, the ladder no longer had ballast and it swayed violently, but he swarmed up, hand over hand, like a sailor. The ladder was quickly drawn up and let down outside the wall.

The men hid the ladder under a nearby cabbage patch, which turned out to be part of the prison Governor's garden: it was a fine 'farewell present'. Making their way to the boat in Liverpool, by the next evening the four men were 'under cover in Murphy's pub', arriving safely in Dublin shortly afterwards.[33]

When the flu arrived at Mountjoy Prison in March 1919, Robert Barton, Press Secretary for Sinn Féin, was among those who had already determined to break out, but his location complicated the escape plan. His cell was on the top storey of the prison, and consequently a coil of rope was going to be necessary for the getaway. An outbreak of influenza among the prisoners in cells adjacent to his, however, gave Barton's companions 'a good excuse for demanding his removal to the ground floor', which was conceded to by the authorities. Once settled in his new cell, Barton took only three nights to saw through one of his window bars with a file smuggled in some time previously, making good his escape on the night of 16 March 1919.[34]

The flu thus had its usefulness at times and was even incorporated into the code language utilised by internees to evade censorship. The prison authorities suspected that the 'usual terms of sickness "flu" etc' stood for 'danger of arrest', with 'hospital' code for prison. The phrase 'flue conferring itself on tongues' was thought to refer to the Irish language ban.[35]

The epidemic also touched the lives of many Volunteers around the country. The RIC reports contain numerous references to Volunteer funerals occurring over the course of winter 1918 (at which point the War of Independence had not yet begun in earnest), and the inspector for Kildare was able to report with satisfaction that in November 1918 there was 'no activity noticed among the IVs (Irish Volunteers) at all, most of its members have been ill with "flue"'.[36] Members of Fianna na hÉireann, Cumann na mBan and the Gaelic League also fell victim to the virus. According to John Cowell, biographer of Brigid Thornton, a medical student and participant in both the Easter Rising and the War of Independence, the Republican Movement in fact 'lost many fine young men. Lacking resistance, they did not take the opportunity to go to bed in time, and many were dead within twenty four hours.' In Wicklow, James Sinnott, 'one of the drill instructors of the Wicklow Corps when it was established', passed away during the winter outbreak. Other Volunteers suffered long-term physical damage.[37]

Years afterwards, former Volunteers depicted the effect the epidemic had had among them. Seán Moylan thought that the flu outbreak had 'numbered among its victims...some of the most promising men in our organisation', while Patrick O'Reilly, a Volunteer in Meath, recorded that 'a couple of months prior to the General election, a flu epidemic had swept the country, which retarded the movement to a great extent'. Thomas Treacy from Kilkenny recalled that 'in October and November 1918 what was known as the Big 'Flu was raging in the country...There was practically no Volunteer work done while the epidemic lasted'. Others remembered the individual comrades lost, which often necessitated changes in the local chain of command.[38]

One theme in Volunteers' memories of the flu revolved around the military-style funerals which marked the passing of their comrades. On these occasions, the RIC usually patrolled the perimeter of cemeteries as volleys of gunfire were shot over the men's graves. It was crucially important that these losses were interpreted as soldiers' deaths, as the epidemic was made to serve a political purpose.[39]

A glance at its effects on individual Volunteers showed the way in which the Great Flu could introduce sudden, irreversible, and unwelcome change into people's lives. For George Geraghty, who had also been interned in Usk, the epidemic helped to deepen his hatred for the British government. When sent to prison, Geraghty had left his children in the care of his sister back in Roscommon. He had already been interned for several months when news reached him that she had contracted the flu. As her condition became more serious, their local parish priest back in Cummins, Roscommon urged the Castle authorities to release Geraghty on parole so that he might visit her before she succumbed to the disease. Following bureaucratic to-ings and fro-ings between the Castle and the Irish Office in London, Geraghty was eventually granted bail. He arrived home too late, however, to see his sister a final time, and returned to Usk before his ten days of parole were up. Back in prison, his bitterness spilled over in his letters home as his writing, which the prison guards usually found to be 'extremely guarded', now openly expressed his hostility and rancour: 'I was arrested without having time to bid my poor sister goodbye, and I never saw her again alive or dead. This only increases my long cherished hate for those responsible for my arrest.'[40]

Geraghty's experience showed how some of the most profound effects of the epidemic could ultimately be seen among families, as 'domestic life in many instances' became 'one of anxious care in the nursing of the sick'. The traditional caring roles were often reversed, as parents found themselves suddenly unable to look after their families. Among Jack Pole's earliest memories was how 'our entire house was stricken with flu. I was the youngest, but I must have got some sort of immunity because I was always running around with hot drinks. We had no antibiotics. Nothing to treat the symptoms.' Of a family in Mohill, County Leitrim, there was only one boy 'strong enough to creep from the bed to the fire to boil water for Bovril for other members' of the sick household. Elsewhere, no members were spared, as 'whole households' and 'whole families' were laid up.[41]

A particular feature of the epidemic was the way in which the disease felled entire households at the same time, and time and again, comments were made by journalists and local officials on how 'whole families' were ill. 'Scarcely a house' escaped in the area from Recess 'all along the villages south of Maam Turk to Maam Cross' in the west, and the Clerk in Tuam Union told the Board of Guardians that 'all families' in Milltown were 'down with the "flue"'. On the western coast, 'practically all on the islands became afflicted with the influenza'. From north Galway to Rathnew, Wicklow, 'whole families' and 'whole households' were 'laid up'. Dr O'Brien, of Kilronan on Inis Mór, wrote to the Galway

Board of Guardians to tell them that 'whole families are stricken down without even a single person to hand them a drink'. In Dundalk, there were 'many instances' in which entire families were forced to take to bed practically at the same time, while 'scarcely a family in Thurles' was thought to have escaped.[42]

Multiple fatalities within households also drew much attention in the local press, and further underlined the effect the Great Flu was having on family life. Several victims from individual families were sometimes put to rest in the same grave, 'the coffins one on top of another', as the high morbidity and mortality rates in Irish homes were consistent with the disease clustering among family members which characterised the pandemic.[43]

During the epidemic, the urge for self-preservation and to protect 'those nearest in' from the flu often made people wary of each other, and in some parts of the country, there was an observable withdrawal into the domestic sphere, as individuals shied away from the public realm and minimised social intercourse. 'Maps of loyalty' became clear, and the first responsibility was unquestionably to the home and family. Thus a rent collector in Rathdrum, County Wicklow, asked the Rathdrum Rural District Council to allow him to refrain from travelling to collect cottage rents, as he feared he might 'carry the infection home to his family'.[44]

Another illustration of the way in which the epidemic affected social relations was the changed attitude towards, and treatment of, the dead. The avoidance and prohibition of wakes in places such as Mitchelstown, Newry, and Enniscorthy pointed to the difficulties posed by the epidemic for communities, as this ritual was 'the most important secular ceremony of rural life', functioning as a crucial representation of solidarity following the rupture caused by death in the locality. The *Down Recorder* linked wakes explicitly with the spread of the disease, casting the flu dead as a source of fear and threat. The paper reported 'a remarkable death roll from influenza' in the county, which was 'consequent on the holding of all night wakes on victims':

> In the western portion of the county the custom prevails of bringing home for burial natives dying from epidemics in Scotland. The remains of influenza victims, three or four days' dead, are for a whole night 'waked' at home, the coffin lid being removed. The far-reaching character of this dangerous procedure can be realised when it is stated that no later than Sunday six coffined dead bodies from Scotland passed through Letterkenny on motor cars.[45]

There were many instances too of reluctance among both relations and neighbours to help with the burial of the flu dead, with people opting instead to leave the task to medical officers or local officials. In the outlying district of Bealadangan, Galway, 'where a death occurred in a family of four affected, the neighbours declined to assist in the interment of the remains', which had to be carried out by the local constabulary. A similar incident was also reported in nearby Rossaveal. The brother of a flu victim in Ballynashannagh, Donegal, refused to assist in the dressing and coffining of the body, 'saying that he had a family and was afraid to take the disease home'. The task eventually fell to one of the locals with assistance coming from the doctor.[46]

During the flu outbreak, domestic space became crowded as social outlets were cut off in many places through people's unwillingness or inability to attend dances, football matches, music recitals, orchestral and drama society meetings.[47] In Sligo, 'all the entertainments' appeared to 'be suffering as a result' of the influenza epidemic, which had been 'working havoc amongst the community', while reports came from Dublin of 'diminished' attendance at theatres, picture houses, and other places of amusement. Visiting the Abbey at the end of October 1918, Lady Gregory recorded in her journal that there was only 'a very small audience because of the influenza'. This was later reflected in the theatre's finance report for the year, which was 'not good owing to influenza chiefly'. The grand Commercial Ball in Tipperary was deferred, 'in homage to his majesty Fing "Flu"', and in Claremorris Union, a blind fiddler who earned a living by playing at local dances had to apply to the Board of Guardians for relief as the epidemic had resulted in the cancellation of so many social events in the area.[48]

Many cinemas also closed for a time, and billiard tournaments too were put on hold. Members of the Kiltimagh Dramatic Club had to find other places to spend their time, as rehearsals were cancelled on account of the epidemic, and in the northwest, the infection conspired with 'fewer trains, bad weather, and other adverse circumstances' to cause low attendance at the practices of the Sligo Orchestral Society. Observers in Cork noted 'a general abandonment of concerts, meetings, and other similar fixtures'. The activities of the Gaelic League ground to a halt in many areas, and it was reported that the League in Roscommon had 'suffered severely' from the flu visitation. The flu was considered by locals to have done irreparable damage to the revivalist movement in Westport, County Mayo.[49]

Other leisure practices hit by the flu included sport – 'for the GAA all over Ireland', the period from summer 1918 to summer 1919 was one of 'exceptional difficulties'. Along with the Government's ban on 'native games', the influenza epidemic was 'another serious interference'. It caused the All-Ireland football semi-final of 1918 between Tipperary and Mayo to be postponed and the hurling final between Wexford and Limerick also had to be deferred owing to the 'illness of some of the Wexford players'. Examples of disturbance at a local level included the necessary abandonment of the North Tipperary hurling championship tie between Newport and Gurtagarry owing to some members of the team being laid up with the virus, while the GAA Dublin College and Schools matches were delayed until the schools reopened.[50]

*   *   *   *

Apart from the general social disruption it caused, in many households, the epidemic constituted that pivotal moment after which nothing was the same. The story of the Great Flu's impact on Irish home-life confirms Guy Beiner's observation that 'a social history of the pandemic is, above all, a harrowing record of ubiquitous despair'. The extent of loss could be sudden and considerable – Barna graveyard saw sixteen interments in ten days, a number representing the total interred previously over a period of several years. With thirty deaths in Hacketstown in November 1918 – almost all of which were attributable to the flu, with half of these including children under the age of seven – one local reporter dubbed the month 'Black November'.[51]

Press reports and obituary notices depicted the startling extent to which multiple deaths within families took place. Just one of the many tragedies was that which befell John Ringland of Ballywoollen, Crossgar, County Down, as the second wave decimated his family, inflicting five deaths on the household. No less tragic was another instance in the west, as the flu stole three sons from one family on the Aran Islands. A father in Clontarf, having just buried his two sons, returned home to find his wife dead. Michael Dempsey, a labourer from Kilcotty, Enniscorthy, sustained four bereavements in one week, 'two daughters succumbing the same day to influenza. Returning home, the funeral party discovered that a son had died, and three days later another boy died from the same illness.' In Durrow, King's County(now Offaly), 'an entire family succumbed, consisting of father, son and daughter', and in Hacketstown, Constable O'Halloran and his wife lost four of their five children within a week. Funerals frequently took place in the absence of family members who were themselves too ill to attend.[52]

For the numerous parents who had to bury teenage and adult sons and daughters, their grief was exacerbated by its growing unexpectedness in the modern age. As historian Emmanuel Sivan has noted, 'it is rare and particularly wrenching due to a long period of attachment suddenly smashed, parenthood status suddenly ended, and the rising fear of impending ageing alone, with no children or grandchildren as solace and assurance of continuity'. For siblings too, the shock could be immense – even decades later, Bill Burgess could recall the feeling of incredulity as a teacher imparted the news that his brother had died from the flu: 'if he had hit me between the eyes he couldn't have done more'.[53]

The epidemic dissolved many marriages, as husbands were suddenly left without their wives and vice versa, and some of their stories hint at the powerful emotional legacy of the epidemic.[54] The brief entry in Kathleen Lynn's diary – 'Mrs Diarmid Coffey dead of 'Flu' – cannot convey how Diarmid remained inconsolable for years following the sudden death of his young wife, artist Cesca Trench, from influenza. A letter to the *Irish Catholic* is suggestive of the kind of disorientation and uncertainty that some experienced in the wake of their unforeseen loss, with the writer relating how he had been 'approached by a young widower of the working class who does not know what to do with his infant lately bereaved of its mother', as the epidemic added to the number of 'motherless babies' already in the city.[55]

There were economic consequences too for those families who lost their breadwinner, with many now forced to rely on charity. Thomas Foran, President of the Irish Transport Workers' Union, in an appeal for support for the Society of St Vincent de Paul, referred to how 'owing to the influenza epidemic and unemployment and various other causes, the bread-winners of many families had been taken away, leaving great numbers of children, young children, without any means of carrying on at all'. He stressed that the need for funds to help these children was 'very urgent'. The *Mayo News* reported that in Castlebar there were 'many families, particularly among the poorer classes' who had 'suffered considerably' as a result of the epidemic, 'and in a few instances they have been deprived of their bread-winners and destitution confronts them'.[56]

While many sectors of society simply experienced disruption of a temporary or medium-term nature, households which suffered deaths at the hands of the epidemic not only had to come to terms with the loss witnessed, but also to reorganise and restructure themselves in an effort to resemble the traditional family makeup. In the case of Atty Dowling's family in Carlow, the 'deadly Spanish Flu' took his mother, leaving his father and a maiden aunt to raise the children. In this way, the effects of the flu were indelibly imprinted on the generation of children who had a parent taken by the virus. In the US, both the life and writing of acclaimed author and former editor of the *New Yorker*, William Maxwell, were informed by his mother's death, which was caused by the influenza in 1918. The loss shaped the themes of his work, and drew him to older literary women as friends and mentors. For millions of families worldwide, the epidemic was the watershed moment after which 'the shine went out of everything'.[57]

In Ireland, the epidemic left many orphans behind. On Lettermullen and Gorumna, there were 'many instances' where both parents succumbed, 'leaving large helpless families'. In 'cases where Catholic orphans were left unprovided for through the death of a parent or parents', the St Vincent de Paul Conference often took charge, dispatching them off to 'suitable Catholic homes'. In Claregalway, a father and mother died, leaving 'seven little children very bad with influenza, three of whom were suffering from septic pneumonia'. The family's solitary cow had to be sold to pay for the funeral, and the children left with their grandmother who was already over 80. Similarly in Ashgrove, Tipperary, the epidemic left four little girls orphaned, who then had to be left with their grandmother who had 'no means of supporting them'.[58]

All of these stories, as well as the many others untold, serve to emphasise the degree of human tragedy the epidemic left in its wake, so frequently obscured by the statistics. They demonstrate clearly too that, as Catherine Rollet has put it, here was a 'real story retold millions of times', as the pandemic, no less than the Great War, left families and individuals all over the world having to reconcile themselves to bereavements, the effects of which were intensified by the swiftness and unexpectedness with which death came.[59]

CHAPTER FOUR

'The flu, God help us':
Fear in the Epidemic

The past fortnight has been one of all-pervading gloom in the parish of Macroom...in numerous cases the families afflicted have had to mourn the loss not only of one of their members, but of two or more. In the early portion of last week the people of the town and district were generally terror-stricken with the appalling results of the malady. At night the main thoroughfares of the town were completely deserted, the people shunned the streets and remained indoors...and every fresh crop of fatal cases added to the nervousness and dread of the people...Wakes and funerals have been sparsely attended, and while the people generally have behaved humanely, in some instances there has been an uncharitable reluctance to offer assistance when it might have saved life. (*Cork Examiner*, 18 November 1918)

The dimensions of sickness and death that distinguished the Great Flu sent ripples of fear and apprehension around the world. Withdrawal from social contact, the raising of personal and national boundaries, and the assignment of blame were common expressions of the fears witnessed by men, women, and communities as they confronted an infection that could appear suddenly and kill quickly. The accounts of those who witnessed the influenza outbreak first-hand are replete with references to the alarm and panic it provoked, and detail people's instinctive reactions to this 'new disease'.

As the flu's reach extended throughout the world, it seemed to bring with it a kind of quiet calm as a widespread impulse to shy away from interaction took hold. In Rio de Janeiro, despite the panic that developed among the inhabitants, the 'streets were almost deserted'. The report of a colonial official on the Gold Coast described the eerie stillness of a local township: 'Lorha is like a deserted village, one sees no one. I hear that some Lobis are wondering if this is the end of the world.' Similarly, in the neighbouring Navrongo District, the people were 'not stirring out of their compounds'.[1]

A world away in New Haven, Connecticut, fear made people wary of each other and kept them in their homes. John Deleno recalled: 'No one was passing around food, talking on the street. Everyone was staying inside.' The son of the town's Health Officer in Meadow, Utah, had a similar memory: 'Nobody was visiting anyone…We were all too scared.' Others felt that the 'fear tore people apart', making 'each man an enemy to his neighbour', and drained their reserves of compassion, withering 'the hearts of people'. In parts of Europe, fears that the flu was a form of plague caused panic: citizens in Stockholm rushed to increase their life insurance, while Greek officials recorded that 'so rapidly fatal were some of the cases that the people believed that the prevailing malady was plague or cholera, and at one time great alarm seized upon the inhabitants'. In Russia, the epidemic triggered 'the flight of thousands of terrified people from their homes', and from Paris came reports that people were 'confused and afraid'.[2]

In 1982, historian Theodore Zeldin observed that a history of the emotions was as yet unborn. By the end of the next decade, however, research on emotions in the past was being heralded as a 'major new approach to the study of history'. Emotions were also coming under the research spotlight in disciplines such as sociology, psychology, and anthropology, with the suggestion that the humanities were experiencing an 'emotional turn'.[3]

Bearing in mind that emotions are a 'basic ingredient of human history', and that history is 'about humanity and it is about emotions', this chapter explores the nature and levels of fear elicited by the Great Flu in Ireland. Almost half a century after the flu had abated, one folklorist would write that the outbreak aroused as much fear as any of 'the ancient pestilences'. How true was this claim? Did the epidemic set off waves of panic that unfolded across the country like the threat of cholera had done in 1832? How did Irish fears of this new flu manifest themselves? Did flu sufferers witness the same stigma and ostracisation that smallpox and typhus patients had suffered in the nineteenth century?[4]

Over the course of the Great Flu, people's fears varied in nature and expression, influencing their actions and routines and transforming their attitudes towards everyday places, objects, and expectations of conduct. In many parts of Ireland, people modified their patterns of interaction, as trust was severed and social norms and bonds disintegrated. Not just the sick, but also the corpses of the flu dead evoked fear, concern and anxiety, and places that were normally seen as safe such as schools and theatres came to represent danger and threat.

The anxious tones that accompanied references to the disease decades later showed how the Great Flu left a residual fear in Irish society, as witnesses of the outbreak continued to utter the phrase, 'the flu, God help us' upon hearing any mention of the virus. The words were another form of the 'pious ejaculations' that accompanied any mention of fever in the years following the Famine – 'God bless us and protect us' – which embodied the enduring fear of these diseases.[5]

That the flu's arrival provoked a certain amount of alarm was reflected in a comment made by Dr George Peacocke in an address to the Royal Academy of Medicine in Ireland in late 1918, as he blamed the press for stirring up widespread anxiety: 'the public have been unduly alarmed by the writings in the press, and something akin to a panic has resulted'. Darrell Figgis, Joint Secretary of Sinn Féin, wrote of a general fear that had gripped the capital: 'Dublin was full of apprehension.' The report of the Council of St Vincent de Paul offered further evidence of the trepidation and unease in the city, describing the 'scares and alarms of many kinds' which had 'disorganised all school associations' in parts of south county Dublin in 1918. Furthermore, Dublin's business-owners complained of a 'trade paralysis', as many people were reluctant or simply unable to leave their homes.[6]

At the time of the epidemic, many nationalists had been interned, some on the pretext of the 'German Plot', while others had committed drilling and other 'offences'. The letters of the internees and their friends and families suggest a certain level of fear of this new form of influenza, with concern manifest in many passages of correspondence. There was a note of urgency to Dora French's counselling of Peter Hourihane in Birmingham Prison: 'Do not get the flu...we can think and talk of nothing else here now, and the Gaels have suffered badly.' Countess Markievicz, interned in Holloway Prison, assured Jenny Wyse Power that in the jail they were 'safer from flu than outside, there is nothing in our condition now to make us ill. Large windows to cells and hot pipes. Authorities have provided us with quite decent winter clothes.' From Usk Prison in South Wales, Tadg Barry wrote that 'there are 9 altogether down with the pestilence...we will consider ourselves lucky to go home at all now'.[7]

The possibility that flu might spread to the jails kept friends and relatives in a state of watchfulness. A letter from one mother reflected the way in which the death of Richard Coleman in Usk Prison had heightened concern for the internees' health: 'We are so anxious particularly on account of the sad occurrence at Usk. Is it not dreadful a young fellow dying in an English prison so far from home and friends.' It was difficult too for the internees themselves to hear of the effects of the epidemic at home, as Liam Manahan's letter showed: 'I'm sorry to hear you got knocked up. I've heard the flu is terrible. I hope you are not the worse of it and all at your home have escaped it.' When Piaras Béaslaí, IRA Director of Propaganda, was sent to Mountjoy prison in 1919, his father protested his son's arrest to the authorities, as he had become 'rather alarmed' upon reading that 'quite a number of the warders and prisoners' were suffering from influenza. In a later letter, he advised his son to guard carefully against the disease.[8]

Many parents feared for their children's well-being during the epidemic. The prevalence of the virus made Lady Gregory loath to leave her family for a trip to Dublin: 'Not a pleasant journey as I hadn't liked leaving the children, with so much influenza about.'[9] A letter from the Chief Secretary of the Commissioners of Education to the Under-Secretary at Dublin Castle was indicative of parents' unwillingness to expose their children to possibilities of infection:

> owing to the unusually high mortality from the disease, and to the peculiar symptoms exhibited in a large number of cases, parents were, from the first, very averse to allowing their children to continue in attendance at school, fearing they would there be exposed to greater risk of infection than at home, and this was the case even before the epidemic reached the particular locality concerned.[10]

And children likewise worried about parents. In the weeks before his death, Pierce McCann had asked his friend Father Hackett not to mention the possibility of a flu outbreak in the prison to his mother:

> the Doctor thinks that it is more than likely that it will spread to the prison, in which case he says the position will be very serious, as some of the men are very run down after their long confinement, and will be bad subjects to resist influenza…Of course if you are writing to Mother don't mention this to her, as the anxiety it would cause her would be terrible, and might even lead to her own collapse.

John Fleming in Belfast Jail also did his best to assure those at home that he was alright, writing to Mary, 'I hope you got my letters of Wed – and that it was the means of keeping ye from worrying about me and the Flue. I feel alright now again I was up today after dinner until 6 o'clock so by that means I hope to be fit for the road of Freedom.'[11]

Around the country, contemporary reports contained many tales of the way in which people abandoned normal activities such as going to market or to town, and gave a wide berth to disease-ridden houses during the outbreaks. In the winter of 1918, markets 'were markets only in name' in Ballymote, Roscommon, as 'country people were nervous going near their town'. From Rathdowney, Laois, where 'scarcely a home in the town' had not been 'visited by this dread disease', came stories that inhabitants of the surrounding areas were similarly 'afraid to come into town to transact their shopping'. In Mohill Union, Leitrim, a scheduled meeting of the local guardians had to be abandoned as not enough members turned up; they were reluctant to brave the town 'fearing they might catch the "Flu"'. Parishioners in the rural districts around Thurles were upbraided by the local priest for their avoidance of the township; Father O'Donoghue lectured them on how they had 'acted very foolishly in shunning the town during the outbreak…There was really no need for such extreme cautiousness'.[12]

The most dramatic account in this vein came from Ballinasloe during the early stages of the first wave, with rumours flying that the town 'was isolated, that no trains would be allowed to stop there, and that a red flag was suspended from the station platform warning all passersby to shun the plague spot'. Although such accounts were dismissed by the local authorities as hyperbole, they nonetheless appear to have had a material effect, with one member of the Urban Council lamenting that they had done 'a terrible lot of harm to the town'.[13]

Fear of the flu was most clearly evident in a common wariness of the sick and an unwillingness to venture near influenza sufferers, as the epidemic eroded the conventions of neighbourliness and mutual support which traditionally underpinned rural life. In Oughterard, the Relieving Officer of the Union reported that 'some people who died from the influenza would not be buried by the inhabitants', while in Mitchelstown, Reverend Ahern scolded his parishioners for their behaviour, stating that some of the things he heard 'showed anything but Christian feeling', and even 'made one ashamed of being an Irishman'. Stories from Claregalway suggested that the alarm was not restricted to a particular class, with local authorities themselves apparently 'so afraid of the disease that they don't like to near it', resulting in neglect of some of the most distressing cases of infection.[14] During his visit to Achill, one of the Union officials had to coffin the remains of a young boy himself, the mother having been rendered incapable of helping with the burial, or of tending to her other

sick child by her 'condition after the death of his brother', while neighbours kept their distance from the house. This reflected popular
associations between disease and place that dated back to the nineteenth
century. Oral histories of the Famine told of how people had strongly believed that fever could lurk in the walls and thatch of houses, remaining an insidious presence in the environment of its victims.[15]

In the year of the Great Flu, fear severely limited people's willingness
to help others as self-preservation took the place of support and empathy
and the epidemic strained social bonds and fractured traditional help
networks. The Limerick Board of Guardians was told of 'one family
of seven who were stricken down, and no one would assist them'. In
Ballytrain, County Monaghan, two brothers, both farmers, 'were stricken
down at the same time', and no neighbour would enter the house to help
them. The Relieving Officer of Oldcastle Union in County Meath had
immense problems in organising the removal of a sick boy in Carrickavee,
reporting to the Board that he 'tried every motor owner but could get
none to go'; in the end he managed to secure the services of a carriage
and horses from Virginia, Cavan. In the Fever Hospital of Rathdrum
Union, the nurses were much overworked due to sickness among the
other members of staff and an inability to find substitutes as 'no attendant
would come near to work in the wards', too many being 'afraid of
the disease'. From Wexford came reports that 'in many country cab-
ins…whole families have been prostrated and the neighbours shun them,
being fearful lest they would become infected', with the poor in the town
facing a similar situation: 'everyone appears to be afraid of catching the
contagion'. With the medium of infection uncertain, contact had to be
limited, even if this meant violating conventional codes of conduct.[16]

Enduring beliefs in the ability of the dead to bring illness to the living
meant that those who died from the flu were not always accorded the
usual respect shown to the deceased. In Dungarvan, the traditional practice of 'having the remains lying in churches overnight' was suspended,
while a memory of a Volunteer from Meath was of the swift burial of flu
victims at this time: 'the victims who died in the morning were buried in
the evening'. In Cork Poor Law Union similarly, the doctor gave directions that 'persons dying in the Hospital from Influenza be buried direct
from the Workhouse Mortuary'; the threat they posed to those around
them meant that even a simple service had to be skipped, as flu victims had
to be prevented from spreading disease and death to those around them.
The *Wicklow People* reported cases in which 'so much were people in fear
of contracting the disease that after being coffined and conveyed to the
graveyard', the remains of a flu patient 'lay there for three days more

before being interred, the local clergyman being instrumental in finding those charitable enough to assist in the interment'. The epidemic meant that the customary homage paid to the dead was curbed sharply.[17]

The few who were willing to undertake jobs which brought them into close proximity with the sick sought payment commensurate with the risks they took, eliciting complaints from disgruntled officials who were reluctant to sanction the unusually high salaries requested. In Dromore West, Sligo, workhouse staff had great difficulty in finding men who were willing to drive the ambulance to transport flu patients to the hospital. In the end, the Guardians were left with little choice but to pay the high wage requests of the few who volunteered, one member of the Board pointing out to his colleagues that 'it was very few they would get to have anything to do with the cases'.[18]

The Lisnaskea Guardians faced similar problems, with wardsmen in the infirmary seeking large sums for their work during the epidemic. Their request also had to be granted; one of the Guardians reminded the Board that 'there are men who would not attend patients suffering with the "Flu" for £1 a night'. The Chairman berated one particularly reticent member, pointing out that 'it is a very serious disease you would not like to go near them for 5s a night'. In this way, the circumstances precipitated by the epidemic served to empower certain, conventionally low profile workers, affording them a bargaining power which they did not possess under normal conditions.[19]

Sometimes, it was easier to persuade people to help if protection was provided. Thus local officials in Portumna were called on by the Local Government Board to justify the appearance of bottles of liquor in their expenses list. The Relieving Officer had to explain that 'no one would go into the house to take out the remains without stimulants being provided', echoing the practice of grave-diggers in the Famine who downed spirits for protection before tending to the dead.[20]

In the course of the Great Flu, many of the sites which were part of everyday life underwent a change of meaning in public perceptions, as the ever-present danger of flu caused a shift in their emotional resonance. Places of work, play, and education were infused with threat, as schools, offices, theatres, and cinemas were transformed into places of menace and risk.

Schools were considered to be 'fertile distributors' of the flu infection. Educational institutions whose sanitary arrangements were unsatisfactory were denounced as a 'positive menace' to the public weal. In the hierarchy of sites of danger though, it was the 'theatres, picture-houses, public offices and other places where microbes most do congregate (*sic*)' that were seen as the most dangerous. Places of entertainment were widely thought to pose one of the most prominent threats to public health during the epidemic, and were branded 'even worse distributing centres for disease germs than the schools', as anti-vice concerns fused with public health issues. A member of Galway Urban Council could scarcely believe that children were permitted into the cinemas, as these were far 'worse than the schools', and a member of Wexford Corporation similarly feared that the picture houses 'constituted an even greater danger than any of the other places of assembly', an observation which met with agreement that 'they were much more dangerous than schools'. The queues seen outside theatres in Dublin during the early stages of the epidemic were both a mystery and a source of anxiety to health-conscious passers-by.[21]

When it came to imagined places of threat though, almost universal agreement prevailed on the need to avoid any place where people were prone to group together, with abundant distrust of the 'crowd' in evidence. In an era seen as distinctive for being 'the most crowded age the world has known', influenza was the quintessential 'crowd disease', with 'crowded assemblies' looming large as the 'most prolific of all sources of infection'.[22]

Anywhere bodies thronged together was thought to be unsafe. Isolation could not 'be too strongly insisted upon', and 'living the life of the recluse...as far as possible' was recommended, with advice proliferating on the wisdom of steering clear of any kind of gathering. Sites of risk included 'places of every kind where people congregated', and in Dublin, people for a time reportedly kept away from any manner of 'crowded place'. 'Close train carriages', 'congestive assemblies', concert halls, 'indoor, over-crowded meetings' were also thought best avoided. Every kind of enclosed physical space posed a threat, with Superintendent Medical Officer of Health for Dublin, Charles Cameron, warning that 'in any case of crowding', there was 'every chance of infection'. The latter found himself 'inundated with letters complaining of the crowded condition of trams at certain hours', with many members of the public evidently fearing the 'overcrowded tramcar' as 'a vehicle for propagating, developing, and spreading the microbes of the deadly influenza and other contagious epidemics'. In north Louth, fears among the locals of being cooped up inside together forced the coroner to 'take evidence in the open' at the inquest of a drowning victim. The abundance of advice about the dangers posed by public gatherings also reflected the unease over the crowd as a sociological phenomenon that had emerged in Europe in the late nineteenth century.[23]

In some parts of the country, fear of the disease escalated into mild panic. In Ballinasloe, Galway – one of the first places where the virus appeared in 1918 – the correspondent of the *Freeman's Journal* covered the initial flare-up of the disease, documenting alarm in the area. When his report was questioned by the local authorities, who felt it had been given a sensationalist slant, he was adamant that 'the malady was there, the panic was there, as both the Urban Council and its Clerk know. Happily the epidemic has practically run its course, and the large numbers affected by it have all recovered from the attack. They regard it as anything but a myth.'[24]

Some newspaper reports at the time suggested that pockets of fear were springing up in rural areas, as the flu spread 'much alarm' and had a 'terrorizing effect' on villagers in Kilkeel and parts of Galway. Meanwhile, panic amidst the Dublin middle classes allegedly precipitated mass departures from the city, as those who could afford it fled to their seaside homes. Ironically though, many who had left 'in the hope of escaping the scourge' reached their destination only to find it there before them, and were 'stricken down immediately on arrival at their holiday quarters'. The impulse to seek refuge at the sea was an expression of the popular perception in western cultures that the seaside environment had healing properties and was 'good for all sorts of lung trouble'. The 'efficacious' effects of the sun had long been propagated by doctors, some of whom saw it as 'nature's method of disinfection'.[25]

Another way in which fear was expressed in 1918/19 was through the mechanism of blame; as Joanna Bourke notes, scapegoating is in effect an externalisation of fears on to 'others'. The urge to thrust responsibility on certain groups was common during the Great Flu, often reflecting already existent tensions among social groups or classes. The powers fighting in the First World War heaped blame on one another, the Germans suggesting that the disease had been 'introduced into the battlefields of Europe by Chinese labourers brought by the British Government to France for employment behind the fighting lines', whereas Americans were happy for the outbreak to be called the 'German plague'. Neutral Spain was a convenient target, and for a time in Argentina, restaurants stopped serving Spanish dishes. The Poles dubbed it 'the Bolshevik Disease', while in Ceylon it was known as 'Bombay Fever'.[26]

Soldiers were popularly associated with the spread of flu in the western world. *Irish Opinion*, the journal of the Labour movement in Dublin, described it as the 'khaki plague', while outbreaks among the military were frequently reported by the press, with accounts casting the soldiers as carriers of disease. The *Derry Journal* floated the idea of a direct connection between the war and the epidemic, noting 'that its appearance in some parts of Ireland followed soon upon the return of soldiers discharged from the seat of war lends an air of probability to that supposition'. The *King's County Chronicle* similarly reported a locally held belief that the epidemic had been brought to the area by 'troops from the west, and there is no doubt that the first cases were among soldiers'.[27] Rather than being a figure of protection or bravery, with the spread of the flu, the soldier had become a potential danger to the community.

Fear was further manifested through the stigmatisation of flu sufferers; their exclusion from full social acceptance reflected the way in which disease could influence behaviour and impact on relationships. That flu victims in 1918 could be subjected to social exclusion was evident in cases such as that reported by the *Mayo News*, when the relative of a flu patient was refused service in a local shop; even those who had simply come into contact with the virus were feared to be carriers of the disease. In Galway, 'bad cases' of the flu were 'stated to create an atmosphere akin to that in which typhus patients are being treated, and it is suggested that the outbreak may be a combined form of typhus and influenza'. Typhus sufferers in nineteenth-century Ireland often experienced acute social exclusion – tradespeople found themselves subject to boycotts when typhus was known to have hit their family, while servants suffering from the disease were sacked and evicted outright. In some municipalities, houses with typhus cases had to signal publicly that sickness had visited their home by flying a yellow flag from the door.[28]

The degree of stigma attached to flu in 1918/19 was traceable to two main sources. Firstly, stigma often hangs over diseases which are marked by a high degree of visibility, apt to cause repulsion or distress.[29] Syphilis or plague sufferers, for instance, can be subject to high degrees of stigmatisation, exhibiting symptoms which are readily perceptible to the observer and which result in an 'exteriorized horror of rotting flesh'. In nineteenth-century outbreaks, smallpox patients also witnessed marginalisation, enduring a disease which similarly caused a graphic and shocking physical transformation. In one case reported by a doctor from the 1871/3 outbreak in Dublin,

> scarcely any part escaped except the trunk and features of the face; the hands and arms, feet and legs, nose and ears, and genital organs, all fell into a state of mortification; the patient turned absolutely black; almost all the cuticle peeled from him, and he exhaled a horrible stench; dark streams of blood exuded from several parts, and he bled from all orifices of the body.[30]

Crucially in 1918, the strain of the virus responsible for the Great Flu exerted much more visceral effects on the body than recent incarnations of the disease. In the nineteenth century, patients with 'aggravated influenza' were characteristically subject to 'prostration of strength and depression of spirits'. The Great Flu was thought, though, to signal a 'sudden and very remarkable change in the behaviour of influenza', displaying a pronounced, and even at times gruesome, symptomology.[31]

The report on the pandemic published by the British Ministry of Health shortly afterwards detailed a host of symptoms not usually associated with influenza. Patients had nosebleeds that could last for 24 hours or longer, 'with the expectoration of bright red liquid blood in amounts varying from half a teaspoonful to several ounces'. Some coughed up 'pure clotted blood', or 'muco-purulent phlegm'. Haematemesis – the vomiting of blood – was 'observed many times', and 'in a few cases it seemed almost certain that the blood was derived from the stomach itself'. Doctors examining flu patients post-mortem found that in some cases stomach muscles had ruptured, resembling 'the breast of a bird that has been shot at close quarters, the muscle being soft, pulpy and infiltrated with dark expectorated blood'. Newspapers reported many cases of people collapsing suddenly in the streets, and the 'ghastly sallow pallor of the cyanosed face, purple lips and ears' was a 'dreadful sight' to behold.[32]

As the death rate climbed, particularly during the second wave in October/November 1918, the infection also fulfilled a second condition for stigmatisation of sufferers – it was a contagious disease, putting those close to the sick in harm's way. No less than the TB patient who neglected to take 'proper precautionary measures', those with flu were feared as a danger to the community.[33]

At the time of the epidemic, doctors accused the press of fostering popular anxiety and fomenting panic, but, in truth, did media portrayals heighten popular fears of the disease? Reports certainly did employ dramatic by-lines in their depictions of the epidemic. The *Limerick Chronicle* stated that flu had been a primary or contributory cause in almost 100,000 deaths in Ireland in the last three months of 1918, a number that flagrantly exaggerated the true extent of flu mortality. The line taken by the *Connacht Tribune* would have done little to calm anxieties, with the paper expressing how this was a disease which did 'its fell work with foul swiftness'. The *Belfast Telegraph* meanwhile painted a chilling picture of the infection: 'it is a remarkable fact which puzzles the medical profession that, although most of the patients die from pneumonia, the symptoms of that disease generally do not develop until after death'.[34]

At the same time, however, the language of those who were dealing first hand with the epidemic consistently conveyed a sense of its severity, and did not differ appreciably from media rhetoric. For example, Kathleen Lynn wrote in her diary in February 1919 that the flu was 'spreading fearfully', while Charles Cameron spoke publicly of the 'horrors of the epidemic'. A letter by the Secretary of Dr Steevens' Hospital in Dublin to the Under Secretary at Dublin Castle contained an urgent request for further supplies of spirits for the hospital in order to meet the doctors' prescriptions, with the Secretary explaining that 'there is now a very severe epidemic of Influenza and Pneumonia raging'. At a meeting of Dublin Corporation, Alderman Thomas Kelly declared that 'they were all...in daily contact now with death' due to 'this terrible infection'. A member of the County Wicklow Joint Technical Instruction Committee similarly observed that 'things were in a terrible state in the town' owing to the 'terrible outbreak of influenza'.[35]

There was distinct urgency too in notes from Councillor M'Carroll (representative of Wicklow town and Rural Electoral District) to the county infirmary: 'the poor are dying the infirmary practically closed...Not a moment to be lost', and from Dr McCormack to the Rathdrum Guardians: 'Epidemic spreading alarming rate. No time write details...more help urgently required.' Dr Raverty, Medical Officer for Bray No. 1 District (where there were 600 cases reported) believed that one could 'only view with horror the consequences of the present epidemic if it continues its course unchecked for any length of time'. At a meeting of the Skibbereen Rural District Council, an official pointed out that 'there was raging amongst them at the present moment a very terrible and a very dreadful malady'. Piaras Béaslaí, writing to his parents in 1918, remarked how those who had 'escaped it altogether' had 'good reason to thank God'.[36]

Many found it hard to believe that this infection could really be influenza, and a variety of sources showed people's difficulty in deciding on a name for the disease: 'what has come to be known as the influenza epidemic'; 'that malady described as "Spanish Flu"'; 'the epidemic of influenza – if influenza it be', and 'that form of influenza – if indeed the name is correctly applicable'. A member of the Urban District Council in Wicklow was deeply uncertain as to the nature of the disease, referring to the epidemic as 'this outbreak of influenza or whatever it might be'. The Chairman of Skibbereen Rural District Council also evinced doubt as to the nature of the disease, describing it as 'the terrible malady, which for want of a better name was called influenza'. Micheál Stapleton, interned at the time in Belfast jail, thought it 'an absurd thing to call it "flu" – or "influenza", for it is in reality a fever of a very dangerous kind'.[37]

Stapleton's comment in particular is indicative of the sudden gulf between expectations and reality that opened during the Great Flu, as this new form of the virus failed to match established ideas of what influenza was: 'influenza proper is merely an acute fever with high temperature, quick pulse, and general prostration…the present outbreak goes far beyond all this'. The brutal effects of the flu in 1918/19 seemed out of all proportion to the familiar disease denoted by the term 'influenza'. If, as Robert Darnton asserts, 'to name is to know', then the problems encountered in putting a name to the disease signalled the doubts and confusion kindled by the epidemic. These in turn were instrumental in fostering fear – as sociologist J.A.M. Meerloo has pointed out, 'mystery, unexpected danger, and unknown threat' always prepare the way for collective fear.[38]

The atmosphere of uncertainty at the time was further evident in the rumours which sped around cities and towns, as stories of ghastly corpses and startling means of contagion further stoked popular fears. Addressing a rotary club dinner in Dublin, Cameron was asked his opinion as to whether 'the bodies of victims rapidly decomposed after death', and if 'it was necessary to have them buried immediately'. Another conviction at the time was that the disease rendered victims so fragile that 'removal to hospital might cause the death of the patient', and tales were passed around which warned of the particular danger of eating fish during the epidemic. The latter story was linked by the *Medical Press and Circular* to commonly held ideas of how 'the dead bodies which are popularly supposed to pave the sea-bed round our coasts' reach 'man by way of his consumption of fish'. Such rumours are suggestive of the disconcerting images and beliefs regarding the flu which were in circulation in the public domain. They also reflect the 'pursuit of meaning' which accompanied the epidemic, as people desperately sought explanations for this widespread sickness.[39]

That flu could suddenly take such an acute form, and inflict such damage, didn't make sense to either doctors or the lay populace and the disease was frequently compared to the fevers which had been among the most destructive diseases in Ireland in the nineteenth century. The Clerk of Clogheen Union used the two terms interchangeably: 'there was a terrible outbreak of the "flu" or fever in Newcastle', while a report by a Medical Officer in Cork noted that 'a few of the very bad cases developed symptoms somewhat resembling malignant typhus, cases of which were found towards the end of the epidemic in 1898'. A doctor from Cloyne described it as 'this contagious malady, which undoubtedly is a fever of the septicaemic or blood-poisoning type'. Use of the term 'fever' to describe the flu suggests the gravity of the epidemic, as the word served as an umbrella term to signify serious disease at this time.[40]

That it was the reality rather than its depiction which contributed to public fears is further evidenced by the way in which the flu of 1918/19 possessed a number of the traits of disease which Margaret Humphreys has described as the 'most prone to generate terror' in societies. Among these she includes age, suddenness, unfamiliarity, preventability, and the symptoms and physicality of the malady in question.[41]

In 1918/19, the youth of the flu's victims caused much incredulity, as the traditional demography of influenza was inverted: instead of striking at the most vulnerable in society, the Great Flu hit hardest at the most robust – the young adult population. James Crowley, a prisoner sent to Belfast Jail under the Defence of the Realm Act, was bewildered by the ability of this flu to strike down those who would usually have offered the most resistance to the disease: 'Truly one wonders at the powerfully strong men going down and out so quickly.' Sinn Féin politicians Arthur Griffith and W.T. Cosgrave were taken aback at the death of Pierce McCann, a founding member of the party, who was considered to have been one of the physically strongest of the internees. McCann was just 36 years old at the time of his death, and Griffith was shocked at the news: he had not 'the slightest idea that he (McCann) would succumb, as he was…a tremendously powerful man'. Cosgrave spoke of how in Gloucester Prison, de Valera and McCann had been 'in a class by themselves' in terms of physical fitness, standing out 'prominently as being remarkable for their fine physique'. He too was stunned at the news of McCann's death: 'I asked "What, Mr M'Cann? Surely it is not possible such a strong man is dead."'[42]

The 'dramatic suddenness' with which the flu could kill also drew the notice of both the medical and lay communities – in Dublin, the majority of flu cases among the Dublin Metropolitan Police were classed as 'sudden and severe', for instance. Unfamiliarity, meanwhile, was demonstrated by the terms in which the disease was referred to in public discourse: the 'mystery disease', the 'strange influenza disease'. It also proved impossible to prevent the disease, or even to arrest its progress. The influenza virus itself was not isolated until 1933, and though some physicians in 1918 reported success with vaccines, there was much disagreement within the medical community as to the preventability of the 'influenza scourge'.[43]

Finally, the flu of 1918 brought with it a host of unsettling symptoms that surpassed the 'pitiful respiratory distress' which Humphreys describes as pertaining to the disease. 'Insomnia, raving, tremor, dry black tongue, with sores on the lips and teeth' were indicative of the 'system-poisoning' caused by the infection. Blood bubbled in froth from the nose and mouth of some victims, as haemorrhages were frequently observed. One Volunteer from Kerry wrote that the victims show 'all sorts of symptoms and do many foolish things'. Delirium, in fact, was frequent, with vomiting 'a distressing and sometimes alarming symptom in many cases'. Michael Costello, another Defence of the Realm Act (DORA) prisoner in Belfast jail, painted a harrowing picture, expressing his belief that it was

> a dangerous form of sickness, nose-bleeding, terrible sweats, weakness, pains in the chest, horrible coughs getting better and then getting worse. My God you would pity the men in the cells beads of sweat standing out upon their faces...I found Murphy lying on the floor one morning at 7 am and I found Pryal bleeding...the latter is the worst case of the lot outside now.[44]

The fact was that seemingly sensational and exaggerated reports – 'many of the patients developed terrible symptoms and died, their bodies becoming black and unrecognisable' – were often part of the 'terrifying realities' of this disease. The 'tendency to haemorrhages' was noted 'by all observers' as being 'a common complication', with some patients also bleeding from the mouth and gums and coughing up a frothy bloody liquid. Doctors described cases in which 'the bed-clothes, wall, and floor have become blood-spattered during a coughing paroxysm' with 'as much as 10 ounces of bright red blood...coughed up in a few minutes'.[45] In many cases too, 'discolouration took place', and for doctors, this 'heliotrope cyanosis' was the most ominous symptom, constituting 'the surest basis on which to pick out those cases in a ward that are likely to be dead in a day or two from those who, unless they themselves develop the same hue later on, will most probably recover'. The markedly increased range and intensity of influenza symptoms formed a sharp contrast with TB, which claimed thousands of victims each year but was 'so undramatic in its methods that it excites no alarm'.[46]

*   *   *   *

In Ireland, fear of the 1918 influenza varied in shape and intensity, ranging from concern and anxiety to alarm and panic, interceded by actions which included withdrawal, flight, and blame. Objects of fear included not just the body itself, but also specific places and social practices – markets and wakes, etc – owing to the omnipresence of the threat of flu. It would seem that the role of the media, though possibly contributory, was not necessarily the primary agent in stirring up anxieties, as Dr George Peacocke had griped. The realities of the disease were in many cases equal to any sensationalism engaged in by the press, as the disturbing nature of this new strain of the disease unsettled expectations of what it meant to be sick with influenza. Although the response to the disease was at times less than noble, the many expressions of fear in 1918/19 were rational and reasonable in light of the realities, effects, and understandings of the flu at the time.

How did the Great Flu compare to previous experiences of disease in terms of the fear evoked? Was the response to the 1918 flu comparable to the terror aroused by epidemics in earlier centuries as Kevin Danaher claimed? A notable feature in 1918/19 was that despite the ubiquity of the disease, there were no large-scale instances of panic or hysteria; in comparison to epidemics in the nineteenth century, the flu outbreak arguably generated a more muted emotional response.[47]

In the previous century, the arrival of cholera could spark entire villages to desert their homes in terror of the disease. When it descended on Inishbofin in the 1830s, people were 'struck with such panic, that they all, men, women and children, abandoned their houses and fled to the mountains'. In 1918 though, there were no comparable instances of widespread abandonment of homes or towns, nor was there a wave of frenzied preventive action, such as that which swept over the country in anticipation of the cholera outbreak of 1832. The Great Flu also lacked any instances of the violence and tumult which accompanied the smallpox epidemic of 1875 at Athenry when the townsfolk attacked and burned the workhouse van used to transport sufferers.[48] Although a certain amount of stigma was attached to the disease, and although it did test social bonds and upset social conventions, the flu of 1918/19 did not evoke a response that was equal in drama or intensity to earlier reactions to epidemic disease.[49]

This is perhaps emblematic of the changes in how disease was being interpreted by 1918. In the nineteenth century, Registrar-General William Wilde recounted the popular beliefs that paranormal forces were instrumental in cases of unexpected and mysterious deaths: 'when death is very sudden and no apparent cause can be assigned for it, nothing will persuade the lower orders...that the person has not been spirited away by supernatural agency'. 'Wasting diseases' in particular were often attributed to fairies or the 'Good People' in the past, and according to Wilde, it was 'this affection' which gave rise to 'the popular ideas respecting the changeling'. The idea that supernatural powers were responsible for sickness heightened popular fears of disease; as Zeldin has noted, 'natural disasters were made much more dreadful by being attributed to supernatural forces'. By 1918 though, these earlier objects of fear had begun to take on the more material form of microbes and germs. This evolution in popular understandings of sickness and the body could help explain the milder response in 1918 in comparison with earlier episodes of disease.[50]

Despite these changes in how sickness and the diseased body were understood, there were also distinct elements of continuity in popular belief systems. This was particularly manifest in the accepted idea that fear and disease were closely linked: fear did not just influence social response to disease, but people believed that it had an important role in the body's response to infection. The *Connacht Tribune* warned its readers that 'certain states of mind encourage disease', and consequently urged people to 'keep away from panic', and to 'maintain a cheery and optimistic outlook'. Interned Volunteer Micheál Stapleton, writing to his sister from his cell in Belfast prison, similarly believed that 'as far as possible, we all should guard against panic, for that, in itself, leaves us liable to fall victim. We should remain calm, cool and confident.' Medical advice also asserted the importance of emotional calm, urging 'the repression of all anxiety and fear of infection', the value of which could 'not be too strongly emphasised' as defiance of fear was fundamental as both a 'preventive and resistive' factor.[51]

Such beliefs drew on a long-standing connection between emotions, imagination, and the body in western medical knowledge. In eighteenth-century Europe, for instance, fear was thought to trigger smallpox and influence a patient's chances of surviving the infection, and this belief held currency among physicians and the public alike. Doctors warned families to cover mirrors in the house, as the sufferer's horror at the sight of his or her own reflection could aggravate the condition. When cholera struck New York in the nineteenth century, official advice warned people sternly that 'exciting causes should not be produced by anxiety or fear. The exercise of equanimity would ward off the evil and render the affliction mild.'[52]

Faith in the power of the imagination and emotions over the body had also been manifest in nineteenth-century Ireland, with doctors asserting that 'fear and the depressing passions' could have a 'powerful and obvious influence' on the body. During an outbreak of cholera, the College of Physicians recommended placing cholera sufferers in separate wards from other patients, in order to prevent the latter from being 'injuriously affected by terror' at the 'alarming appearance' of the symptoms of the disease; the frightening sight of cholera victims was thought to be enough to render people liable to an attack of the infection. Even in the late nineteenth century, assertions continued to be confidently made that 'the infection of fright' was 'itself a disease'.[53]

Similar beliefs were also in evidence among the lay population in this period. During a cholera outbreak in Sligo in 1832, a man 'placarded his house and the town thus, "fear is cholera, and cholera is fear"', preaching his doctrine in the streets and 'warning the people against entertaining fear'; fear and cholera were inextricable. Even during the epidemic of Russian flu towards the end of the century, the Local Government Board itself attempted to impress on people the link between mind and body: 'the liability to contract influenza and the danger of an attack are increased by depressing conditions...whether mental or physical'. In 1918, fear was significant not just in terms of the social response to the flu, but also for the role it was accorded in the mechanisms of infection, demonstrating how the earlier acceptance of a close connection between body and mind endured into the twentieth century.[54]

Despite the evolution in understandings of disease which was taking place at this time, the flu outbreak was marked by strong echoes of the nineteenth century. Although not as dramatic as popular reactions to outbreaks in the past, there were distinct elements of continuity in terms of how people reacted to epidemic disease. This was especially evident in the temporary disintegration of social norms, the avoidance of flu-stricken houses, the disruption of burial rituals, and the difficulty in getting people to care for the sick and to bury the dead. The complaints of local officials in 1918 mirrored the difficulties witnessed during the Famine when 'large wages' would not 'induce men to bury' their bodies. The common wariness of influenza victims illustrated the spiritual challenge posed by the Great Flu: the way in which wakes were avoided in some parts of rural Ireland meant that the deceased was not shown the traditional respect accorded to the departed, a violation of belief systems and a show of disrespect to the family. Fears of the potential dangers contained in the flu corpse moreover made for many hurried burials and prevented the ceremonies taking place which traditionally preceded burial of the deceased. Protecting the living during the Great Flu often meant neglecting the dead.[55]

> The medical doctors of Sligo – as in many other parts of Ireland – had to face one of the greatest epidemics that had come to the country in the past half century. During that crisis they were working night and day...As a result of their continuous administration to the poor, many lives were saved. In fact half the country would have been dead only for the efforts of their doctors. (*Irish Supplement to the Medical Press and Circular*, 12 November 1919, p.3)

CHAPTER FIVE

'That terrible time': Medical Response to the Outbreak[1]

In November 1919, a year after the peak of the Great Flu, the Sligo Board of Guardians listened to the above speech from Alderman Lynch as he called for an immediate increase in the salaries of the Union's Medical Officers. The conditions he described were witnessed by doctors and nurses all over the country during the outbreak as they laboured through non-stop days of house-calls, and worked long shifts in hospitals that were teeming with coughing, fevered, and bleeding patients. They found themselves facing a disease that they thought they knew well – influenza – but that now seemed to resemble cholera, typhoid, dysentery, and even forms of plague.

The inability of medical researchers to pinpoint the cause of influenza was unsettling for a profession whose status and assurance had grown considerably in the half century preceding the pandemic. Progress in bacteriology had allowed for the identification of the causative organisms of a slew of diseases, including typhoid, diphtheria, pneumonia, leprosy, plague, and syphilis. And perhaps more importantly, bacteriology offered the prospect of cures for these infections; the discovery of vaccines for anthrax (1879), rabies (1885), and the development of antitoxin therapy for diphtheria (1890) and tetanus (1914) raised the hope that all diseases might eventually be overcome.

One of the acute ironies of the Great Flu was that it coincided with this period which had seemed to be the 'golden age' of medicine. Alongside the rush of advances in medical theory, the prestige of the medical profession across the western world had risen substantially. The pandemic punctured the rising confidence of both physicians and researchers as they found themselves having to completely revise their thinking on the infection they had known as flu, admitting that 'the recent epidemic of influenza has altered our conception of this disease'.

The outbreak provided an untimely interruption to the narrative of progress that had characterised medicine and public health up to 1918.[2]

In Ireland, the story of the medical response to the flu epidemic resonated audibly with the devastating experience of the Famine years, that 'late disastrous epidemic'. The acute pressure on health resources, people dying from 'want of medical attendance', full and overcrowded hospitals and workhouses, as well as inadequate understanding of the disease(s) in question, all served as features common to both events. The burden of care and responsibility shouldered by the medical sector in 1918/19 forms the main focus of this chapter, as it looks at the ways in which the medical profession reacted to 'the most virulent outbreak of influenza then on record'.[3]

In many ways, the medical experience of the Great Flu was much more extreme than that of the rest of society, the effects of the three waves of sickness amplified, as doctors and nurses met with case after case of this baffling infection, and saw up close the kind of brutal effects it could have, particularly 'among the sick poor'. The problems posed by the dimensions of sickness were compounded by the kinds of symptoms which patients presented, as 'haemorrhages and pneumonia and other inflammatory and alarming complications' added 'grave terrors to a form of influenza incredibly serious already'. In many of the most critical cases, bodies streamed blood, their extremities sometimes changing colour, displaying a confusing array of physical signs which reminded physicians of typhus, diphtheria, meningitis, and pneumonic plague. The results constituted a period which doctors and nurses found difficult to forget.[4]

The purpose of the following pages is to impart a sense of the gruelling physical and emotional conditions of the Great Flu, as doctors and nurses did their best to help the great numbers of families and individuals stricken by the infection. While the word 'failure' has been mentioned in reference to how their British counterparts coped with the epidemic, the Irish case would suggest that such an assessment may underestimate both the demands placed on, as well as the efforts made by, health professionals to cope with what was a 'gigantic natural disaster'.[5]

'ON FOOT NIGHT AND DAY' AND 'OVERPOWERED WITH WORK'[6]

In November 1918, at the height of the epidemic, a doctor in Croydon, in the southeast of England, was pulled over by a sergeant of the Special Constabulary for having only one light on his vehicle. The doctor, rather than objecting to the inconvenience, replied wearily that 'he hoped he would be sent to prison, because it would give him a rest'. This anecdote, related in the pages of one of the most widely read medical journals in circulation in Britain and Ireland at this time, encapsulates the immense strain placed on doctors and nurses by the flu outbreak.[7]

Analyses of the pandemic consistently refer to the immense and unanticipated demands it placed on the health sector. Geoffrey Rice and Edwina Palmer describe it as a 'major public health crisis that was shared simultaneously by nearly every country in the world'. In Australia, it simply 'swamped the capacity of the hospital and medical system', while in Britain, 'the logistics of disease and death on such a scale overwhelmed the medical profession' with services almost 'crippled by demand and by the incapacity of personnel through disease'. In her study of the epidemic in the US, Nancy Bristow deemed the flu outbreak to have been 'a medical catastrophe unrivalled in its time'. Such descriptions could equally be used in reference to the Irish experience of the Great Flu, as around the country, hospitals and workhouse infirmaries heaved with the sudden influx of flu sufferers. 'Medical men' found themselves 'run off their feet', with the result that people often had to wait several days before being seen by a doctor. Physicians and nurses alike worked through sleepless nights, disease, and exhaustion in order to tend to the sick.[8]

For those whose families experienced the epidemic, the incredible demand for medical attendance formed part of the memory of the Great Flu. In Longford, Brigid Lyons Thornton fell victim to the virus and recalled that

> at one stage, my three cousins and myself were hit at the same time. Then Aunt Frank's staff went ill. Finally, she had to give in and close the business. This was the general picture everywhere, and the doctors were so busy it took two days before they could visit you.[9]

Jeremiah Murphy, growing up in Kerry at the time, similarly recalled that his sick father had to wait several days before he 'was able to get a much overworked doctor to see him'. Memories of Cumann na mBan members also point to the pressure endured by the health professions: 'the bad 'Flu raged so violently that nurses and doctors were scarce', 'it became impossible to get nurses or admission to hospital', 'doctors and nurses were taxed to capacity'.[10]

In Dublin, the Mater Hospital shuffled ward allocations in order to accommodate the increased numbers of flu patients arriving, and apart from one gynaecological, one male and one female surgical ward which had to be 'kept open for emergencies', all the rest 'became temporarily medical or, if you like, fever wards'. A junior doctor recalled being 'literally run off my feet at this time' and the 'great difficulty of getting a doctor if one was ill', due 'in the first place to the fact that so many folk were seriously ill simultaneously, and secondly, because many doctors were down with the disease themselves'.[11]

In Waterford, the shortage of medical services was such that Dr Vincent White, 'the sole dispensary doctor in Waterford City at the time', was on his feet 'night and day…answering what seemed to be an endless line of calls'. In this stronghold of the Irish Parliamentary Party, White would later become a parliamentary candidate for the Sinn Féin party, but his political allegiance came to matter little during the epidemic, as he treated victims of the flu around the city's backstreets:

> Hushed now were the political jibes which had been flung at me as I went into houses in lanes and alley-ways seeking to bring succour to the many victims of that terrible malady which was raging throughout Europe and was leaving behind it a grim tale of many deaths.

White even found himself called to attend the wives of ex-soldiers, who quickly reverted to open expressions of contempt for his politics in the run-up to the General Election: '…I was often amused to see the wives of ex-soldiers, to whom I had ministered during the 'flu epidemic, with their lungs now so fully restored that they were able to yell after me as I passed: "To hell with White! Up Redmond every time."'[12]

The epidemic heaped immense caseloads on doctors all over Ireland. In Wicklow, the Killeen Medical Officer sent an urgent wire to the Relieving Officer of the Dunshaughlin Board of Guardians stating simply that he was 'overwhelmed with work and asking for assistance'. The Relieving Officer of Claremorris Union reported to the Board of Guardians that Dr Smith of Ballyhaunis had had to attend 800 cases in his district. The Clones Guardians heard that Dr Fitzgerald of New-townbutler 'had to get the help of Dr Timoney for the past three weeks, being overpowered with work'. In Dripsey District, County Cork, Dr Ryan tried to give the same guardians a sense of what he was up against – the widespread sickness in the community, and the worrying gravity of some of his cases – as he faced a caseload which he feared would quickly become too demanding for a single physician:

I regret to report to you that a serious epidemic of influenza (of a virulent type) has broken out in my district within the past few days, I had this day to ask Mr Walsh, Relieving Officer, to get a trained nurse to carry out my recommendations, as in some cases all the members of the family are laid up...several of the cases are very bad and have to be seen by me twice a day; ...should the cases continue increasing as at present, I am afraid I will have to requisition the services of another doctor.[13]

In the year of the epidemic, the number of cases in which dispensary relief was afforded to patients in their homes increased by over 100,000 – going from 137,658 up to 238,386 – a figure which may not even reflect the full extent of the outbreak, due to the tendency of under-registration among dispensary doctors; amid the chaos of the flu outbreak, there was little time for paperwork. This sizeable increase in the number of 'scarlet runners' (dispensary tickets given to the most serious cases which entitled them to receive medical treatment at home) issued indicates that substantial numbers of the worst flu cases received treatment at home, with families reluctant or simply unable to move them to the hospital.[14]

In the months before the epidemic, Dr Kathleen Lynn, a prominent member of Sinn Féin, had been on the run from the authorities, having evaded arrest in the wake of the 'German Plot' sweep. As the flu outbreak worsened and the need for doctors became evident, she was granted permission to return home and to practise medicine on condition that she would not leave Dublin city. Her diary also conveys the pressures the Great Flu placed on physicians. In late October, she wrote simply, 'Epidemics (Pneu Plague) fearful'. The following weeks were dominated by work, and Lynn had little respite until she herself became ill:

Hard work all day with 'Flu...Busy all day with Plague pts...Patients increasing...Another day of battle with disease...busy day as usual, Poor Feerey dead...busy day in Hosp...Many pts here yet...In bed with 'Flu...nearly fainted when sat up in bed, everyone very kind.

The ubiquity of the third wave was conveyed by two words: 'flu everywhere'.[15]

The island counties off the western shorelines offered an example of what were among the most trying experiences of the Great Flu for

doctors. On the Aran Islands, the disease was 'universal', with consequently 'no neighbour to lend a hand', and the district 'much handicapped
for lack of a nurse or attendant'. There were considerable problems in
securing a second doctor, one of the Galway Guardians commenting
that 'there's many a doctor and nurse wouldn't go there for a hundred
guineas'. Further north up the coast, the island of Arranmore, Donegal,
could not get even one doctor to come, despite being 'in a bad way
with Influenza'. According to a frantic note sent by a general merchant
on the island,

> if all in the island died they could not get a Doctor for any
> money. The B. Port Doctor is down with the 'Flu' and then
> the Dungloe Doctors won't come, saying they have enough
> to do...There is a fine young man for death today, no doctor
> to be had and no stimulants of any kind on the island.[16]

The bleakness of the medical experience of the epidemic, especially
that of Poor Law medical officers, was laid fully bare in a strongly
worded letter by Dr T. Hennessy, Medical Secretary to the Irish Office
of the British Medical Association, which appeared in several of the
major newspapers. Hennessy's letter forcefully criticised the inadequacy
of the Poor Law medical salaries, and the epidemic was held up as
further proof of the need for salary reform, a campaign for which was
already underway before the Great Flu hit. Hennessy had received
letters from doctors in 'every part of Ireland' who were '"run off" their
feet'. They told him how they were 'trying to do their work while
suffering themselves', and 'that their miserable salaries absolutely pre-
clude them from providing the necessary locomotive means to cope
with the ravages of the disease and that as a result of all three causes,
people are dying from want of medical assistance'.[17]

Due to the continual demand for their attention, physicians found
themselves unable to devote as much time and care to each
patient as they would have liked. They were uneasy over the 'hurried
visits' and 'the hasty diagnoses' necessitated by the outbreak, reflecting
the standards required by the increased professionalisation of medicine
in the nineteenth century. The epidemic was simply 'a rush for most of
those who have to deal with the victims', and as Dr McCormack
admitted to the Wicklow Guardians, 'I cannot pretend that the patients
received that attention all of us would wish, but the best help possible
was given under the abnormal circumstances'.[18]

Exposed to disease on a daily basis during the outbreak, it was
common for doctors to contract the flu, and a minority succumbed to

the infection. There are no definitive mortality statistics for health professionals available, but references to the sickness and death of doctors and nurses from the epidemic appear frequently in workhouse minutes, local newspapers, and medical journals, providing some impression of the extent to which their physical health was affected by the flu outbreak. With so many medical men sick, some districts had to go without any physician for a period as 'nine out of every ten rural districts' were 'one-doctor areas' at this time.[19]

Even for those who managed to escape the infection, the epidemic could still result in a breakdown in health, as the 'heavy duties', long hours, and 'arduous' work left many physically drained and in need themselves of recovery. Dr McCormack, who had attended the badly stricken Wicklow Dispensary District, applied for a month's leave of absence from 1 December 1918, pointing out 'that the strain and over-work experienced there at present and for some time past had been most severe, and he trusted it would be possible to provide for the leave'. Similarly Dr Moore, who manned the Strangford and Killough districts in Downpatrick, imparted to the Board of Guardians that the epidemic 'had entailed an unprecedented number of calls, night and day' for a period of six weeks, with the 'result that he was quite exhausted'. The Medical Officer from Cork No. 3 Urban District also requested annual holiday leave as 'the recent Influenza was a great strain', and he would be 'glad to get away for a rest'.[20]

The stresses and strains experienced by doctors during the epidemic were also witnessed by the nurses, and the shortage of nursing staff constituted a universal problem throughout the epidemic. Local authorities and doctors referred repeatedly to the difficulties encountered in attempting to find nurses during the flu. The Medical Officer of Sligo Prison, in a report to the prison authorities, recorded that it was 'impossible to secure nurses here'. The Navan Guardians 'applied to a Dublin Nursing Home for temporary help but could get none', while in Trim, the 'dearth of nurses was keenly felt'. In Cork, 'so general' was the 'call for nurses that the infirmaries and kindred institutions could not possibly supply all who were required as their staffs...[were]) taxed to the utmost to attend to the cases brought to the institutions'. The seriousness of the problem was magnified by the fact that in the absence of a cure for flu, nursing was one of the few measures that could make a material difference to patients.[21]

The shortage of nurses meant that institutions and communities were often left to rely on the services of medical students and volunteers from the community – particularly nuns – to care for flu patients, while the available nurses endured overwork, with many caring for patients while ill themselves. The full extent of their contribution is difficult to ascertain as their voices are not as audible in the source material – it is rather the local doctor's input that is quoted at the meetings of local authorities and workhouse officials.

One effect of the Great Flu was to illuminate the everyday realities of healthcare provision in Ireland at this time. In addition to being a physically demanding experience, the efforts of doctors to respond to the epidemic were often frustrated by a range of factors. Some of the most common problems included transportation difficulties and navigating the local terrain in order to get to the homes of patients which could often be located in 'rather inaccessible places'.[22]

Other fundamental problems during the outbreak included the difficulty of filling prescriptions due to shortages of medicines and spirits. 'The scarcity of the stimulants for medical treatment' was 'greatly felt', with doctors also paying for vaccines out of their own pocket at times. A further problem was that of how to ensure that their patients had sufficient nutrition. Dr Garland, Medical Officer for Dunganstown Dispensary District, chided that 'one of the greatest scandals' during the epidemic had been 'the difficulty in obtaining milk in places'. A traditional part of the rural diet in Ireland, milk was also viewed by both the lay and medical communities as therapeutically beneficial and constituted an integral ingredient in hospital diets.[23]

One of the biggest problems posed by the flu for physicians was establishing the nature of the threat they faced in 1918/19. Doctors and researchers witnessed great difficulty in isolating the pathogen responsible for the outbreak, prompting doubt and confusion as to whether the disease was in fact flu at all. At a meeting of the Royal Academy of Medicine in Ireland in December 1918, Dr Boxwell 'said that from the beginning he had regarded the more severe types as cases of profound septic intoxication'. Medical journals reverberated with this uncertainty, as doctors admitted that 'there is no precise evidence we are dealing with influenza'. Those at a conference of the British War Office in October 1918 heard how most physicians were of the 'opinion that the existence of some as yet undiscovered virus must be possible', and all over the world, medics 'were assailed by doubts and queries' to the point that many were reluctant to even write the word 'influenza'.[24]

Although Irish doctors broadly agreed that what they were facing was a widespread outbreak of flu, physicians nonetheless found themselves on unstable theoretical ground during the epidemic, due especially to the difficulties this new strain of flu posed to clinical diagnosis. A milder pandemic of influenza had taken place in the early 1890s, hinting at the potential virulence of the infection, but in the decades that followed, flu continued to be viewed as a relatively minor ailment. In the years leading up to the Great Flu, doctors still classed 'influenza proper' as 'merely an acute fever with high temperature, quick pulse, and general prostration', describing how the infection 'was unquestionably recognisable as a tax upon personal comfort and efficiency but hardly admissible as a cause of death'.[25]

The flu of 1918/19, however, inflicted an often perplexing symptomology which gave rise to 'a whole series of possible interpretations of the illness'. Doctors not only encountered patients with breathing difficulties, fever, sudden weakness – considered to be the usual characteristics of influenza – but who were bleeding from all over their bodies. A doctor from Arklow, in a letter to *The Lancet*, referred to the epistaxis (bleeding from the nose) and haemoptysis (the coughing up of blood from the respiratory tract) which had been 'so common in the present epidemic of influenza'. In some cases, a feature of the disease was 'heavy bleeding from the ears'.[26]

The peculiar smells emitted by flu patients also attracted attention. Dr John Moore, Physician to the Meath Hospital and County Dublin Infirmary, remarked on the 'heavy or even foetid' breath exhaled by flu sufferers. Cases of pneumonia meanwhile produced sputum containing 'foul pus'. In accounts of the epidemic in America, Dr John Walters noted that many physicians mentioned a 'peculiar stench… instantly recognised as influenzal'. This curious smell puzzled medics, defying 'rational explanation'. Some considered war to offer the only comparable odour, drawing a parallel with the smells emanating from 'rotting corpses on the battlefield'. No one could locate its origins – 'the sputum or breath were not its cause, nor was flatus'. Doctors writing in *The Lancet* were baffled by this 'real stench' which came not from the mouth or the sputum, but rather 'from the patient's living body generally'.[27]

Physicians were also taken aback at the severe levels of internal damage administered by this strain of flu. Post-mortems revealed hearts which were in a 'flabby condition', sometimes dilated. Lungs had been subjected to 'widespread mischief', and were found congested and haemorrhaged, leaking 'purulent material' from the bronchioles. Livers also showed signs of internal bleeding as well as 'marked general congestion', and kidneys were frequently inflamed. The disease proved difficult to localise, with autopsies exposing 'many new morbid conditions not connected with ordinary influenza at all'. This flu seemed to intoxicate the entire body, issuing a compelling reminder of how 'severe a disease influenza can be'.[28]

There was the additional problem that the 'dread symptoms' of this influenza seemed to overlap with those usually characteristic of other diseases. Irish doctors treated many flu patients who had symptoms that were more typical of diphtheria and typhus than of flu.[29] They were also struck by the ability of the infection to produce 'severe meningeal complications', particularly in children. In some cases, this flu even bore a strong clinical resemblance to typhoid, suggesting that some of the many outbreaks of this fever which occurred both in Ireland and Great Britain at the time of the Great Flu may in fact have been part of the epidemic: *The Lancet* asserted that the 'experience of the present epidemic throws light upon the nature of many obscure cases (of typhoid) which occurred during the past summer', and commented on 'the likeness of influenza to typhoid fever'.[30]

One of the most problematic aspects of 'this insidious disease' for doctors, however, was the speed with which it could act, and its swiftness was a noted feature with stories of how 'a mother spends an hour at the bedside of her suffering son, falls ill the next day, and is dead three days later'. Dr John Moore remarked that 'the present epidemic has killed its victims with appalling speed in many cases', while Dr Speares at the Royal Academy of Medicine in Ireland referred to the way in which 'the onset has been in many cases remarkably sudden'. Cases which seemed on the way to recovery could suddenly take a 'bad turn', leaving doctors having to justify their initially favourable diagnosis to angry and grief-stricken families.[31]

The speed of the disease and the transient nature of the epidemic deprived physicians of the opportunity to try out different remedies or to extensively examine the disease before it had abated, contributing further to their sense of ineffectiveness and aggravation. Speares, for instance, pointed out in frustration that 'the evolution of the illness was too rapid to allow of satisfactory vaccine treatment, which took time'.[32] Further distinguishing this strain of flu from earlier visitations, words such as 'severe' and 'virulent' were scattered throughout doctors' descriptions of the disease. They saw an infection which had the ability to exert alarming effects on the body, leaving it open to a range of complications, including pleurisy, bronchitis, septic pneumonia, and even neuritis. In some districts in Ireland, the 'visitation of influenza was also accompanied by outbreaks of enteritis'. A common feature of these secondary infections was internal swelling and inflammation – of the pleura (the membrane lining the lungs), of the nerves (neuritis), of the small intestine (enteritis) – as the body's white blood cells strove to provide protection against the virus, but inadvertently caused damage to its own tissue. A disturbing characteristic of this strain of flu was the way in which it triggered the body to turn on itself.[33]

The doctor working as a locum on Inishbofin, just off the Galway coast, wrote to the Clifden Guardians of the daunting effects of the disease as he witnessed it:

> ...I found that the Flu had attacked about 60 families, the type here picks out the very strongest at 20 to 50 years of age – the attack is complicated with Pleuresy (*sic*), Pneumonia, Peritonitis, etc. it is also particularly severe on the central nervous system. I consider it a virulent type – it is infectious and infective.[34]

A Wicklow Medical Officer, in describing his own experience of the infection, also commented on the range of symptoms displayed by his patients: 'the type of the disease varied in a remarkable degree, even when several members of a family were infected'.[35]

When it comes to the medical experience of the Great Flu, what also emerges is that it was not simply a case of the 'weary, over-worked dispensary doctor' making 'the shortest diagnosis', administering medicine and leaving to move on to the next case; by and large, the physical exertion was often compounded by an emotional toll. Dr Kathleen Lynn for instance expressed the painful sense of impotence she felt during the epidemic: 'the 'flu rages, I can do so little, poor children and all dying around'. In rural Ireland, the epidemic visited many households which teetered on the brink of the poverty line, which doctors were at pains to impress on the local authorities. Dr Cusack told the Galway Guardians of the case of a family where both parents and all five children were 'seriously ill from pneumonia'. He found the children all 'lying in one bed, and it was necessary to climb over them to give them attention...The people were very badly off.'[36]

Dr McGinley in Donegal witnessed 'many pathetic cases in all three dispensary districts – young hired boys and girls in the throes of this flu dying in outhouses of farms'.[37] *The Lancet*, meanwhile, printed first-hand accounts by doctors which detailed the 'heart-rending' sight of

> heliotrope-cyanosed lusty great men breathing 50 to the minute, and obviously bound to die within a brief hour or two...not complaining and not obviously in physical distress, yet fully conscious of what is about to happen to them by reason of what they know has happened to their

fellows from the same regiment a day or two before.[38]

One of the most arresting pictures of the effects of the epidemic was portrayed by Dr Costello in his report to the Galway Guardians:

> You have no conception of the state of affairs that existed. I went into one house at half past three in the morning, and found a woman lying dead on the kitchen floor. Two children were staggering about hardly able to stand, and two more children were dead. By the aid of my electric head-light I made my way into the room, and there I found a man lying dead across a bed. There was no light or anything in the house. You have no conception hwo (*sic*) bad things were. You got the nurse to help these people and it was a good thing. The epidemic was an exceptional one.

Responding to the Guardians' concern that patients pay for the medical attendance received, the doctor stressed the level of poverty in the area: 'Even if you tried the most you could recover would be a few shillings from those patients.'[39]

The rural practitioner did considerably more than simply diagnose and prescribe for his patients. At times, he remained in houses 'several hours when all there were sick', 'lifting the patients about' and doing the nursing himself. Responsibility for coffining the dead also fell to doctors and nurses at times, a consequence of the basic lack of able bodies due to the epidemic and of popular fears of the disease: in Fálcarrach, Donegal, the local doctor and priest 'had to take a corpse to the graveyard on a wheelbarrow' as all the relations were too weak to help.[40]

A Dublin doctor's memory of the event was suffused with the disheartening nature of the task facing physicians: 'it was a depressing job administering to patients with such a disease, with death at every corner of every ward'. He recalled the need for distraction the epidemic provoked, and the desire to forget the reality created by the Great Flu: 'the only really convenient escape one had from all the work and worry was an occasional dash of an evening to the then comparatively new Bohemian Picture House'. Here 'the cares and worries of the day would slip temporarily from our shoulders, as we were lost in love of Mary Pickford or the Gishes', so that 'even the aura of death all around the city could not curb our enjoyment'.[41]

The urge to escape from the oppressive world of the influenza outbreak was similarly apparent among medics abroad and found explicit expression in a letter written by a doctor working in the Base Hospital at Camp Devens, Massachusetts. The doctor outlined the shocking potency of this form of influenza as well as the immense physical toll the epidemic was taking on him and his colleagues, and conveyed his eagerness to put the outbreak from his mind for any brief period, even if this might only be possible by means of a few lines from a friend:

> These men start with what appears to be an ordinary attack of La Grippe or Influenza, and when brought to the Hospital they very rapidly develop the most vicious type of Pneumonia that has ever been seen...We have no relief here, you get up in the morning at 5.30 and work steady till about 9.30 pm, sleep, then go out again. Some of the men of course have been here all the time, and they are TIRED...The men here are all good fellows, but I get so damned sick of Pneumonia that when I go to eat I want to find some fellow who will not "Talk Shop" but there ain't none no how. We eat it, sleep it, and dream it, to say nothing of breathing it 16 hours a day. I would be very grateful indeed if you would drop me a line or two once in a while, and I will promise you that if you ever get into a fix like this, I will do the same for you.[42]

A further indication of the ways in which doctors were affected by what they saw was suggested by the recurrence of certain images in medical accounts. Dublin physicians John Moore and George Peacocke both selected cases of young girls drowning and choking on their own fluids and blood to illustrate the virulence of the disease. The death of these girls was quick, with the doctors able to do little for them, and a sense of futility pervades both narratives. Peacocke felt his case deserved 'special mention' due to the 'dramatic suddenness' with which death ensued:

> A young woman, 24 years of age, complained on a Wednesday night of feeling sick. Her temperature was slightly elevated. The next morning she was not so well, and fainted on getting out of bed. During the day her condition grew worse; she was removed to hospital and when I saw her, at 7 pm on Thursday evening, she was dying. Râles were audible all over her chest; she was unconscious; her pulse was imperceptible and she was coughing up fluid of the kind I have just described (blood-tinged, frothy sputum). She died at 10 pm the same evening.[43]

Moore referred to 'the haemorrhages so often observed', describing how 'in one instance, a girl of fifteen years died in my presence, positively drowned in her own blood, which bubbled in froth from her nose and mouth as she passed away'.[44]

Depictions of the deaths of young women from the disease were not unique to Irish accounts, and similar imagery also featured in the accounts of physicians overseas. In one Japanese doctor's narration of a typical day at the height of the epidemic in his district, he recounted how

> When I got to one of the stricken houses that had called for me, I found that the young bride had caught the flu two or three days previously. She was pregnant, and had miscarried and died. Because the family were all sick, the young woman's own family had had to arrange her funeral...For the past several days all the doctors had joined in treating her...I saw her and guessed that she wouldn't last out the night. Then I went to the other house to which I'd been called.[45]

Isaac Starr, a medical student in Philadelphia during the epidemic, remembered the Jewish family whose 18-year-old daughter was desperately ill. 'She was flushed with fever, and to my eye she was very beautiful. Father, mother, brothers and sisters had gathered around, and they would not leave her. After suffering for a few days, it was she who left them.'[46]

These recurring descriptions of the suffering and deaths of young women at the hands of the flu read as a metaphor for the sense of ineffectiveness and inadequacy witnessed by the medical profession during the epidemic. This corresponds with Nancy Bristow's analysis of the American medical experience of the Great Flu, as 'a sense of helplessness as individuals, and of humility as members of a profession' was perceptible in doctors' accounts of the event.[47]

The emotionally punishing nature of the epidemic also registered with nurses. Annie Smithson, a district nurse in Milltown, Dublin, at the time, wrote in her memoir, 'the influenza was frightful. I was on duty night and day. I saw four in a bed often – all very ill. Next day one would probably have died. On the last day that I was on duty before collapsing myself, I had visited 35 cases.' Her sombre recollections contrast markedly with the memories of many American nurses, who often articulated their experiences in the epidemic in positive terms, stressing the opportunity it held for 'meaningful ministration', affording them a way to show the difference they could make to their patients.[48]

It is the recollections of the Cumann na mBan members who

volunteered as nurses during the epidemic that are more consistent with the sense of material contribution manifest in the American nurses' accounts. For instance, Máirín Beaumont, a member of the Cumann na mBan Executive at the time, considered that 'our girls did excellent work...after their day's lectures and studies by staying up at night nursing and relieving those members of families who had been on duty with the sick all day'. Another Cumann na mBan volunteer remembered how

> whole families were prostrated by it (the epidemic), especially in the congested areas of Dublin so that there was nobody to attend to the sick. Cumann na mBan was asked to step into the breach and they did very good work among the poor. They visited them in their homes, cleaned their places, cooked for them etc.[49]

These representations of nursing during the epidemic correspond with the feeling of contribution and accomplishment which Bristow found in the self-perceptions of American nurses during the Great Flu. The experience for doctors in the US had been defined by disappointment and was frequently recalled as an 'exercise in horror and humility', whereas nurses found in the epidemic 'a meaningful opportunity for service' that served to strengthen their confidence as both women and health professionals. Although the flu outbreak was an emotive and challenging time for Irish nurses, some of the women felt that it had also allowed them to demonstrate their abilities and that it had given them a chance to show that they could significantly contribute to society. In this way, the epidemic constituted a complicated and nuanced experience for nurses, harrowing but also at times affirming in nature.[50]

The way in which the Great Flu affected doctors and nurses, both in Ireland and overseas, was further evident in their conviction that it would endure in memory. Starr summed up the events of the epidemic as 'unforgettable medical experiences', and Smithson portrayed the outbreak in similar terms: 'that epidemic swept through Milltown in a devastating manner and is remembered to this day'. Belief in the lasting medical legacy of the epidemic also marked Patrick Meenan's address on influenza to the Royal Academy of Medicine in Ireland in 1957. He dismissed the 'need to describe that episode (the Great Flu) in any detail. It is within the memory of some of you, and the knowledge of all...at the back of every physician's mind is the memory of 1918–19.'[51]

Many of the medical accounts examined by Bristow were also imbued with the doctors' certainty that the images of the epidemic had been deeply imprinted on their consciousness. Victor C. Vaughan, an eminent epidemiologist at the time, witnessed the flu's destructive effects on American military camps, and in his memoirs described how in the mornings, the dead bodies would be 'stacked about the morgue like cord wood'. The picture, he thought, was painted on his 'memory cells'. American nurses also referred to the way in which the flu outbreak had deeply scored their memory: '...The wards were quiet with the stillness of death. It was a spectacle never to be forgotten.' Dr John Sundwell, working at the University of Minnesota at the time, wrote afterwards that

> two things in connection with the pandemic are indelibly impressed on my memory. The one was the characteristic chain of symptoms – sudden onset; fever; extreme prostration; pains in back, head, and extremities; involvement of the respiratory system, and early pneumonia in a large percentage of cases. The other impression was the helplessness of the medical sciences.

Though the epidemic may have been subject to a 'public commemorative silence', the generation of doctors and nurses who experienced it first-hand considered the Great Flu to have been a powerfully memorable event.[52]

*   *   *   *

The response of the British medical profession to the Great Flu has been described variously as 'passive, confused and ineffective', and as ambivalent or even obstructionist. Such descriptions, however, may fail to encapsulate the overwhelming reality of what doctors faced in 1918/19. The magnitude of the task which met doctors and nurses – never-ending lines of patients, a vastly over-burdened medical system, lack of resources – was echoed almost everywhere. In Ireland, the vast majority of medical professionals battled to cope as best they could, visiting as many cases as possible, labouring through exhaustion and sickness, and sharing a sense of powerlessness and frustration at their inability to do more to help their patients. They received much praise for their efforts, suggesting the epidemic may have served to enhance the status of the medical profession. The hardworking, physically drained doctors of the flu outbreak contrasted sharply with images of the drunken, gambling medics found in nineteenth-century Ireland.[53]

The epidemic also provides an insight into the full extent of the role of the Poor Law Medical Officer in the rural community. During the flu, apart from attending to their health emergencies, medics would often try to secure food for families in need, and would impress on the Guardians the need to look into cases of severe distress. Moreover, they were ready to tend to the dead when no one else was willing or able to do so. The epidemic also highlighted the stark contrast between the theoretical debates on aetiology and treatments which took place among the physicians in the Royal Academy of Medicine in Ireland, and the demands on the Poor Law Medical Officer, who travelled his district on horse and cart, acting as social worker as much as health professional.

A major problem for doctors during the Great Flu was that the laboratory on which they had grown reliant was now unable to provide the answers they needed: to either identify the cause of the flu disease or to fashion a cure in the form of a vaccine or antibiotic. It would be another fifteen years before the influenza virus was isolated. And while eminent physicians argued about causes, aetiology, and potential silver bullets, the reality of the pandemic was that nurses were more important than doctors, as no medical treatment to cure influenza or pneumonia yet existed. This was eventually admitted by the doctors who compiled the Ministry of Health report, as they acknowledged that 'from experience extending over thousands of cases, the general conclusion was that nursing was of infinitely greater importance than the drugs administered'.[54]

Both in Ireland and abroad, the epidemic left a deep impression on health professionals. Patrick Meenan's reference to the way in which the epidemic was at the back of every physician's mind was shared by many nurses and doctors overseas. A nurse at a military camp in Washington summed it up as a time 'which we would not like to live over again', while the Principal Medical Officer on the Gold Coast admitted that 'we shall not soon forget the...almost entire cessation of all activities save those connected with the care of the sick and the disposal of the dead'. Emerging from the experience physically and often emotionally spent, those who tended to the sick found it difficult to forget the intense and gruelling period of the Great Flu, as in the western world, the epidemic left in its wake a shaken and chastened medical profession:

> Intoxicated by the victories achieved over the plague...over the enteric group, over typhus...and over smallpox, we are too apt to suppose that the campaign has ended in our favour, that we have little more to fear from the typically

epidemic diseases…That we have just passed through one of the great sicknesses of history, a plague which within a few months has destroyed more lives than were directly sacrificed in four years of a destructive war, is an experience which should dispel any easy optimism of the kind.[55]

'The responsible authority': Responsibility and Accountability During the Epidemic [1]

When the flu struck in 1918, practically all governments and public health systems found themselves ill-equipped to deal with its ferocity. Official responses varied widely: from strongly interventionist, to disorganised, detached, and ineffective. In a brief assessment of overall trends, Richard Collier has described how the epidemic widely exposed 'appalling deficits in organisation'. Persistent themes in the literature of response included lack of preparation, the distinct absence of coherent relief plans, and the consequently vital role played by civil society: in Collier's view, 'rarely in the history of mankind had so many volunteers toiled so long or so patiently in the service of humanity'.[2]

This chapter examines how central and local authorities in Ireland attempted to manage the flu outbreak, and their readiness to assume the mantle of 'custodians of public health'. How did they seek to cope with the arrival of the 'terrible and rather mysterious epidemic'? Outlining firstly the actions of the Local Government Board (LGB), the central health authority of the time, this chapter focuses subsequently on those of local authorities, revealing, as in the case of Britain, a highly decentralised response to the Great Flu.[3]

In studies of the flu abroad, its relatively short time span and the need to 'carry on' in the face of war have been cited as important influences on official response.[4] In Ireland, these were of secondary importance in comparison to the unwieldy and fragmented system of health administration in place at the time. The result was that during a crisis like the flu epidemic, it was not clear precisely who should take the lead in directing preventive measures or aid efforts. This in turn fostered a conspicuously uneven response to the flu's arrival, as some areas benefited from officially sanctioned and community involved relief, whereas in others, it was the exhausted Medical Officer or the overworked nurses who provided the only form of state support experienced by the flu-stricken household.

In its annual report for 1918, the Local Government Board (LGB) announced that 'the most important event from a public health' point of view had been the 'outbreak of Influenza in an epidemic form, appearing in three distinct waves in June and October 1918, and February 1919'. It noted that the second wave in particular had been 'very widespread' in nature, and had inflicted 'a large number of deaths'. The Board gave a satisfied account of its response to the epidemic, conveying the image of a concerned, energetic body, deeply anxious over the health of the population:

> the question of the addition of Influenza to the list of notifiable diseases received careful consideration...we afforded local authorities all possible facilities for the employment of additional medical and nursing assistance...the utility of protective inoculation engaged our constant attention...we closely followed any available information with regard to experiments with prophylactic vaccine treatment.[5]

In contrast with this picture of activity and prompt responsiveness, the most concrete action of the LGB was late in coming and focussed on containment rather than relief. In spring 1919, when the third wave of the disease was well established, the Board finally made 'acute primary pneumonia' and 'acute influenzal pneumonia' notifiable diseases, with the effect that doctors could have patients removed to hospital and their homes disinfected. Although late in arriving, the legislation was, in principle, consistent with the role of the Board as the central health authority, explicitly placing the needs of the community over those of the individual.[6]

In taking this step, the actions of the LGB also corresponded with public health doctrines of the day, based on belief in the importance of tracking and quantifying the distribution of disease. For officials, it was vital to know where the disease was and its direction of movement. The *Medical Press* approved of the legislation, regretting only that the measure did not go far enough – it wanted influenza itself made notifiable. *The Irish Times* reported that the Board circulated a memorandum on influenza 'containing a summary of the most recent information on the subject', but the local records of several counties make no reference to such a document, and the extent of its distribution is unclear.[7]

Late legislation and memos were not enough to calm an uneasy public, and the Board came in for much criticism at the time, with widespread accusations of official inaction and ineffectiveness. Although virtually no government had been prepared for the onslaught of pandemic influenza, the LGB and sanitary authorities in Ireland were thought to have been 'very much to blame for not having foreseen the epidemic and taken precautions against its ravages'. The *Catholic Bulletin* scolded that compared with 'alleged secret societies or German plots', the nation's health was a considerably more 'legitimate matter for official concern, especially when we are faced with the frequent recurrence of decimating epidemics'.[8]

Dr Kathleen Lynn was scathing of the sluggishness and inefficiency of both the LGB and Dublin Corporation: 'my experience is that the epidemic would be over before they had done considering the matter'. Members of Strabane Urban Council were also struck by the inactivity and lack of initiative demonstrated by the LGB during the epidemic: 'in other outbreaks, the Local Government Board wrote to see what was being done, but in this case there was not a word from them'. Dr E.C. Thompson, in a letter to the Omagh Board of Guardians, wrote that 'so far as I know nothing is being done to mitigate or control its severity. The Government should be able to establish a well-equipped hospital camp near Omagh and send nurses.'[9]

Wires were sent to the LGB telling of the desperate circumstances in some localities and calling for help: 'terrible influenza epidemic...500 alone in Bray affected; union full; several deaths; immediate action of Local Government Board requested'. The Board in turn dispatched a circular, suggesting that Boards of Guardians 'enlist the cooperation of any voluntary workers in their districts, who would visit the houses where there were patients, and advise them as to the necessary precautions'. The measure elicited only scorn from the Chairman of the Rathdown Board of Guardians: 'very kind of them to send us advice; but they don't send us a doctor'. The *Down Recorder* declared simply that the LGB members had 'done nothing in their history to justify the public in committing to them a larger trust'. The popular reading of the situation was of the LGB's inadequacy and apathy, in keeping with how the Board had operated in the past. Even the *Medical Press and Circular* commented that 'the Board has nothing in its history to justify the public in committing to it a larger trust than that which it has abused in the past'.[10]

And yet, what could the LGB have done? Niall Johnson has noted that it is questionable whether a 'large, centralised authority' could have reduced the toll of the outbreak. To have combated the Great Flu with any degree of success would have required a 'large, well-resourced medical workforce distributed at the local level, and even that would have been hard-pressed to do much more than alleviate some of the suffering'. Moreover, the LGB was constrained by limited powers and by continuing tensions between central and local government; it was also subject to the financial checks imposed by war-time exigencies. Sir Henry Robinson, Vice-President of the LGB, admitted that the Board exercised 'very little control over general administration', as its power by this time was limited to sanctioning loan applications, auditing accounts, restricting expenditure on road works, and arbitrating when disputes arose between county and district councils. The lack of leadership shown by the LGB reflected the way in which the body by now resembled a 'drowned rat', subject to repeated 'hammerings' from Irish deputies in parliament.[11]

The response of the Local Government Board in Ireland appears in many ways to have mirrored its British equivalent. Sandra Tomkins has concluded that 'the official response at the central level took no account of the realities of the situation', and primary source material shows that a similar situation pertained in Ireland. The Board emerges repeatedly as a body which lacked a fundamental awareness of the problems witnessed by rural communities in their attempts to cope with the flu.[12]

For instance, both the Downpatrick and Letterkenny Boards of Guardians were deeply frustrated by the LGB's insistence on waiting until the end of the war before sanctioning the appointment of permanent Medical Officers for their districts, with similar situations existing in Aclare, County Sligo, as well as in the Dublin Union. In the Downpatrick district, the temporary MO was 'not within the reach of many of the people' who needed medical assistance, with one Guardian despairing completely of the central authority: 'the Local Government Board are entirely wrong in their attitude. It is no wonder there is a rebellion in the country.'[13]

Other examples of this detachment were provided by the individuals who were at the frontline of the epidemic. In March 1919, the LGB asked doctors to provide the documentation necessary for the Board's annual report. Their demand prompted a terse response from a struggling, and now infuriated, Enniskillen doctor:

> I regret that the matter should not have received my attention earlier, but since the influenza epidemic commenced some months ago it has been rampant in the two districts of Tempo and Lisbellaw. It is raging at present,

and if the Local Government Board will wait until after the 15th inst. (March), I will furnish them with all particulars. I am unfit for the two districts so I am resigning the appointment in Lisbellaw as I am nearly killed trying to work both districts.[14]

An irate letter from the parish priest on the Aran Islands also attests to the apparent distance between the LGB and rural life, with the clergyman berating the Board's Inspector for not having

> visited the Islands during the Influenza outbreak and seen the condition of affairs for himself. The epidemic should have been reported a fortnight before it was. The appointment of Dr Lyons did a good deal, but should have been done long before…some very sad casualties occurred, and nourishment was scarce, milk being almost improcurable.[15]

The Irish central authorities thus appear to have been able to do little to help curb or relieve the effects of the epidemic, a prominent theme in official response observed by historians of the Great Flu, as few governments could claim to have achieved anything 'significant worth mentioning in this regard': the pandemic highlighted the way in which modern states in the early twentieth century had little involvement in the delivery and organisation of medical care. And as in Britain, responsibility was rather passed on to the local authorities and communities of cities, towns, and rural areas.[16]

In local government circles, the meaning of public health was largely translated as disease prevention rather than relief provision. In the cities, this meant cleansing the metropolitan landscape, consistent with public health ideas and activity in the nineteenth century when measures were grounded in the theory that dirt caused infection. In 1918/19, the focus was on making public space healthy by keeping the city's streets clean, and in Spain, Italy, and France, precautionary measures such as large-scale use of disinfectants, street sweeping, and refuse disposal all featured in authorities' attempts to temper the flu's onslaught. Dublin city, meanwhile, was placarded with notices outlining directions on how to avoid the flu, while the corporation's disinfecting cart could also be heard rumbling through the streets applying a 'strong disinfectant' to the thoroughfares. Almost 'every square inch of the city was a potential source of danger' and had to be flushed with carbolic acid. Trams were disinfected, as they were in Belfast too, with Dr Bailie, Superintendent Medical Officer of Health for the city, also arranging for the 'thorough ventilation and disinfecting of all buildings in which public meetings or entertainments' were held.[17]

Around the country, the practice of such large-scale sanitation measures varied greatly. According to Surgeon-Colonel D. Edgar Flinn, the sanitary authorities were, 'with very rare exceptions, lamentably apathetic', failing 'absolutely to recognise their responsibilities as guardians of the public health'. The citizens of Tralee were left to rely on their 'famous "dreadnought" Urban Sanitary Authority that only meets once in a blue moon and never does anything by chance'.[18]

In contrast though, Bray Urban District Council looked into the disinfection of houses and the cleaning of lanes, drains, and sewers in an effort to stop the spread of the flu. In Kilkenny, the streets were 'daily washed with disinfectants', whereas in Westport, the Urban District Council decided that the lime washing of houses and removal of manure heaps would be 'the best means to adopt to cope with the present epidemic of influenza'. In an era when disease was still considered to be inseparable from dirt, purifying the environment was among the best measures the authorities could hope to take in attempting to arrest an outbreak of infection.[19]

When it came to relief measures, the response of local government bodies was again subject to variation, ranging from genuine concern and high activity levels, to failure to meet for several weeks at a time, and reluctance to provide even the basic running costs of doctors. While some local officials engaged readily in efforts to prevent disease and to provide relief, others demonstrated more concern for the ratepayers than the sick. Reactions at the level of local government ranged widely: from energetic and industrious, to inactive and unhelpful.[20]

In Macroom, for example, 'very laudable and desirable measures' were initiated by the Urban Council in an attempt to 'mitigate the suffering and distress consequent upon the ravages of the influenza epidemic amongst the poorer classes'. The Chairman helped set up a fund in aid of 'the destitute sick', and subcommittees visited different parts of the district, providing 'suitable articles of dietary' and even 'physical attendance where whole families are incapacitated'. Similarly in Youghal, it was members of the Urban District Council who went to the country 'to arrange with certain farmers to send milk into the town for sale and distribution amongst the poor'. The Corporation took the lead in Clonmel, issuing 'supplies of new milk to afflicted houses', a move praised in the press as a 'great boon' in light of the fact that 'death in some instances was due to sheer poverty and neglect'. Relief was a collaborative effort between volunteers and officials; 'were it not for the efforts of the neighbours and charitable visitors' who nursed the sick 'and procured food and fuel the number of deaths would undoubtedly have been considerably larger',[21] especially in the poorer quarters.

Officially sanctioned aid efforts were not so common in smaller towns, or in the more remote or sparsely populated rural districts. In the small village of Kilmacthomas, County Waterford, where the disease was reportedly 'very virulent', there was little evidence of relief activity, only that the officials viewed the 'state of things with apprehension'. In Loughrea, County Galway, all the Town Commissioners appear to have done was to pass a motion of sympathy with the families of the victims of 'the awful scourge which had brought grief and misery to so many houses in the country'. In a wire to the Westport Board of Guardians, the parish priest in Newport chastised the local authorities for their inaction: 'People of Mulranny and district in lamentable condition with epidemic whole families stricken; about 140 cases. No nurse or doctor in district. The abandonment of these poor people is criminal on the part of those responsible.'[22]

Nonetheless, the size of a town was not a guarantee that official assistance would be forthcoming. Even in a large town such as Strabane, a member of the Urban Council criticised 'the treatment of the sick poor...by the Board of Guardians, no hospital being provided for urgent cases, despite the fact that an epidemic was raging'. He also observed that 'the fever hospital was available and all the Guardians had to do was to provide the nurses', and attributed 'three deaths in the town to neglect – one poor boy had no other bedding than straw and rags'. In the end, the Council resolved to 'ask the local Board of Guardians to convene a special meeting to deal with the question'. In Wexford, the local press sympathised with the town's poor about the 'corporation's inactivity when so many people are laid low by the cruel epidemic of influenza'.[23]

In Britain, war conditions have been cited as one reason why official reaction lacked conviction, whereas in Ireland, there were deep structural problems in the health system which militated against a coherent official response. The *Church of Ireland Gazette* was in little doubt that the problematic structure of health administration had played a decisive part when it came to official response to the flu outbreak:

> Certain matters with reference to public health come under the control of the Local Government Board, some under the Board of Education, others under the Board of Agriculture. All this spells insufficiency and confusion. Maternity, hospitals, and the treatment of disease are largely

in charge of private enterprise and charity, while sanitation, food inspection and the prevention of disease generally are under the control of unco-ordinated officials and departments...The want of elasticity in our medical system has been exemplified in the total failure to meet the influenza epidemic.[24]

The *Fermanagh Times* similarly posited that 'if arguments were needed for the institution of a Ministry of Health, the confusion of the authorities with regard to the present influenza plague would provide one...we see little but divergent views, divided authority, and lack of co-ordination'. The second flu wave prompted *The Irish Times* to point out the urgent need for health reform, going so far as to suggest that if a Ministry of Health Bill 'had been put into operation a year ago, it is almost certain that the epidemic of influenza would not have reached such serious proportions'. With no central coordination, 'local health authorities were quite unprepared to combat the disease when it broke out'. One Dublin citizen was fuming at how influenza was being allowed to play 'havoc with the population', the authorities taking 'no serious steps...to cope with the epidemic'. He understood 'that there are at present no fewer than eight central Government departments concerned with matters affecting public health. Surely it would be reasonable to think that this epidemic is sufficiently important to attract the attention of one or other of these departments?'[25]

The issue of public health was further complicated by ongoing tensions between local authorities and the LGB, which had been evident since the nineteenth century. The question of how to deal with the Great Flu illustrated the continuing contestation of power between central and local government, with discussions on the epidemic among local politicians liable to veer off topic, descending into fervent indictments of the Board.[26]

At the time of the influenza outbreak, the Irish healthcare system was in structural disarray, with responsibility for public health diffused in a complicated way between central and local bodies. This was laid fully bare in a report produced by the Public Health Council of Ireland in 1920 and submitted to the British Government. It had been commissioned to establish how the government could go about setting up an Irish Ministry of Health, similar to that being established in Britain as part of Lloyd George's post-war reconstruction plans.[27]

The document clarified how the duties of medical provision had been carved up and divided between a mixture of central and local authorities in a confusing manner which limited any scope for effectiveness. Stressing the critical need for change in the health system, the Council pointed explicitly to the organisational shortcomings which had resulted in 'a considerable lack of coordination, and a certain amount of overlapping, both in the central control and in the local administration' of the public health and medical services. The product was an elaborate system which eluded the understanding of virtually all concerned.[28]

Reflecting this acute need for structural reform, the epidemic revealed confusion over who was ultimately accountable when it came to the people's health, with criticism shared around liberally. While local government bodies accused the LGB of having 'very little sense of their responsibilities to the poor', the Chief Secretary, Ian Macpherson, explained to Parliament that breakdowns in the health system were due to the local officials and the electorate that had put them in power in the first place. For Macpherson, 'a great responsibility was on the electorate of Ireland who had the selection of the County Councils and District Councils which had failed to put the provisions which existed – defective they might be – into operation'.[29]

Unable to assume that either central or local officials would take responsibility for directing help for the sick, it was often the doctors themselves who took on the duty of providing as best they could for the health of their districts. They stressed to local authorities the need to supplement nursing provision, helped mobilise local charitable organisations, and highlighted the necessity of augmenting local healthcare facilities. In Clonmel, it was 'the medical men' who got the local Red Cross Organisation to help in the flu relief work, while in Buncrana, when 'fuel and milk for the poor were almost improcurable', it was through the agency of the 'medical authorities' and the 'Spiritual Director' that milk was collected daily from 'outlying districts from those who could help'. At a meeting of Derry Corporation, it was once more the doctor who 'moved that the necessary steps' be taken to prepare rooms in Gwyn's Institution 'for the reception and treatment of influenza cases'.[30]

Along with doctors, civil society was at the centre of relief activity during the flu, with aid provision and philanthropic initiatives set up and undertaken by a variety of groups. In Dublin, the 'invitation of the Dublin Public Health Department for volunteer nurses from the various Volunteer Aid Associations' was apparently 'very well received', with the Women's National Health Association rendering 'excellent assistance'. Under the direction of Kathleen Lynn, women from the Citizen Army helped to clean up 'a wing of 37 Charlemont St' for use as an 'emergency hospital for Influenza'. Although it was by Lynn's own admission a 'very scratch affair', this ultimately paved the way for the eventual establishment of the city's first infant hospital, St Ultan's.[31]

Informed by the conviction that 'the relief of the poor is the first of Christian duties', the branches of St Vincent de Paul around Ireland provided much-needed assistance to flu-stricken families. They also galvanised the wider community to do likewise, with little mention of the usually sought commitment to spiritual or moral improvement from the families or individuals. 'Immediately on the appearance of the influenza epidemic' in Thurles, a 'special meeting of the Conference was called, and the visiting Committee were instructed to visit every house in the district'. In normal circumstances, philanthropy was an instrument of social discipline and reform, with material support intended to act as an incentive to good, Christian behaviour. During the epidemic, though, aid was provided freely and willingly to those who needed it most, with little evidence of proselytism.[32]

In parts of the country, the Volunteers also provided much assistance and relief to households suffering the flu. Michael O'Suilleabhain described the help provided by Volunteers and Cumann na mBan to stricken families in Cork:

> The Volunteers and Cumann na mBan had helped the peo-
> ple immensely. Where an entire household became ill, or
> were otherwise handicapped, units from each organisation
> took over the duties of nursing, heating and food supply
> until the family was on its feet again...and where necessary
> they helped to coffin and bury the dead.

The involvement of the Volunteers in relief efforts corresponds with sociologist Robert Putnam's assertion that political knowledge and interest in public affairs can act as important preconditions for more active forms of community involvement.[33]

Cumann na mBan were keenly active in aid efforts, with the Dublin District Council offering 'the services of their members to help in the nursing of the stricken, especially the poor', and opening aid stations in Harcourt Street, Parnell Square and Winetavern Street. Concerned at the spread of flu in Shandon, the Cork District Council sought out the local Cumann na mBan branch to help the sick. Such gestures expanded the largely political focus of the Cumann's activities, and suggested a willingness to take on a supportive role in the community.[34]

As was the case in Spain, female religious orders played a pivotal role in relief work. A member of Bray Trades' Council stressed the contribution made by the Sisters of Charity, stating that were it not for them 'coming to the rescue in the present epidemic…turning the school-house into a hospital, he did not know where Bray would have been for the last fortnight'. The Sisters of Mercy did duty at a short-staffed Macroom hospital, thereby helping to relieve a 'critical' situation, and at night, nuns at the nearby convent often came to help attend flu victims at the overrun Navan Workhouse. In Tuam, the nuns were warmly praised for going to nurse patients in their homes, and in Dublin, the Sisters of Charity filled in for the sick attendants of the hospital at Crooksling Sanatorium.[35]

The 'ladies' of various towns were also instrumental in caring for the sick and in mobilising local resources for aid provision. In Dublin, they 'acted as collectors' for the St Vincent de Paul flag days, and were most 'energetic in bringing the charity to the notice of the citizens and visitors to the city'. 'A number of ladies' in Dundalk, responding to an invitation by the Rev. J. McKeone, established 'committees for the relief of the many cases of poor people suffering from influenza in the town…one of these is providing daily a supply of beef tea and other nourishing foods suited for invalids'; and, 'at a meeting of ladies' in Wexford town in late October, 'arrangements were made for securing milk from the country districts' to give to the 'sick poor of the town'.[36]

These examples of charity also point to the element of class in relief efforts. For instance, during the epidemic in Rathvilly, County Carlow, the Rathdonnells from 'the big house up above' at Lisnavagh provided relief to the families of Phelan's Lane: 'at midday, every day, they sent down a big phaeton [an old-fashioned pony and trap] with two men driving and two big churns of soup. Everyone would be out with their tubs and their cans and that. Boiling hot soup! Only for that, we were all gone.'[37]

The fact that organised relief efforts were more common in the medium to larger-sized towns is reflective of the important role of the middle and upper classes in initiating aid attempts. As Richard Simpson notes, larger settlements are more likely to have a coherent group of higher-status people with the 'readily available sources of elite leader-ship' that are necessary to rouse collective relief efforts. During the epidemic in Ireland, such collective attempts to relieve suffering appear to have been absent in the hard-hit peripheral communities such as Arranmore in Donegal, or Lettermullen and Gorumna in the west.[38]

In early twentieth-century Ireland, there was also a widely held expectation that it was a responsibility of the middle and upper classes to help the less fortunate. The *Kilkenny People* declared that helping the sick members of the lower classes was 'not a question of charity', but rather 'a plain obligation of duty imposed on those who can afford it to succour and relieve those who cannot'. Father Ahern in Mitchelstown advocated the strengthening of help networks within classes, and also referred explicitly to the obligations of the wealthy to help the disadvantaged: 'the country people should see to it that none of their afflicted neighbours should suffer from want of milk, and the well to do townspeople should succour their poorer brethren as they had done in Clonmel'. The way in which the middle and upper classes came together to provide aid in many towns indicates the importance of a 'sense of one's place' in Irish community life at this time.[39] With privilege came responsibility, and philanthropy was an expression as well as a requirement of social position. Helping those less fortunate was a way of confirming one's social status, and at the same time, one's social status made it a duty to help.

Although charity operated in many towns in a top-down direction, expressions of altruism and compassion also took place within classes, and went unrecorded by official reports and statistics. For instance, during their bout of flu, Jeremiah Clarke's family received help from their neighbours in looking after the farm: 'it was impossible to get any work done but our neighbours took care of the farm stock and chores'. This demonstrated how relief could take place outside of formal, organisational contexts, unfolding on the basis of the reciprocity principles which underlay social networks. Similar instances are cited in Donegal, with neighbours tending to the cattle of ill families, with other manifestations of informal helping also in evidence – in Patrick Cahill's home area, the community pulled together and had 'one of the largest dances ever held at the Hall on Saturday night last, receipts to the amount of £80 (were) handed over to the widow of Bill Naughton who...succumbed to an attack of Flue and left six very young children'. In Downpatrick, the problem of feeding the sick was solved by the 'many kind friends' who supplied the Downpatrick Nursing Society 'with bottles of oxo and nourishment of various kinds in a portable shape' which the nurse was able to 'carry with her on her rounds'.[40]

Such acts of charity are indicative of the way in which generalised reciprocity bound rural communities at this time. Support was commonly given without expecting anything specific in exchange, based on the idea that a helping hand would be extended when needed, not necessarily by the original recipient, but by someone else or indeed by the community: 'I'll do this for you now, without expecting anything immediately in return and perhaps without even knowing you, confident that down the road you or someone else will return the favour.' As Jack Pole put it: 'we shared everything in the country. If you killed a pig...you brought pork to the neighbours and if they killed one, they reciprocated. There was very close contact and co-operation between farmers and neighbours. It's not necessary now...it was a different way of life back then.'[41]

A general trend appears to have been that officially generated relief efforts and also community-driven aid provision were more common in the more densely populated areas. Meanwhile, it was the doctors, nurses, and sometimes the Relieving Officers of the Board of Guardians who shouldered the responsibility for relief and care in districts where population distribution was more thinly scattered. This may have been due to the way in which rural communities have less potential to generate 'social pressure' in comparison to areas with more clustered settlement patterns. In such districts, there is more scope for people to 'see what other people are doing' and for the dynamics of social pressure to grind into gear as a sense develops that helping is 'the thing to do'.[42]

The amount of material resources available constituted another key factor: when resources are stretched, primary group loyalties – such as to the family – overcome 'humanitarian identification with sufferers generally'. As sociologist Allen Barton points out, 'irrespective of his desire to help, someone who is disabled cannot help others; the homeless cannot give shelter, nor can the starving feed the starving'.[43] Thus, aid efforts were more likely to be initiated in areas where families had the means at their disposal which were surplus to their own needs. Therefore, community-based relief efforts were more likely to come from areas which had a distinct middle-class stratum.

*   *   *   *

When it came to responsibility and accountability during the flu outbreak, the reaction from Irish authorities had a number of features in common with government response abroad. These included: lack of preparation, the secondary role played by central government in comparison with local authorities and communities, and the apparent disconnection between central authorities and the grim realities and chaos of epidemic disease.

The importance of governmental response during the epidemic is a contested issue. While historians such as Myron Echenberg assert that 'even the most diligent actions' of public health authorities would not have been able to curb the effects of the flu, Alfred Crosby found that good management could mitigate the death rate. In their study of influenza in the US, Martin Bootsma and Neil Ferguson similarly found that cities which introduced measures early in their epidemics managed to achieve moderate but significant decreases in overall mortality, concluding that public health response was a key factor in explaining the 'very different influenza patterns' evident across US cities in 1918/19.[44]

That official response has the potential to influence the severity of an epidemic experience highlights the acute need for health reform existent in the Irish system in 1918. While it seemed that almost every facet of the public health machine was blamed for inadequacy, the reality was that each could legitimately bear some of the blame. Rural and Urban District Councils (RDCs and UDCs), for instance, were the sanitary authority for their area, and thus had the power to initiate clean-up operations – largely ineffective measures against the flu, but the best ones possible in the context of the know-ledge available at the time. Levels of activity varied widely, and although some councils were prompt and unsparing in their attempts to curb the outbreak, not all were as assiduous in their activity.

It was also the RDCs and UDCs which had the ability to authorise outdoor relief to be administered by boards of guardians in times of exceptional distress. But with guardians in some areas failing to even attend meetings during the epidemic, it was difficult to discharge this responsibility – administration of relief required cooperation between the local bodies. Matters were further complicated by the fact that spending permission ultimately came from the Local Government Board, whose own hands were tied by wartime budget constraints. The result of such interdependence was that it was difficult for any part of the public health system to operate effectively or to provide relief to a suffering population.[45]

In places such as New Zealand, the failure of the healthcare system to cope with the epidemic was recognised and led to a complete overhaul of public health. In Ireland, there were small steps in this direction, as represented by the major review of the health services commissioned in 1919. However, these were soon swallowed up by the tumult of political violence and civil war, with the result that much-needed reform was further delayed, although many of the Irish Public Health Council's recommendations would later be implemented by the Free State.[46]

The decentralised, improvisory, and highly variable nature of official response to the Great Flu in Ireland meant that in some areas doctors, nurses, volunteers, and neighbours provided the only form of relief that families experienced, particularly those in the more isolated areas. Despite popular fears of the disease, there was a widespread philanthropic response to the outbreak, as civil society assumed much of the responsibility for the problems posed by the epidemic.

The ineffectiveness of central state organisations in Ireland compared to the contribution made by civil society touches on an issue that Rajnarayan Chandavarkar has raised in relation to health care and the state in India: was official response to the epidemic indicative that 'public health occupied a low place on the imperial list of priorities'?[47]

In Britain and its colonies, the epidemic highlighted the disparity between central authorities and local realities. Tomkins has criticised authorities in British Africa, noting that local administrators 'proved more sensitive to the threat than did the metropolitan authority', characterising the response of the Colonial Office as 'passive in the extreme'. In the Gold Coast, meanwhile, the colonial government made little effort to inform the population about the epidemic or to issue advice on how best to care for flu victims. In her study of the flu outbreak in the Bombay Presidency in India, Mridula Ramanna found that official response was defined by confusion and inconsistency. It was the non-governmental organisations which provided the main form of aid, suggesting that health did not figure highly on the agenda of the imperial government.[48]

In the years prior to the epidemic in Ireland meanwhile, public health had been neglected, especially in comparison to improvements made in Britain. In a paper read before the Social and Statistical Inquiry Society of Ireland in February 1919, a doctor pointed out that Ireland had had no Public Health Act since 1872, whereas England and Scotland had had several acts 'for the improvement of their population in rural and civic areas'. He added that 'the death rate has been lowered by 35 per cent in England and by 30 per cent in Scotland, whilst in Ireland there has been an increase in the death rate of two per cent'. Shortly before this, the Medical Secretary of the British Medical Association's Irish office had reproached the government for attaching 'more importance to the repair of Irish roads' than to the 'repair or care of 50 per cent of the Irish people'. In the wake of the epidemic, the *Medical Press* complained that 'in the minds of those in authority everything comes before the health of the people'.[49]

Although the colonial apparatus was shown to be inadequate to the challenge of the pandemic, the Great Flu cannot be cited as an instance of the centre neglecting its peripheries. The British government's attempts to combat the flu domestically also left it open to much criticism, leading one historian to dismiss its reaction as 'one of the least effective responses to the epidemic'. This placed it at one end of an international spectrum that ranged from America, which 'put considerable effort into public health interventions', to Germany, where authorities at both national and state level did their best to either deny or to significantly downplay the threat posed by the flu's arrival.[50]

It should also be noted that at the same time, in Ireland, the epidemic did not figure prominently on the Sinn Féin agenda, reflecting perhaps what Ruth Barrington has described as the 'low priority afforded in Irish public life to medical relief of the poor'. The minutes of the First Dáil contain no references to the flu, despite the fact that the spread of the third wave coincided with its opening sessions. Kathleen Lynn reported on the flu epidemic at the Sinn Féin Ard-Fheis in March 1919, but did not expect that her speech would make an impact, writing in her diary: 'I reported on 'Flu epidemic, hope they will mind my words.' The subordination of health to politics was perhaps most clearly illustrated by the fact that the only collective effort engaged in by the Boards of Guardians of the various Poor Law Unions in response to the flu was to circulate a petition for the release of the doctors who had been interned by the British Government. It was only when the epidemic overlapped with the national question that any kind of organised political action was undertaken.[51]

The epidemic revealed that there could be a substantial difference between who was meant to be responsible, and who in fact took responsibility, when epidemic disease broke out. Technically, responsibility for public health was divided between the Local Government Board, Rural and Urban District Councils (and Corporations), and Boards of Guardians. Sinn Féin, presenting themselves as a shadow government, could also have been expected to take an interest in how thousands of people were coping with this onslaught of disease. The epidemic revealed a Local Government Board that was detached from the lives of many of the populace, and local authorities whose responsiveness varied, although many did the best they could within the boundaries of contemporary epidemiological thinking. Cleaning streets and clearing refuse may not have made much difference, but accepted beliefs meant that these were the best measures possible at this time. Those who accepted the bulk of the responsibility during the epidemic, however, were the doctors and nurses, nuns and 'ladies', charities and volunteers, and neighbours and friends around the country. It was these men and women who proved to be the main providers of relief and the most reliable custodians of public health in Ireland during the Great Flu.

CHAPTER SEVEN

Putting Order on Disease: Naming and Understanding the Great Flu [1]

As this aggressive form of flu spread around the country in 1918/19, people had great difficulty in reconciling their previous experiences of influenza with the disease that was now causing such disarray. In a desperate wire sent by the parish priest on the Aran Islands to the Galway Board of Guardians, he attempted to impress upon the officials how the flu was 'making havoc', appealing to the Board for any kind of help – 'Can you do anything?' In other parts of the country, the epidemic elicited countless expressions of bewilderment and disquieted confusion. [2]

Medics and local authorities were forced to publicly confess their lack of understanding, admitting the cause of the epidemic to be 'unknown'. Its initial advance in the west prompted the 'most weird accounts' of what was cast as a 'terrible and curious form of influenza'. In witnesses' reflections on the epidemic, the verb 'rage' appears repeatedly, reflecting the popular sense that this disease had an ability to spread that eluded control. That such words appeared so often in depictions of the influenza epidemic is suggestive of the way in which the event not only caused material disorder, but how this disorder also pervaded discourse on the 'new influenza', suffusing the ways in which people constructed and portrayed the 'terrible epidemic'. This chapter traces the ways in which people tried to understand the Great Flu, charting the 'epidemic of explanation' that accompanied the outbreak. It asks how people tried to make sense of, and to rationalise this 'mysterious malady' which brought death rates to a point where corpses could not be 'interred as fast as they arrived' in cemeteries, and overwhelmed victims' bodies to such an extent that those around them took them to be as good as dead. [3]

THE 'MYSTERIOUS MALADY': FINDING A FEW NAME FOR 'FLU'[4]

For many people, 'flu', 'influenza', or the 'old hin', as it was colloquially known in some parts, does not seem to have been thought appropriate for the infection which ripped through the country in 1918/19. The host of names given to the disease showed the problems people witnessed as they tried to understand and to impose logic on the epidemic – as sociologist Pierre Bourdieu notes, the process of naming is fundamental to the 'production of common sense'.[5] The varied and uncertain nomenclature reflected the mystery surrounding the disease and did little to assuage fears of the infection.[6]

Historiography consistently asserts that contemporaries referred to the pandemic as 'Spanish flu' due to the lack of censorship in Spain which allowed reports of the disease to circulate. In Ireland, however, there was much less consensus over the proper name for this malady. Niall Johnson has also shown that most countries settled on names for the outbreak that were appropriate to their own cultures and ways of understanding sickness and health.[7]

There was unmistakable doubt and disbelief that the disease spreading around Ireland with such injurious effects could be influenza. Uncertainty over the nature of the threat persisted throughout the epidemic's three-wave visitation, and was evident in the wide variety of names given to the infection. Whereas during the Russian flu pandemic of the early 1890s, the disease was referred to consistently as 'flu' or 'influenza', in 1918/19 it was seldom labelled in such direct, unambiguous terms, reflecting the 'disorientation of collective anxiety' that existed during the epidemic.[8] The infection was regularly called the 'mysterious malady', 'the mysterious influenza epidemic', or 'that mysterious form of influenza'. Schoolmaster Thomas Hayes, in a letter to the *Freeman's Journal*, expressed his concern at how citizens were 'dying in scores from a mysterious malady'. The terms 'influenza' or 'flu' were often found to be insufficient to describe the realities of the sickness and the effects it was having. The Chairman of Skibbereen Rural District Council referred to it rather as 'the terrible malady, which for want of some better name was called influenza', while the *Tipperary Star* wondered if the Irish language even had an appropriate name for this abhorrent disease which was being denoted by 'flu' in English. It was not influenza, but only 'so-called influenza'.[9]

There was a sense of disconnection between flu outbreaks in the past and the form of the disease as witnessed in this epidemic. 'Flu' and 'influenza' were no longer adequate when it came to capturing the bleak reality of sickness which erupted in 1918 and 1919, as this 'highly infectious and decidedly virulent form' of influenza differed starkly from the 'homely malady' with which people had 'been long familiar in Ireland'. Departing so substantially from previous experiences of the infection, the flu of 1918 was variously dubbed 'the New Influenza', 'the modern influenza', 'the new flue', 'the new malady', or 'an tinneas nua' (the new fever/sickness).[10]

Other naming strategies focussed on the disease's source and believed 'foreignness', reflecting popular perceptions of where guilt for the pandemic lay. Although historians have asserted that the term 'Spanish Flu' was common, in Ireland at least, the flu was rarely assigned an Iberian origin. References to 'Spanish Flu' were relatively infrequent in Irish sources, and autobiographies and retrospective accounts seldom employ this term, using instead a variety of other names to refer to the epidemic. This is consistent with Eugenia Tognotti's finding that there was a lack of consensus over the proper name for the disease at the time, and that contemporaries may have found the moniker 'Spanish Flu' inappropriate. Although foreignness was assumed, the flu virus was seen rather as linked with the Great War than with any particular country, and both 'Flander's Flu' – also employed in the US at times – and 'war plague' featured.[11]

The vast dimensions and incredible ferocity of the disease were other aspects which cropped up frequently in popular representations of the Great Flu. For example, the *Freeman's Journal* referred to the flu outbreak as 'the great sickness', while an official in Galway Union thought that it was nothing short of a 'world-wide epidemic'. A belief in the scale of the pandemic also informs a series of names used in Irish autobiographies and local history studies, with writers recounting it as the 'Great Flu'. An impression of its magnitude is also a motif in the stories told of the epidemic in the Bureau of Military History archives, and several references are made to 'the "Great Flu"', and 'the "Big 'Flu"'.[12] That portrayals of the dimensions of the epidemic should feature in public discourse is consistent with 'the hard to grasp magnitude of its toll which could not be credibly attributed to as everyday a disease as influenza'.

The disease was often denoted by its severity, as phrases like 'the bad epidemic of influenza', 'the bad 'Flu', 'a serious outbreak', and 'the horrible epidemic' all featured in both contemporary accounts and recollections. Described too as 'nothing less' than a 'fever', this reflected the way in which the various names given to the disease frequently related to specific local conditions, as fevers had been among the most dreaded of the Famine diseases.[13]

The tendency to label the disease on the basis of its symptoms and physical effects was most evident in retrospective accounts of the epidemic, as it was recalled variously as the 'Black Flu', the 'falling sickness', and 'gastric flu'. Descriptions of the infection as 'Black Flu' denoted the change of skin tone that sometimes occurred in the bodies of those that died from the disease. The heliotrope cyanosis was 'the most dreaded symptom', with only a fraction of cases managing to recover after developing the 'dusky blue' colour, the 'great majority' succumbing.[14]

Use of the term 'falling sickness', meanwhile, represented the numbers of cases in which 'the onset was so sudden that people used to fall down in the street while going to or coming from work'. The official report by the British Ministry of Health described this abrupt and uncontrollable weakness as being among the characteristic symptoms of the new influenza: 'the patient would be seized rapidly, or most suddenly, with a sense of such prostration as to be utterly unable to carry on what he might be doing'. In Canada, one of the persistent memories of the epidemic was how people were prone to collapse, liable to drop 'just like a shot. Even the children...they just fell down and died. Like that. They...just fall right down.'[15]

Naming the infection according to how it felt and its physicality resonates with survivors' keen recollection of the effects of the flu on their bodies. One of the things that seemed to stay with people most clearly was how this strain of influenza *felt*, as it left an intensely visceral memory with many survivors. Comments on the acute prostration – 'the revolting "grogginess" that persisted for weeks, and sometimes even for months in those lucky enough to recover', the profound debilitation and long recovery period, and the soaring body temperature, which reached 105 or 106°F in some cases, all suggested that a vivid sense of the physicality of the disease lasted among those who lived through it.[16]

Frank Drohan recorded, for example, how he was 'in a kind of trance for about three days, delirium I suppose. I remember I was going through halls and all kinds of grand places during that time...' Tipperary Volunteer Seamus Babbington recalled the acute weakness brought by the virus – he was scarcely able to take his 'clothes off with sickness'. He had 'it bad and was in bed for a month', with deep cyanosis: 'the blackest man in Africa was not blacker'. Seán Moylan from Cork, who would later become a TD, lay in bed for a month 'lifeless, dead in body and mind'. Even when he recovered, his energy 'had completely disappeared', and it was a further month before he 'was back in fighting trim again'. Mathew MacMahon, of Trentagh, Donegal, who was just a boy at the time, recalled being sent to the shop for bread, beginning to feel weak on his way back, and 'as everything began to turn green and swim about him he sat down on a stone, recovered eventually and managed to reach home'.[17]

Among the memories of the epidemic that stayed with Ernest Blythe, leader of the political prisoners in Belfast Jail, were the speed and prevalence of the infection, and the symptoms it exhibited:

> Very few escaped the 'flu. Up to a certain point we had full parades every day. Then there came a morning when half a dozen were sick. By the time the evening parade was reached the half dozen had grown to twenty. At last, out of the two hundred men in the prison barely thirty were on their feet...A lot of the prisoners were pretty bad, with a great deal of bleeding from the nose. Two men went off their heads and had to be removed to a mental institution.[18]

The term 'plague' appeared repeatedly, usually to indicate the numbers of sick and dying the flu was leaving behind. *The Kerryman* used it to signal the scale of mortality recorded world-wide: 'it is roughly estimated that over six million have succumbed to the ravages of this plague, or whatever you like to call it'. In the *Tipperary Star*, 'the "Flu" Plague' headed an article which was concerned with the 'terrible toll' taken by the infection on Clonmel, while in Tipperary town and district, 'the Plague' had reportedly caused within the space of a few days 'five or six deaths'.[19]

The plague metaphor was often embedded in contexts of quantification, with writers using it to convey this infection's ability to spread and kill in large numbers. Use of the word in this sense had a precedent, having often been invoked in a similar way in accounts of disease in the past. For instance, in the nineteenth century cholera had been represented as 'plague' ('pláigh') due to the many people lost to the disease and an awareness of its potential to inflict extensive mortality. The term had also been used to express the increased seriousness of influenza observed during the Russian flu pandemic of the 1890s – 'the present plague of influenza has been more *fatal* and *prevalent* during the last portions of our autumn' (emphasis added). The metaphor functioned as the 'benchmark of a severe epidemic', its use calculated to convey gravity and threat.[20]

The variety of names given to the disease, and the multitude of ways in which people chose to describe and define the epidemic, suggests that the impression given in historiography that 'it was known as Spanish flu as it was believed that it originated in Spain' somewhat glosses over the diversity of labels used at the time and the uncertainty accompanying the epidemic. It also has the effect of simplifying the ways in which people tried to organise and express their thoughts on this 'mysterious and deadly epidemic'.[21]

'WHAT IS THIS SPANISH INFLUENZA THAT EVERYONE IS TALKING ABOUT?'[22]

The urge to assuage the confusion and disorder wrought by the epidemic was further evident in the abundance of explanations for the 'mysterious malady' which circulated during the outbreak. From contaminated monkeys to putrescent mouth infections, causality was articulated in a variety of ways, reflecting how the search for the causes of illness has been an enduring aspect of the sickness experience and an intrinsic part of epidemic medicine.[23] Though a range of explanations for the Great Flu were offered over the course of the outbreak, there were a number which surfaced consistently, situating the event in socio-political, religious, scientific, and historical interpretive frameworks respectively.

Although historians have disagreed over the connection between the First World War and the Great Flu, those alive at the time were much more certain that there was a close link between the two. In Italy, the public blamed the flu on the German launch of a bacteriological offensive, whereas in Canada, the epidemic was remembered as a sequel to the conflict: 'After the war was over…then came the flu. Thats where it came from…(sic)' In France, contemporary writers also saddled the war with culpability, positive that it was the fighting that had caused a usually innocuous illness to mutate into a 'devastating scourge', while in South Africa, English patriots were sure that the Germans were behind the outbreak. Physicians also connected the two, with some doctors believing the initial wave to have been 'occasioned and spread by war conditions'.[24]

In Ireland at this time, ideas of a clear causal link between the war and the pandemic frequently circulated in the public sphere, loading perceptions of the flu with moral and ethical significance. Rather than perceiving the Great Flu as having originated in Spain, genesis of the disease was traced more decisively to central Europe, with guilt often laid specifically at the door of the German army.

In one of the earliest reports on the epidemic, a delay in the renewal of the German offensive was attributed to a 'very severe epidemic of influenza' thought to have broken out 'in the ranks of the enemy forces'. The *Fermanagh Times* was not surprised, and commented knowingly that 'mutinies and epidemics are very significant causes which would make the enemy hesitate'. Jeremiah Murphy from Kerry, still a boy at the time, believed that 'it began in Europe and was spread all over the world by the discharge of troops to all countries'. 'War bread' was even thought to have ushered in this 'dreaded visitor', with 'malnutrition and the general weakening of nerve power known as war-weariness' providing the 'necessary conditions' for the epidemic. That an outbreak of disease would follow the war was not wholly unexpected, and the perceived connection between the two events was consistent with the 'popular coupling of wars and epidemics in the western world'.[25]

Another hypothesis in Ireland was that the Great War had upset the relationship between humanity and nature. The slaughter during the military campaigns had reached 'a scale unprecedented in human history', and since the dead bodies had remained 'overground longer than was desirable', infection had spread, providing a lesson that 'nature always brings her nemesis'. The Great War had unsettled the precarious balance between man and the natural world, and now the world's population was paying the price. One of the parish priests in Boyle, Roscommon, was quoted as having 'often said that this war will wind up with a Great Plague', with the flu seen as having borne out his wisdom.[26]

The role of the war dead in bringing about the pandemic was a recurrent theme in speculation on the Great Flu. In Seamus Babington's account of the epidemic, he mentions how the flu was supposed to have originated in Europe, a consequence of the 'thousands of unburied bodies' left lying on the ground and in the trenches. Dr Kathleen Lynn similarly proposed that the outbreak was due to a miasma produced by the bodies of dead soldiers:

> ...in France and Flanders the poisonous matter from millions of unburied bodies is constantly rising up into the air, which is blown all over the world by the winds. Hence the Influenza plague is universal, though, it is said, most severe in France.[27]

Holding to a similar theory, the Spanish authorities thought that 'the present plague originated as a result of the fighting in the early stages of the war in the Carpathian Mountains, when hundreds of thousands of corpses were allowed to remain unburied for months', and in fact 'were never buried'. The melting of the snows hastened the decomposition of these dead soldiers, 'lying, as many of them were, in great heaps, carried together by mountain streams'. It was this mass decaying of bodies which brought about the Great Flu, illustrating Deborah Lupton's observation of how in the past 'the miasmas issuing from diseased, dead and decomposing bodies' were seen as especially dangerous and liable to cause sickness.[28]

Ideas of the threat posed by dead bodies to the living were not confined to Europe, but stretched also to parts of Africa. Terence Ranger's research on belief systems in Southern Rhodesia during the epidemic unearthed the following account: '...[None] of the ngangas [traditional healers] could do anything. They told the people that the disease came from the white folk. It was not sent by the midzimu [ancestors], or by the Mwari [high god], but by the white people. So many were killed in the great war of the white people that the blood of the dead had caused this great sickness.'[29]

The way in which the epidemic was tied to the war and its dead in turn shows the moral meanings being read into the First World War at the time. This scale of collective death had implications, and the association made between the war and the Great Flu suggested a widespread and concerned awareness of the war's unprecedented levels of bloodshed. Notions of blame are etched deeply into this framework of explanation, finding scapegoats in the Germans and in the event of the war itself. In these war-based understandings, responsibility for the pandemic lay in man's hands. The explicit connection drawn between the Great War and the Great Flu illustrated the ability of disease to take on 'a wider social, political and cultural significance': the pandemic made sense in the context of war; it was the price of conflict and a necessary atonement for man's destructiveness.[30]

Religious interpretations of the Great Flu were also informed by themes of morality, punishment and penitence. In calling on faith to help interpret the influenza outbreak, people were invoking longstanding explanatory frameworks for epidemic disease. Providentialist explanations for outbreaks of sickness had in fact been relatively widespread in Ireland in the nineteenth century, with even doctors believing that illness was imbued with spiritual and moral significance. Events such as the cholera scare of 1832 reflected the widespread and ardent belief that the disease could be prevented by prayer and by distributing 'blessed' turf and straws, and the cult of the Marian shrines several decades later also highlighted popular acceptance of the role of God in sickness and healing.[31]

Though such ideas had largely faded from medical discourse by the end of the nineteenth century, as theories about disease came increasingly to centre around germ theory and bacteriology, in 1918, lay people continued to link sickness with God's will. Reflecting on the deaths of two colleagues at the hands of the epidemic, Mr Doyle of Wicklow Urban Council thought it was 'a sad thing to think that since their last monthly meeting, it had pleased God to visit them with a severe epidemic that had been brought home to them very forcibly as…today they had to mourn the loss of two most amiable, good, and trustworthy officials'. The Chairman concurred, regretting that though 'it was very sad to have these two young men taken away in the prime of life…God's Will must be done'.[32]

Priests explained the epidemic as 'the will of God', and comforted families with reminders that the dying were simply answering the 'Great Call', responding to the 'Divine Will', and bravely demonstrating a readiness to place themselves in 'God's hands'.[33] Religious translations of the epidemic allowed for the deaths of flu victims to be assigned a comforting meaning – they were being called to God and the loss of life was an expression of His will, imbuing the deaths with sense and purpose.

For many, God not only decided the fate of flu victims but was also a protector and healer. James Crowley, interned in Belfast Jail when the flu hit, marvelled that none of the many political prisoners in Belfast died from the disease, concluding that 'the Good God must have been looking down on the boys with a kindly eye'. As the second wave of the epidemic in Dublin faded away, it was gratefully said that 'the people's prayers' had finally been heard. Officials at Castlebar Petty Sessions similarly attributed diminution of the epidemic in the area to 'Providence and the able medical men of Castlebar', and the Ballyhaunis Parish Church was 'packed' on 12 December 1918 in order to celebrate a thanksgiving High Mass for 'the aversion of (the) dread scourge from Ireland'.[34]

Religion offered a way to bargain for health: if people were devout enough, God would keep them safe. Thus, newspaper notices were commissioned to thank the Lord for ensuring that families remained safe and recovered from the flu – 'I wish to return my most sincere thanks to the Sacred Heart of Jesus for my recovery from influenza'; 'heart-felt thanks to the Sacred Heart…and the Holy Souls for preserving our family from the influenza'. In the same vein, masses were offered around the country in the hope of alleviating the suffering. In times of epidemic disease, health was contingent on a bartering process:

if sufficient prayers were tendered, God would hear and relieve the communities' physical ills.[35]

The flu epidemic, moreover, showed a continuing belief in Ireland that the age of miracles was not yet past. One particular column in the *Freeman's Journal* advised everyone to wear a Sacred Heart badge, as this had a proven track record in disease prevention. Such instances of trust in the power of religion and faith tie in with Laurence Geary's identification of a strong belief in faith healing in nineteenth-century Ireland, which lasted well into the twentieth century.[36]

The Great Flu highlighted the acceptance in Irish culture of the close links between the body and spirit, showing that in turn-of-the-century Ireland, illness and healing were interpreted holistically, with widespread acceptance that there was a connection between the 'worlds of matter and spirit, the seen and unseen'. Religion offered not just comfort in a time of crisis but a way of dealing with sickness – health could be ensured through religious devotion and moral goodness. Illness in Ireland was 'spiritualised', and the unhealthy body bore a distinct religious meaning, reflecting lack of religious fortitude.[37]

In addition to war and religion, another body of knowledge drawn on to interpret the epidemic was supplied by the world of science, as nineteenth-century public health ideas, as well as bacteriology and germ theory, were called on in popular interpretations of the 'mysterious disease' and its origins.[38]

In the nineteenth century, sanitarianism had been one of the dominant creeds in both medical thought and public health theories in Europe. It stressed the role of the environment and social conditions in the spread of disease, and that infection could be kept at bay by ensuring sterile surroundings and efficient waste disposal. The presumed link between disease and an unclean environment was among the main themes in lay discourse on the flu epidemic in 1918/19, as people repeatedly called for cleansed physical surroundings in their efforts to prevent and curb the disease.

Calling attention to the outbreak of influenza in the town, the Chairman of Arklow Urban Council attempted to impress on his colleagues the urgent need to have the public thoroughfares cleaned up. He was also concerned by the danger posed by a local sewer: 'it wants to be cleaned out immediately', as they 'could not be too careful for if the present epidemic went ahead in the town they did not know where it was going to end'. A number of local residents were in agreement with these sanitation principles, writing to the council to point out 'the disgraceful condition of an ashpit' in Meadow's Laneway, Arklow, which during the 'present time of sickness' they considered 'dangerous', asking that it be removed.[39] In Trim, the Chairman of the School Board thought that in order to prevent 'recurrent attacks of the epidemic', it was vital to pay 'prompt attention' to the 'sanitary arrangements' of the institution.[40]

Although these ideas suggested a large measure of continuity with nineteenth-century sanitarian discourse, awareness of the newly emergent discipline of bacteriology was also apparent, with ideas on the epidemic often expressed in the vernacular of 'germ theory' and borrowing from the developing vocabulary of disease pathology. Micro-organisms, bacteria, and germs were increasingly coming to constitute the disease threats that comets and fire from heaven had once done in the past. Even at the turn of the century, the idea that diseases were traceable to 'bacilli' was being absorbed into lay understandings of disease, with illnesses such as influenza, cholera, and consumption coming to be seen as 'the work of invisible living pests'.[41]

Ways of 'germ thinking' were frequently evident in the language people used to express their thoughts about the 'dreaded "flu"'. Con O'Donovan, writing to a friend from Usk Prison, hoped that 'you and yours continue in the enjoyment of perfect health and spirits despite the prevalence of influenza and other microbes'. Influenza was described as lowering the 'natural power of resistance to disease', leaving persons liable to attacks by the 'germs of pneumonia among others'. In Sligo and Galway, there was a 'big run' on chemists' shops as large numbers of people rushed to buy disinfectants, to cleanse their surroundings of the harmful microbes, and to render the home a place of safety once again.[42]

In certain parts of the country, sales of quinine soared, possibly due to the belief that 'the germs of influenza' were 'said not to be able to live' in the substance. In order to fend off the flu microbes, people were advised to practise personal hygiene – 'keep your mouth, nose and hands clean', as concern moved from the environment to the human body. It was no longer just the physical environment that had to be feared; germ theory showed how infections could skulk in the body's pores and crevices, as sputa and breath passed on bacteria and made cutlery, cups, clothes, and even library books into carriers of disease.[43]

Advertising was one sphere of public discourse in which bacteriology was particularly prevalent, as producers of all manner of disinfectants and patent medicines clamoured to profit from the epidemic. The proliferation of ads for flu therapies spawned by the epidemic can be seen as representative of a growing commercialisation of the self-help tradition (already underway in Britain by the end of the nineteenth century), as the outbreak was enthusiastically expressed in the 'language of consumerism'. Companies were willing to bank on the 'germ sell' being one of the most effective ways to shift their products.[44]

In these ads, the cause of the disease was reduced to a single factor – a microbial invader – with the malady curable by means of a number of convenient correctives – a few pills or a teaspoon of medicine. These were the 'magic bullets' which promised to eliminate the disease quickly and easily. Safety from flu and protection of health were transformed into hassle-free purchasable commodities. *Genasprin*, for instance – 'a powerful antiseptic' – promised to kill any flu microbes in the blood, while *Kue pills* were another product which would perform the same function. Further miracle drugs were available in the form of quinine and cinnamon influenza tablets and *Gelsemium Pillules*, the latter being marketed as 'a homeopathic remedy for adults and children'. *Formamint* boasted of being 'the germ killing throat tablet', while *Taylor's Influenza Mixture* was another simple cure.[45]

'*Vaporising*' *Bacterol* staked its reputation on being 'the most potent non-poisonous germ destroyer known', providing comforting assurances of its ability to sterilise the air 'scientifically', acting as a 'perfect deodoriser', while at the same time preventing the 'spread of Influenza'.[46] These products, whose abilities were expressed in language redolent with ability, purpose, and potency, were calculated to allay anxieties, promising to eradicate the threat of this ubiquitous disease. The spirit of commercial opportunism was also evident in the way in which disease fears were played on to promote a variety of other items, including life assurance, lemonade, clothing – you could 'avoid the "flu" by keeping yourself warm', and at Duignan's store there was 'plenty of warm clothing' – and meat. People were warned of the tendency of hair to fall out during a bout of the flu, but luckily *Ashmore's Pilocarpine Lotion* was available as a cure. Even *Dunlop Tyres* could play their part in keeping the flu infection at bay. With undertones of the nineteenth-century vitalistic doctrines which had espoused a strong connection between exercise and health, one advertisement asserted that 'very few of the people who've had influenza are regular cyclists', since those who took to the roads on their bikes were exposed to the healthy air of the outdoors – 'the clean sweet air on the road is far healthier than the stuffy atmosphere inside the tram, the bus or the train'.[47]

The abundance of flu advertisements during the epidemic raises the issue of how scientific knowledge may have been diffused to the public in early twentieth-century Ireland. Nancy Tomes has shown that in America at this time, the lively promotion of medical products in the form of 'epidemic entertainments' played an important role in spreading and popularising bacteriology and scientific information. The way in which science suffused the ad campaigns of so many flu products during the epidemic suggests that advertising may have been fulfilling a similar purpose in Ireland in this period.[48]

Another theme in the popular response to the flu echoed that identified by Jay Winter in the reaction to the Great War, namely a 'backward gaze' – a tendency to look to the past in search of meaning in the present. In Ireland, there were many instances of people trawling recent history for any events comparable to the flu outbreak, and an impulse to seek analogies for the epidemic in living memory was frequently evident over the course of the epidemic. An official of Longford Union spoke of the condition of the town brought about by the flu's arrival as 'the gravest ever I remember (*sic*)…there was a vast quantity of illness and sickness', with another describing it unhesitatingly as 'the greatest necessity that has arisen in our lifetime'. The Clerk of the New Ross Board of Guardians similarly reported that the number 'on the sick list was the largest he ever remembered there', as the local press estimated 1,500 cases of influenza in Wexford alone.[49]

Reports, however, repeatedly stressed the exceptional quality of the epidemic, with recent decades unable to offer any comparable experiences. People at the time felt strongly that this outbreak was unique and remarkable in nature – in Birr, Offaly, 'the exigencies of the time' brought about by the flu were considered unequalled 'for upwards of half a century', while Kilkenny was described as 'passing through an ordeal unparalleled in its severity and devastating in its effects'. In Thurles, Tipperary, 'not for many years' had the 'dead' bell 'been heard so constantly', and in Nenagh, the old Abbey bell had never been 'so frequently tolled, and not since its erection did St Mary's of the Rosary contain at the same time so many corpses'.[50]

These efforts to find a precedent for the epidemic showed how people tried to seek meaning and order through the orientational power of the past, reflecting a more general cultural pattern discerned by Stephen Kern in this era, as those living at the turn of the century were inclined to look to history 'for stability in the face of rapid, technological change'. Sociologist Barry Schwartz has explored this ability of memory to provide signposts for present experience, asserting that it can act as an 'ordered system of symbols that makes experience meaningful'. The importance of memory for making sense of present experience is also noted by Michael Schudson who observes that by invoking the past, people are seeking to 'know what is right, what is true...some kind of direction...some kind of anchor when they are adrift'.[51]

Examination of lay discourse on the flu in 1918/19 reveals that people frequently attempted to draw on memory of any event in the past that was similar to the epidemic. Vague references were made to a period of roughly half a century previously, implicitly comparing the hardship of the epidemic to that witnessed in the aftermath of the Famine years or 'Drochshaol' (literally: 'Bad/Awful life'). The Chairman of Strabane Urban District Council, for instance, commented that 'not for over fifty years had such a scourge as the influenza come among the poor', and Dr Costello of Tuam Union declared to the Board of Guardians that 'this epidemic may never occur again. The like of it has not occurred for fifty or sixty years.' One of a handful of explicit parallels was to be found in the Ministry of Health report on the pandemic which compared the severity of the flu outbreak to the 'famine typhus of Ireland'.[52]

Attempts to link or 'key' the event with any similar one in the familiar past were largely unsuccessful though, with few clear comparisons made. 'Keying' is described by Schwartz as a 'mechanism of memory work', and involves juxtaposing events so that one narrative can be used as a means to interpret another event. Scholar Paul Fussell, for instance, has documented the way in which soldiers fighting in the Second World War used the First World War as a framework for expressing their experiences.[53]

In 1918/19 there were few parallels which could be drawn with the outbreak, and what emerges more persistently is a sense at the time of the historical uniqueness of the Great Flu. A letter to the *Freeman's Journal* searched for, but was unable to find, a precedent for the epidemic, considering it to be 'a visitation of a kind utterly unlike, both by reason of its character and intensity, anything that has come before'. The *Wicklow People* alleged that in Tinahely 'not within the memory of the oldest inhabitant' had such a 'large number of people been ill at the same time'. The *Sligo Champion* reported that 'Death's harvest' had 'never in living memory' been as heavy as during the winter of the epidemic. The Clerk of Rathdrum Guardians similarly commented to the Board that 'they had not had an epidemic like that for many years', while during the first wave in Belfast Union, Dr Gardner Robb, the Medical Officer of Health, stated that 'never in his recollection had the strain been so great on the staff as during this past few weeks'.[54]

Living memory was unable to provide the points of reference or the orientation sought for during this visitation of flu 'in its new form'. The Great Flu was considered by members of Wicklow Urban District Council to be a 'special outbreak of illness', while the clerk of Youghal Board of Guardians described it as 'the most appalling' epidemic the Board 'had ever to deal with'. In the northwest, the 1918 outbreak of flu was reported to be 'the most virulent on record', while *The Irish Times* judged that 'the gravity of the epidemic was beyond all recent experience'. The Ministry of Health report also described how it had 'far surpassed anything previously experienced', with the toll taken on the young adult population being 'without any known West European or American precedent'. One of the Wexford Guardians described it as 'not an ordinary visitation': it was 'one so terrible that it demanded every precaution'.[55]

Doctors in particular were struck by the unfamiliar and distinctive character of the flu outbreak. Dr King, of Coollattin Dispensary District, considered it to have been an 'exceptional epidemic', while a local doctor attempted to impress on the Tuam Board of Guardians its severity, classing it as an 'emergency that didn't happen before', and which he hoped 'would never occur again'. Those who examined the internal organs of flu sufferers noted the new ways in which the disease damaged tissues and cells. A physician who worked on the Ministry of Health's official report was tempted 'to coin a new word altogether to express so complete a type of lung-inflammation'. The infection had reduced the lungs to the consistency of 'Gruyère cheese', causing changes in the anatomy that were 'entirely unlike what is met with in any ordinary forms of pneumonia'.[56]

Even seasoned chemists and physicians such as Sir Charles Cameron, and Sir John Moore, senior physician at the Adelaide Hospital, Dublin, were hard-pressed to find a prior instance of disease comparable to the Great Flu, with the former describing it as 'the most dangerous epidemic of the kind that has ever visited Dublin'. Moore's extensive experience proved likewise unable to yield any enlightening parallels:

> It has fallen to my lot to witness a cholera epidemic in 1866, small-pox epidemics…and last, not least, the epidemic (or rather pandemic) of influenza in 1889–90. But, in my opinion, none of these visitations equalled the present outbreak in extent, virulence, or treacherous course.[57]

Other doctors also found it difficult to reconcile this new form of influenza and its effects with their understandings of and encounters with infection in the past. The speakers at a clinical meeting of the British Medical Association freely used expressions such as 'unparalleled in medical history' and 'like nothing we have met before' in order to describe their experiences. One surgeon at the meeting who had been serving with the navy declared simply, 'there is nothing in the history of medicine like these epidemics, and I doubt very much if we should apply the name influenza to the diseases'. Dr Kathleen Lynn, attempting to impress the gravity of the situation on a Sinn Féin convention, stated that 'the October and February outbreaks were of a violence almost unparalleled in the history of medicine'.[58]

The period of the Great Flu seemed to some almost like a time apart, a few months that were out of sync with the normal passage of time as the fear, death, and urgency which accompanied the epidemic meant that it served as a bleak contrast with the routine unfolding of everyday life. One judge in Limerick described how it had been 'a time of real emergency', and in Ballyhaunis, the 'general feeling' was that the epidemic had given rise to 'one of the most un-Christmas-like Christmases we have had for some time': 'the presence of this scourge in our midst since early October up almost to the eve of Xmas, bringing sorrow to many homes, in great measure accounted for the absence of such festive rejoicing during the Christmas season of 1918'. The Master of Ballinrobe workhouse referred to the epidemic as a time 'of great difficulty', and the *Tipperary Star* preferred the term 'a time of the utmost emergency'.[59]

Observers noted the seemingly incessant funeral processions to Glasnevin cemetery in Dublin, which at one point in October 1918 numbered 240 over eight days, and which were a vast departure from 'ordinary times' when the daily average was more likely to be in the region of 12 or 13. Responding to a charge of negligence from a patient's family, one doctor was resolute and unapologetic in his explanation, making clear the distinction between the working conditions in 'normal times' and those occasioned by the epidemic:

> It is difficult for persons unacquainted with the conditions of the recent influenza epidemic to realise the enormity of the work thrown on medical men. My ordinary work was, during that time, increased twenty-fold. I worked my best and longest, and if everybody have (*sic*) not received the full attention they were entitled to in normal times I cannot help it.[60]

Obituaries were imbued with a sense of 'time lost', as loved ones grappled with the same issues confronting families and friends who were mourning the loss of men and boys in the Great War – 'questions about the truncation of millions of lives, about promise unfulfilled'. The youthful demographic claimed by the epidemic meant that innumerable lives had been ended precipitously, their deaths being 'premature', and 'untimely', coming when many of the victims were still at 'an early age', barely having entered the 'prime of life', and still having the 'prospect of many years to come'. The unexpected ending of so many young lives meant that 'shock', 'unexpected tidings', and 'painful surprise' became predictable phrases in the death notices of this time, underscored by sadness over the potential that would never be realised and the hopes that would never be fulfilled.[61]

*　　*　　*　　*

When the Great Flu struck, people turned variously to the Great War, to religion, to science, and to historical memory in their efforts to understand and reconcile themselves with the disease's onslaught. The ways in which they confronted the reality of the epidemic – the disease itself, its origins, transmission, and treatment – revealed themselves to be a palimpsest of ideas on sickness and health from previous centuries. In 1918, men and women drew on concepts and beliefs that had long been a part of wider health discourses such as man's relation to the world around him, the link between body and mind, the role of God and Providence in health, and ideals of balance and temperance, which hinted at the strong element of continuity in people's evolving understandings of infection and of their bodies. Although science (in particular bacteriology) may have been altering how people perceived sickness, as fears came to focus on micro-organisms rather than the supernatural, it did not fully displace older ideas about health and the body. Instead, it formed another layer on top of pre-existing ideas and frameworks of understanding, consistent with how, as Jacques Le Goff expressed it, 'mentalities change slower than anything else'. This also corresponds with the continuity that Deborah Brunton asserts characterised the medical world in Europe during the same period. Unlike in parts of Africa, where religious revivals and millenarianism blossomed in reaction to the flu's arrival, there is no evidence in Ireland that the epidemic precipitated any long-term change or developments in belief systems.[62]

That more than one interpretive framework was drawn on reflected in turn the plurality of models of illness used by people at this time, with faith, science, and man's relation to the cosmos all serving as categories of explanation. Sickness could take on multiple meanings, and during the epidemic, it was seen variously as a manifestation of divine will, a consequence of man's infringement of the delicate balance between nature and humanity, or simply as the work of microbial life. There were a number of different ways of thinking about the body available to, and practised by, people in early twentieth-century Ireland.[63]

One of the major problems which people witnessed as they struggled to impose meaning and logic on the outbreak, though, was the unusual and 'abnormal' nature of the visitation. With the Famine just beyond the memory of most, both the lay population and the medical community had difficulty in finding outbreaks of disease in the recent past that were comparable in severity or intensity to the Great Flu, with the result that, for many, the flu epidemic was felt or imagined to have no parallels. A wide variety of names were bestowed on the malady, demonstrating the widespread sense of disorientation and collective anxiety witnessed at the time as people had problems believing that this destructive disease could be the influenza with which they were familiar. Words and expressions such as 'exceptional', 'special', 'abnormal', 'remarkable', and 'not of the ordinary' punctuated discourse on the outbreak, as people found themselves unable to use their past experiences of disease to help them understand an extraordinary present.[64]

CHAPTER EIGHT

'The plague will long be remembered'?

Kenneth Crotty was only 11 years old when the flu struck his neighbourhood in Framingham, just outside Boston, Massachusetts. Almost ninety years later, Crotty could still remember how death was a constant presence during the epidemic: 'it was scary, because every morning when you got up, you asked, "Who died during the night?" You knew death was there all the time.' Jimmy Brady, from Glenveigh, Donegal, remembered the Great Flu in almost the same way, recalling 'how on rising every day the question was how many had died since the day before'. At Norway House, a community in the Canadian subarctic, the scale of death was also a distinctive memory for one of the locals: 'there were so many people, you know, they can't bury them all and after that, when they all gathered and they were buried in a box…they have an awful…difficult time, to gather all the people and to bury them…'. Along with broken bodies and homes, the Great Flu bequeathed harrowing and troubling memories.[1]

The recollections of doctors and nurses were particularly profound, studded with haunting images of the never-ending numbers of flu dead: 'the morgues were packed almost to the ceiling with bodies stacked one on top of another…You could never turn around without seeing a big red truck loaded with caskets for the train station so bodies could be sent home.' Historian Christopher Langford judges that the shock of the pandemic never faded for doctors and nurses, deeming it 'fair to say that the medical world is still haunted by the memory of 1918–19'.[2]

For some, silence was the only appropriate response. American historian William H. McNeill found that for his parents, it was an experience 'so searing' that they 'almost never spoke of it afterwards'. Journalist Gina Kolata similarly discovered that the horror of the outbreak made people reluctant to try to even put their experience into words: they said 'it was so horrible that they would not even talk about it', with the result that scholars assumed that the Great Flu had simply been forgotten.[3]

Literature on the pandemic is littered with claims that people forgot what had happened, that 'as soon as the dying stopped, the forgetting began'. In 1965, author H.L. Mencken wrote of how 'the epidemic is seldom mentioned and most Americans have apparently forgotten it'. Professor John Oxford, one of the foremost medical authorities on the Great Flu, has called it 'a forgotten pandemic'. Studying the flu in Britain, Niall Johnson concluded that the outbreak 'lacked long-term resonance' and that 'many western nations' have 'little collective recollection of this massive pandemic'.[4]

In parts of Africa and Asia, though, memory of the epidemic remained alive well into the latter decades of the twentieth century. In Southern Rhodesia (modern Zimbabwe), Terence Ranger found that 'the sudden onset of the disease, the bodies left lying unburied, the fate of whole homesteads' were aspects of the epidemic which had been branded on the rural imagination. Remembrance was also ensured through the names given to the babies born as adults died – the numerous 'Frazers' in Zimbabwe owe their titles to 'freza', the flu. In the northern parts of the Gold Coast, meanwhile, even decades after 1918, the smallest villages could still remember the outbreak: it had become 'an historical date because, everywhere, so many people died'. And in areas of Indonesia, Colin Brown found that memory of the epidemic still pulsated, having been incorporated into folklore and kept 'still very much alive'.[5]

Although the flu was largely absent from the meta-narrative of twentieth-century Ireland, it crops up frequently in biographies, memoirs, works of local history, and oral history sources such as the Bureau of Military History Archive, suggesting that rather than being forgotten, the epidemic was preserved in seams of memory at an individual and local level. Survivors could often remember and portray the outbreak with a considerable degree of clarity and vividness, and showed a common belief in its gravity and intensity, which contrast with the claims of how the epidemic was forgotten elsewhere. For many who witnessed it first hand, the Great Flu had a prominent place in the story of the individual's life, in the family history, or in the history of the community.

Teasing out the nature of those recollections provides some clues as to why these clusters of memory never developed into a collective memory or a national will to remember. Loss, death, and a sense of uncontrollable catastrophe were just some of the associations made with the outbreak, deterring the story-telling and open discussion which are crucial for remembering 'from below' and which are necessary to ensure that memory of an event is preserved collectively and in the long-term. More importantly, some believed that even talking about this fearsome disease might in fact bring it back.

At the time of the Great Flu, media rhetoric and popular assessments of the influenza outbreaks carried a confidence that the event would survive in people's memories long after the disease itself had subsided. The *Tipperary Star* judged that the outbreak would leave in its wake a widely shared memory, inscribing itself particularly on those who had suffered the deaths of loved ones: 'By all those who lived through it the plague will long be remembered, but particularly by those who, on its account, mourn the loss of those who were nearest and dearest to them in life.'[6]

The *King's County Chronicle* was similarly convinced that the epidemic would continue to resound tragically with those who had witnessed its effects first-hand, with the 'influenza and pneumonia plague' staying with many Tullamore families 'as a bitter memory, as they journey through life bereft of those whose happiness and welfare were everything to them'. The *Down Recorder* predicted that the flu would leave an immutable and widely shared memory trace, having ruptured family life to such a terrible extent: 'in the Killyleagh district, as in many parts of the country, the mysterious influenza waves of 1919 will long be remembered. They have broken down many a home.'[7]

Writing almost half a century afterwards, folklorist Kevin Danaher was sure that the flu epidemic had endured in the recollections of the generation that had lived through it: 'Older people will remember the great influenza epidemic which swept over the world at the end of the first Great War and killed, according to some authorities, more people than died from shell, bomb and bullet from 1914 to 1918.' Nurse Annie Smithson was similarly convinced that memory of the flu had lasted, and recalled the outbreak as ranking alongside the General Election and the Armistice of 1918 in terms of significance, describing 'the terrible epidemic of influenza which raged in Dublin and the General Election when Sinn Féin swept all before them'. These were the 'public events' she could still 'recollect vividly' almost thirty years later – 'more so even than the end of the war which came in November of that year'. Darrell Figgis, Joint Secretary of Sinn Féin, also presumed that the epidemic would be part of how the years 1918/19 would be remembered and that people would recall 'that at this time the epidemic known as post-war influenza raged in Europe, causing many deaths'.[8]

First-hand memories of the Great Flu could last for several decades after the outbreaks had subsided, with 'commonly held representations' of the epidemic to be found in oral and written reflections on Ireland in 1918 and 1919. Similar phrases were consistently used to portray the flu outbreak, and the persistence of expressions such as 'the bad epidemic of influenza', 'the bad 'Flu', and 'a serious outbreak', suggested a common sense of this influenza's severity and dimensions. Edward O'Malley, who had been a Volunteer in Mayo at the time, referred to it as 'the disastrous 'flu epidemic'. Joseph Sweeney, a university student in Galway during the flu, spoke of how a bout of 'the very bad influenza in 1918' prevented him from sitting his exams that year and necessitated his return home to west Donegal. Other terms employed in retrospect were the 'Great Flu' and the 'Big Flu', with Kathleen Behan recounting it as the 'great influenza epidemic of 1918'. In the written account of their escape from Usk Prison in Wales, Frank Shouldice and George Geraghty called it simply 'the terrible 1918 influenza'.[9]

Many accounts of the epidemic begin with depictions of its world-wide scale, indicating that survivors may have been drawing on what historian Niall Ó Cíosáin has termed a 'global memory' of the Great Flu. Ó Cíosáin defines 'global memory' as a particular type of knowledge which appears in reflections on a specific event, and which suggests that subjects are drawing on a 'level of information which is abstract' and national, and may derive from other written accounts of the incident in question.[10]

A clear theme in memories of the epidemic was a belief in the flu's reach, and the sense that it had been very much an international tragedy. Kathleen Behan portrayed it as 'the biggest epidemic the world has ever known...A terrible thing – I believe more died of the influenza than died in the war itself.' David Hogan, a journalist working with Robert Brennan in the Publicity Department of Sinn Féin when the flu struck, recalled that the Armistice coincided with 'the time of the Great 'Flu...throughout the world it swept away in six months more young lives than war had taken in four years. In Ireland before it was over there were few who had not lost a relative.' Recalling his time spent interned in Belfast Jail, Fionán Lynch described the 'bout we had of the influenza that was sweeping through the world and killing millions' as 'the most significant thing' he could remember about that time. Seamus Babington noted that 'though millions were lost in the 4½ years war, in two months twice as many died from this 'flu supposed to originate in Europe'.[11]

What stayed with people were their impressions of the Great Flu's vast dimensions, and the sense that it was a global, collective experience that eclipsed even the First World War in terms of scale and damage. The similarity in the substance of the memories, and the sweeping imagery so frequently used, suggest that witnesses were able to draw on a relatively well-known contemporary narrative of the pandemic, indicating that those who lived through it shared a base level of common knowledge about the event.

References to the ubiquity and prevalence of the disease were common motifs in depictions of the influenza epidemic. Bill Kelly wrote of the 'great 'flu which was raging' at the time the first Dáil convened, while Seán Moylan recounted that 'the influenza epidemic of 1918 struck the country like a plague'. Micheál MacCárthaigh recalled that in Tipperary, 'it hit us hard. It was everywhere...'[12]

One verb frequently chosen for portrayals of the epidemic was 'rage' – the flu was 'raging' in winter 1918, it 'raged so violently', 'the flu epidemic now raged', 'I now developed the flu which was raging at the time', 'I remember having the 'flu (which was raging at the time) and being confined to bed on Christmas night on that year', 'from June 1918 on, the bad epidemic of influenza began to rage all over the country'. Witnesses retained a common sense of the omnipresence, speed, and uncontrollable spread of the flu waves, while the expressive, dramatic language which they selected to portray their experiences suggests that the epidemic had the ability to leave a deeply ingrained memory on those who witnessed its worst effects.[13]

Images of debility, loss and mourning arose frequently, with repeated references to the way in which the disease felled entire households and to the inescapable presence of death. Kathleen Behan thought that 'in Dublin, one died in every house', while others mentioned how 'most families were stricken down and many lost three or four', and 'whole families were prostrated by it'. Seán O'Casey described how undertakers had piles of coffins outside their premises, 'towering barricades of them already sold, yet many more were needed for those who died'. D.W. Macnamara, who had been a junior doctor in the Mater in 1918, referred to 'the cavalcade of funerals trotting quietly and inevitably towards Glasnevin', while Thomas Treacy told of how in Kilkenny 'the daily funerals of young and old were numerous'.[14]

While it has been suggested that the Great War may have crowded out the epidemic from popular memory in the west, accounts of the flu in Ireland suggest rather a continued and close association between the Great Flu and the First World War that had been evident at the time of the outbreak itself. Art O'Donnell, Commandant of the West Clare Brigade during the War of Independence, recalled in 1955 that 'probably conditions there [in the war] caused a 'flu epidemic throughout Europe and America and eventually it reached Belfast Gaol', where he was interned at the time. Meanwhile, 'war flu' was among the various names used years later to describe the disease.[15]

The epidemic was also recalled as part of the backdrop to nationalist activity in these years, showing once more the interweaving nature of social and political history at this time. In his account of the period spent interned in Belfast Jail during 1918/19, Neilus Connolly's description of the Great Flu dominated the opening passage:

> On 1 December the dreaded 'flu struck the prison, and within a week most of the Irish Volunteers were victims. Some were critical and the prison chaplain asked that the cell doors be left open so that the prisoners could help each other. Most of the warders were also on the sick list and there was a general relaxation. The doctor in attendance did all he could to change the diet. Luckily we had no casualties and most of us were on our feet for Christmas.[16]

Biographers of figures who had been active in the Nationalist movement also refer to the Great Flu and its impact on their subjects. Florence O'Donoghue recorded how 'the severe influenza epidemic' of 1918 laid low the later Mayor of Cork Tomás MacCurtain for several weeks that winter when he came to Dublin following a Brigade Council meeting in Cork city. In his biography of Harry Boland, Jim Maher notes that when the General Election rolled around, there was a relatively good turnout of 69 per cent considering that 'there was an epidemic of the deadly 1918 flu at the time'.[17]

Many regional studies of nationalism in Ireland also make reference to the epidemic, reflecting the way in which it continued to be perceived locally as an event of historical significance. Documenting revolutionary activity in Laois, Michael J. Rafter comments on how the campaign to elect the new MP in December 1918 took place 'against the backdrop of a 'Flu epidemic'. In his examination of political activism and conflict in Meath, Oliver Coogan also describes how 'the last three months of 1918 saw the great flu epidemic of that year raging through the county', providing a 'deathly background' against which the 'election drama was played out'. In Sligo in the same period, Michael Farry represented the epidemic in similar terms, referring to the 'virulent strain of flu' which hit Ireland and laid low many in the county in November 1918.[18]

That the sickness experience stayed with people was clear in the way in which survivors of the disease, even years afterward, were able to give graphic portrayals of their symptoms and to communicate their experience with a degree of detail – down to the temperature of their fevers – that showed a strong belief in the accuracy of their memory of that time. The detail recounted served to indicate the deep impression left by the experience on those who felt the effects of the flu first hand.

Michael O'Donoghue, an engineer with the Volunteers' Second Battalion in Cork, thought that he had been 'among the first victims in Cork' in late October 1918: 'despite touching death's door for a week or two (temperature 105°F for 3 days) copious quinine saved me and I was out and around again for the historic Armistice night of 1918'. Thomas Wallace, who was among the internees in Belfast Jail in winter 1918 when the epidemic struck, recalled his removal to the prison hospital: 'this was at the end of October. Shaw, a Dublin lad, and myself were carried from there to the Workhouse on stretchers. I was 106° temperature, but contrived to walk in.' Curious as to what caused the nurse to make an 'involuntary exclamation when she noticed the temperature', Frank Drohan, an internee in Gloucester Prison, 'climbed up to have a look at the chart and saw that it registered 104'. Unusually high fevers were a noted feature of the 1918/19 flu strain.[19]

This enduring and visceral sense of the disease was a frequent feature of subsequent accounts of the Great Flu. Almost thirty years afterwards, Annie Smithson could still recall the day she contracted the flu, coming home and 'feeling deadly ill, only able to push my bicycle. I almost fainted when I got indoors, and crawled upstairs to bed.' Gearóid Ua h-Uallacháin recollected leaving a céilí early to go home as he 'was feeling so seedy', but on the way considered stopping at a friend's house as his body was weakening so quickly. Deciding in the end to push on, he made it back, clambouring into bed 'and was delirious' by the time his mother found him. Those around the stricken Seán Loughlin and Seán Moylan thought the men so sick that death was a certainty. 'Nobody expected' Moylan to recover, while Loughlin's trip to Whitworth Hospital in North Brunswick Street was thought to be in vain: 'I was conveyed…in a dying condition believed by those who took me there.' Charles Gildea of Tubbercurry, Sligo, remembered the acute debilitation wrought by the disease which left him physically drained for several months after his bout of flu.[20]

The timing of the Great Flu seemed to pose difficulties for memory, and although it was most often associated with the winter of 1918, some placed it before or after the period in which it took place. Daniel Mulvihill from Kerry told of how his 'second eldest [brother] died in December 1919 from flu-pneumonia after having qualified as a Doctor', while Martin McGowan from Sligo, 28 years old at the time, recorded that 'my brother was President of the [Sinn Féin]) Club until his death, caused by Flu in 1917'. Patrick Ormond from Waterford thought that 'it was early in the month of December 1920, when I became ill with influenza and came home to Waterford', although he remembered the General Election as being in December 1918. John Feehan, of Leenane, County Galway, thought that the epidemic had occurred before it had reached the country – 'in the spring of 1918, the 'flu was raging'. This could reflect the fact that Galway was one of the earliest centres of the flu when it eventually reached Ireland in June 1918, and suggests the influence that local experience could exert on subsequent perceptions of the event. The close association of the flu with winter 1918 indicates that it was the brutal second wave which left the strongest imprint on people's memories.[21]

Subsequent reflections – especially those which took a written form – on the Great Flu typically depicted the experience using similar themes and language, suggesting a memory of the epidemic that was shared by many who lived through the outbreak. Macnamara referred to it as 'a time of great drama' and the evocative words, images, and phrases used by others who experienced it first hand would seem to confirm that he was not alone in thinking of the epidemic in such terms. Hogan wrote that it was 'the deadliest epidemic in the memory of man', while Seán Moylan described how 'the influenza epidemic of 1918 struck the country like a plague'. Thomas Treacy's story of the epidemic took the form of a heroic narrative, outlining how the disease had severely tested its victims' will to live, as he recalled that 'some members of the Irish Volunteers died with it. Many who got it were strong enough to survive.'[22]

The dramatic language used to tell the story of the Great Flu suggests that it was felt to have been an intense and dreadful time. Reflecting on his youth in Kerry, for instance, Jeremiah Murphy's impression of the outbreak was of widespread local suffering and damaging social consequences:

> the great influenza epidemic at the end of the war was disastrous. It weakened the lungs, making a person subject to pneumonia, which was fatal in many cases to people who had any respiratory disease...Very few people escaped the 'flu'...The saddest example was the death of a young man and his wife leaving four orphaned children...One of my brothers complained of pains in his legs which was regarded as a general symptom. After several days my father was able to get a much overworked doctor to see him....The doctor was forced to open my brother's leg with a penknife in order to relieve the pressure.[23]

Memory of the Great Flu also survived in those households which had experienced losses at the hands of the outbreak. In Micheál Ó Muircheartaigh's family, they were told of how his 'father's sister Ellie caught the Great Flu of 1918 in New York and died of it in the year in which she was due to get married'. In the Bardon family, 'hushed tones' accompanied references to George's memory, the son who had gone to fight in the Great War contracting the infection while in combat. When granted leave, he went to Dublin to visit relatives, his sister Alice later telling of what the family had said at the time: 'He was sick with Spanish influenza when he got there. But he would go on those double-decker buses because he wanted to see everything when he was there. He was only there a few days and he was dead.' Stories of the Great Flu were also passed on in Kieran Fagan's family, with the latter hearing of how 'in Dublin my grandfather Willy Fagan was sent home from the Rotunda hospital to die of it in December 1918. "We can do no more for him", his young wife, my granny, was told.' Even if governments chose not to, families continued to remember the epidemic.[24]

Details of the epidemic were also preserved in, and were portrayed as part of, the history of several hospitals, with chronicles of Dublin's Meath Hospital, the Adelaide, Baggot Street, and St Vincent's all depicting the overwhelming effects of the Great Flu. Peter Gatenby illustrated the acute shortage of staff precipitated by the epidemic at the Meath, which had only 'half the usual number of nurses available' to run the hospital and to tend to the 141 '"bad" cases' of flu that were in need of treatment there. David Mitchell describes a similar acuity of circumstances in the Adelaide Hospital, quoting from the annual report for 1918 which portrayed a taxing period in the institution's past:

> Large numbers of nurses were attacked, some very seriously. The wards were crowded with very ill patients, especially of pneumonia. Many died within hours of admission. This placed great strain on the few Nurses able to remain on duty. It was fortunate that no member of the medical or nursing staffs died.[25]

Local history works suggest that the epidemic was assimilated to narratives of the regional past in areas which had been affected badly by the outbreaks. Micheál MacCárthaigh outlined the effects of the epidemic in a single Tipperary parish, emphasising the heroics of the local doctor during 'the dreaded flu' which merited his insertion into the 'great tradition' of the priests and dispensary doctors 'who died on duty in the famine years'. In *Memories of Macroom*, James Kelleher describes the

Sisters of Mercy Order as being 'particularly remembered for their Tro-
jan work during the Great "Flu" in 1918 when, with Sister Aloysius as
Matron, they nursed so many people back to health, so saving many lives'.
In 1990, a flu outbreak 'revived memories of the dreadful epidemic
of 1918' in Wicklow, where it was said that only one girl in the area
recovered from the pneumonia prevalent at the time. The Irish Folklore
Commission Schools' Survey recorded tales of how faith in the ability
of garlic to stave off the flu motivated people in Sligo to carry a piece
around in their pockets as protection.[26]

The Great Flu remained part of the stories of families, localities,
individuals, and institutions, with familiarity retained in individual
memories and local knowledge. Despite the fact that it was an event of
national proportions, touching all of the thirty-two counties, and claim-
ing more than 20,000 lives in the space of a few months – more than
the Easter Rising, War of Independence, and Civil War combined – the
influenza epidemic has rarely been presented as part of the history of
early twentieth-century Ireland. Even Ruth Barrington's survey of
the health services from 1900 to 1970 devotes only a few words to the
epidemic. Journalist Pete Davies comments that the pandemic simply
'fell off history's map' and in Ireland too, the outbreak has seldom been
incorporated into histories of the twentieth century, and until relatively
recently was largely absent from public discourse on the Irish past.[27]

The reasons for this absence may be partially traced to the challenges
which the epidemic posed to historiography. When it came to explaining and ordering the past both in Ireland and abroad, politics dominated
the historical narrative right up until the mid-twentieth century. In the
years immediately following the epidemic in Ireland, history lessons
were geared towards liberating 'the Irish from the supposed effects of
British domination', and towards legitimating the new state. Senia
Paseta has commented on the myopia that this caused, noting that 'the
attention lavished on one particular mind – republican – has obscured
numerous other political and social developments' in Irish history.
Politics had presented more immediate concerns for history to deal with
than a social disaster like the Great Flu.[28]

In the early twentieth century, moreover, ill-health and sickness were
still a routine part of everyday life in Ireland, which made them a less
pressing issue for the historical record. TB was an endemic problem, with
Ireland among a minority of developed countries which saw incidence of
the disease continuing to increase at the turn of the century even as it
declined in the rest of the British Isles. This was a time too when outbreaks of various 'fevers' still took place, and smallpox continued to

pay sporadic visits. The abundance of material concerning sickness and popular cures which was gathered by the Irish Folklore Commission in the 1930s is further indicative of the way in which disease was a habitual intruder on community and family life in the early twentieth century. The customary presence of illness in general at this time may have had the effect of dulling historical recognition of the effects and intensity of the Great Flu in its immediate aftermath – as Bruce Ross puts it: 'since the commonplace is dismissed as unimportant background, it tends to disappear from history'.[29]

The 'glossing over' of the pandemic by historians in turn helps to explain why there is little sense today of the epidemic as being a part of the collective past in Ireland, giving the impression that a 'seeming loss of folk memory' has taken place. History is vital in shaping people's awareness and understanding of the past: historians are variously cast as 'remembrancers' – 'guardians of awkward facts of the social memory', and 'practitioners of the collective past', keeping, interpreting and transmitting social memories. Jacques Le Goff places them among anthropologists, journalists, and sociologists as 'professional specialists in memory', while Anita Shapira similarly views historians as being among the 'memory agents' of a society. Historical neglect of the epidemic greatly diminished the chances that the Great Flu would become part of a shared understanding of the past, at both a national and international level.[30]

The state also plays a crucial role in the conditioning of social memory. D. George Boyce notes that 'without some means of transmitting memory, every generation would forget the experiences of the one before. The state mediates these memories, encouraging some, discouraging or suppressing others.' The flu did not generate serious political interest, however, either during the outbreak or subsequently. Irish politicians first mentioned the flu in parliament only when it offered a chance to score some political capital, having become rife among the nationalist prisoners interned in Belfast in November 1918.[31]

The epidemic was politicised to an extent: the deaths from flu of two Irish internees were depicted by the nationalist press as arousing a 'wave of emotion' comparable to that which swelled in the wake of the Easter Rising executions, and the British Government was widely blamed for their deaths. But this seems to have died out quickly and the Great Flu was not appropriated to the revolutionary narrative in the long term. This contrasted with, for example, the Famine – a catastrophe which proved assimilable to the story of the Irish nation, expressed as another instance of British misgovernment. It was much more difficult to appropriate the flu to the political narrative, though, especially as Britain suffered higher casualty rates and mounted a similarly lacklustre official response domestically.[32]

That the epidemic should fail to sustain the interest of Irish politicians was by no means an isolated trend. Governments abroad had little interest in remembering the lack of preparation and over-strained resources highlighted by the flu pandemic – 'no one had much to be proud of'. Politicians could have little motivation in promoting remembrance of an event which showed how state healthcare systems around the world had been almost uniformly overwhelmed by the pandemic.[33]

Remembering the epidemic at a collective level was also made difficult by the challenging nature of those memories it did leave behind. In order for 'collective memories' to develop, it is necessary for individuals to articulate their own memories of an event and to pass these on. As Iwona Irwin-Zarecka explains, it is 'the telling itself, the ongoing articulation of the "reality of the past" that forms and informs a community'. Talking about the past is 'the most basic and accessible means for memory articulation and maintenance'.[34]

Evidence of this articulation and transmission of memory is apparent, for instance, in the folklore of nationalism contained in the Bureau of Military History witness statements. Patrick Connaughton, whose father had been a member of the Land League and was interned in Galway Jail for six months in 1882, frequently heard him speak 'of the fight against the landlords and the hardships of that period', while Patrick O'Reilly recalled hearing stories of the Famine, of Parnell and Davitt, and 'of the landlords who rack-rented the people and spent their hard-earned money across the water in England and France on wild orgies of drinking and immorality'. Charles Gildea, meanwhile, traced his determination to 'join and support an organisation that would assist in gaining freedom for Ireland' to the 'long conversations with some old men in the district who had a very good national outlook'.[35]

By contrast, the kinds of memories left by the epidemic would seem to suggest that the outbreak was perhaps not deemed an appropriate topic in a social environment. The anxious atmosphere of the period appeared to be easily re-imagined, with references to 'the terrible fear that was everywhere, which gripped people like a vice'. Doctors could see up to fifteen bodies in the hospital mortuary at the one time, almost three times the usual number, and found that patients could die within hours of admission. The junior doctor at the Mater, D.W. Macnamara, remembered examining 'a freshly admitted case at 4 pm' and finding 'another patient in the same bed three hours later, the first patient having died and been removed to the mortuary, only to make room for the second in that short space of time'.[36]

The epidemic often appears in the memory of individuals as a time of strain, shortage, and hopelessness – 'the medical profession seemed power-less against it' – with comments made on the acute pressures faced by doctors, and the absence of medical treatment and resources. David Hogan described how the doctors in Dublin were 'unable to cope with the calls on them', while Gearóid Ua h-Uallacháin also referred to the exertions of health professionals at this time. Bill Burgess, a teenager in 1918, recalled that most of his siblings contracted the flu but 'there was no antibiotic and no whiskey either. There was nothing to be had. No up-to-date medicines. No pick-me-ups. Nothing. Dr Kidd in Tullow recommended we get some whiskey or poitín but even that was hard to find.' Micheál MacCárthaigh noted that 'at that time there was very little hospital accommodation. Dr McKeogh of Dundrum was night and day on the road'.[37]

For those who had shunned the sick, or avoided the wake or burial of an ill neighbour or relative, the epidemic may have served to awaken shame or guilt, especially as the inability of a society to give proper burials to its dead can leave 'a deep scar on the imagination of the people', as Carmel Quinlan found when examining memories of the treatment of the Famine dead. Although not as widespread a problem during the epidemic, there is much evidence that death rituals were disrupted and even abandoned in 1918/19. The necessity for self-sufficiency so noted during the Famine when 'every man had to do for himself' because 'when a person died not even his nearest neighbour would darken his door', surfaced once more during the later waves of flu, tarnishing memories of that time with remorse.[38]

Moreover, the loss of so many in so short a period – 20,000 extra deaths in less than a year, possibly in as little as five or six months – meant that the epidemic was a time of great sadness and mourning as people struggled to cope with the sudden emptiness and disorientation left by the flu deaths. The epidemic was characterised by the 'mournful appearance' of towns, with houses closed up 'due either to the death of an occupant or in sympathy with relatives'. A painful reminder of the shock of sudden loss, there was little incentive to protect or pass on the memory of the flu epidemic.[39]

The trauma of the Great Flu was intensified by the fact that so many of its victims came from age groups whose deaths were considered 'untimely' in Irish society, and thus bore particular social and emotional resonance for communities – more than 4,000 children and young teenagers, and over 8,000 young adults died directly from influenza in 1918 and 1919. The toll taken by the Great Flu on the young adult population may be especially important when it comes to trying to unravel the 'peculiar puzzle of the forgetting of the pandemic', as the virus inflicted its heaviest damages on the age groups which would have been the most likely to retain and transmit its memory – as Jeffrey Olick observes, 'historical events are more memorable to people still in their formative years'.[40]

Belief in the uniqueness of the Great Flu (see Chapter 7) presented further problems for its remembrance. Historians Natalie Zemon Davis and Randolph Starn have commented on memory's 'delight in similarity', while sociologists David Wickham and Charles Fentress explain that events can be more easily remembered if they fit into 'the forms of narrative that the social group already has at its disposal'. Chris Morash has highlighted that certain images which were used to portray the Great Famine – the grass-eating man, the dead mother, the walking skeleton – had all acted as signifiers of famine prior to the 1840s. It was not easy, however, for people to incorporate the epidemic into other social or political narratives, as evidenced by the difficulties experienced by witnesses in attempting to find a precedent – in medical journals for instance, the pidemic was heralded as 'the story of a new disease'.[41]

The question of memory of the Great Flu also raises the issues of class and power. Sociologist Maurice Halbwachs argued that the lasting power of collectively retained memories is linked closely to the 'social power' of the group that holds them, while Fentress and Wickham explain that since the arrival of capitalism in each country, the upper middle classes and the intelligentsia are 'the bearers of national memory'. Nonetheless, a glance at the epidemic's mortality statistics in cities such as Kristiania or Dublin (see Chapter 2) reveals the imprint of class on the influenza and pneumonia death rates. That the Great Flu is so frequently assumed to have been forgotten may be a further reflection that a sizeable proportion of deaths came from the lower classes which had no one to fight for their remembrance.[42]

Another factor which militated against a widely retained and long-standing memory of the Great Flu was the sense of impotence and powerlessness which accompanied the outbreak, as official measures and medical efforts had little success in curbing the impact of the disease. The infection eluded the understanding of scientists and the medical profession, prohibiting effective preventive action – doctors in Belfast and Omagh could only describe it as 'more or less a plague', such was the scale of death, and so 'violent and deadly [were]…its effects in many instances'. A member of Belfast Corporation protested that it was a 'misnomer' to even call the disease 'influenza'. It was portrayed in the press as a 'mysterious and deadly epidemic', against which the medical profession was helpless', as the flu defeated the 'combined efforts of the world to control it'. There was difficulty in trying to ascribe long-term meaning to this public health crisis, a stark contrast with the widespread efforts (in Ireland and abroad) to memorialise and impose meaning on soldiers' deaths in the Great War.[43]

*　　*　　*　　*

Though painful to remember, the Great Flu was not easily forgotten by those who witnessed its effects first hand and the outbreak left a 'general impression of the whole thing' that was relatively consistent through subsequent accounts. Reflections on the epidemic were often structured around similar themes and expressed in uniformly grave tones and dramatic language, suggesting that a 'popular memory' of the epidemic may have existed for some time afterwards. The 'commonly held representations' of the event which can be found in written and oral accounts suggest that people drew on a common reservoir of images and expressions when speaking and writing about the epidemic.[44]

The dramatic language and striking imagery frequently employed in subsequent portrayals suggest moreover that when it was revisited in memory, the epidemic was felt to have been a deeply unsettling and trying experience. In Ireland, the violence of the epidemic was reflected in how people at the time tried to articulate what was happening, as words like 'rage', 'terrible', and 'severe' cropped up repeatedly in descriptions of the outbreak. One of the political prisoners received a letter from home telling him how the epidemic had caused people to become 'indifferent to war, death and all things', leaving an emotional numbness which echoed that bequeathed by the Famine when 'people were so benumbed that they took no interest in anything'. The empirical data on the pandemic – the voluminous graphs, charts, maps and tables it has generated – are limited in what they can convey, and fail to capture the 'personal dimension of the suffering' as thousands of families witnessed the tragedy of unexpected loss inflicted by an 'incomprehensible disaster'. The time of the flu epidemic was readily identified with loss, exigency, and a sense of futility and impotence. Richard Collier's compilation of hundreds of anecdotes about the Great Flu from around the world illuminates the way in which bereavement featured heavily in private memories, with the accounts creating a 'modern folklore of affliction'.[45]

Depictions of the epidemic as a plague are consistent with contemporary reporting on the flu, but they also suggest the anxiety aroused by a rampant and lethal disease, with the plague metaphor providing 'visual expression' for the intensity of the lived experience of the Great Flu. The quietened voices that spoke of the family members who had died and the way in which people winced at the mention of influenza even decades after the epidemic further intimate that although it was remembered, most may have preferred not to speak of the 'dread disease' and its shattering effects.[46]

The vague parallels occasionally drawn between the flu and the Famine (see Chapter 7) illustrate the crucial importance of audience and narrativity when it comes to social memory. Stories of the Famine found a ready audience among the emigrant population, ensuring that memory of the event would endure to some extent at least. In addition, it was also possible to appropriate the Famine to a metanarrative – the story of the Irish nation – as it could be held up as a further representation of British misrule. The Great Flu, on the other hand, lacked an audience that was keen to perpetuate its memory, while belief in the event's uniqueness, and the fact that there was not a definite focus for blame, also made it difficult to insert into a familiar social or political narrative, producing further problems for long-term remembrance.[47]

The consignment of the Great Flu to the 'dustbin of history' for much of the twentieth century, combined with lack of recognition from the state, further diminished the possibility that the epidemic would become part of 'public discourses about the past...that speak in the name of collectivities'. The result was that though the Great Flu left dense memories with individuals, families, and communities, and was recorded in memoirs, autobiographies, and local histories, awareness of the event did not extend beyond these sources to become part of a 'shared past'.[48]

American historian Beverly Gage has suggested that in order for an event to be remembered as a 'significant historical moment, there must be a group of people both concerned with preserving the memory, and capable of inserting that memory into a public discussion'. In the case of the flu epidemic though, it would seem that individuals, historians and the state itself may have simply been content to allow the shelf-life of the Great Flu to expire. The almost universally negative nature of its memory – for individuals, families, communities, doctors, and officials – meant that there was no real wish to make the Great Flu part of subsequent generations' shared sense of the past. It was not so much that a 'forgetting' took place, but for many, silence was preferable to preserving what was so often a saddening, disquieting memory.[49]

CHAPTER NINE

Consequences

The Great Flu's effects on Irish society were varied and pervasive: it diminished the year's profits for the Abbey Theatre, infringed on election activity, delayed All-Ireland matches, and at the GPO, postal workers were dismayed to find that annual leave for the year had to be suspended, owing to sickness among the staff. For numerous families, its intrusion left an enduring legacy as families did their best to cope with sudden absences. Although the epidemic is often characterised as forgotten, in Ireland at least, it insisted on remembrance among individuals who witnessed it first hand, among families that were altered by their losses, and in communities hit by its disruption. This chapter teases out the consequences of this 'calamitous' surge of disease, and assesses whether the Great Flu represented continuity or change in the context of previous epidemics. Was it the case that the epidemic really '"made any difference" or not'?[1]

Turning first to its demographic implications, it would seem that the irony that interlaced the narrative of the Great Flu also extended to its consequences. In his study of the outbreak, the Registrar-General William Thompson concluded that 'it may be considered worthy of note that if the mortality from influenza in 1918 had only reached the normal, the number of deaths from other causes being the same as is shown in my Annual Report, a record for low mortality in Ireland would have been the result'. As the Local Government Board had to concede, 'the abnormal mortality from Influenza and consequent respiratory complications...had the effect of raising the death rate from all causes in the Irish towns to 22.3 per thousand of the estimated population, or 27 per cent in advance of 1917'. Although the incidence of infectious disease on the whole had in fact been 'below the average', because of the 'epidemic prevalence of Influenza', for every four people who had died in 1917, five died in 1918.[2]

In addition to causing a sharp rise in the death rate, the epidemic also shifted the usual patterns of death in Ireland. Not only did the numbers of flu deaths rise, but the Great Flu affected the distribution of other diseases, with the result that casualties from heart disease, pulmonary TB, kidney disease, and bronchitis variously dropped by up to 11 per cent over the course of the flu visitation. As was the case overseas, in Ireland too, the epidemic carried off 'many chronic invalids, such as those suffering from pulmonary tubercle, organic disease of the heart, acute nephritis and Bright's disease'.[3]

In 1919, deaths from heart disease increased in Ireland, which may have been yet another side effect of the epidemic. The report by the Ministry of Health, for instance, had deemed it 'noteworthy that in the months which succeeded the epidemic and indeed throughout the year 1919, one was constantly meeting with cases of the chronic type of infective endocarditis, whose origin was obscure'. The swift climb in deaths from heart disease may have been the 'aftermath of the virulent infections of the acute influenzal epidemic types'. In addition, the year of the flu outbreak saw uncertified deaths fall 11 per cent below the average for the years 1914–17, suggesting that the epidemic may have carried off some of those whose deaths would usually have gone unnoticed and unaccounted for, further reflecting the influence of class on flu mortality rates.[4]

In terms of the epidemic's influence on birth rates, live births in 1918 actually saw a rise compared to 1917, suggesting that the increased morbidity and mortality among pregnant women at the hands of influenza did not lead to a sizeable number of abortions or still births in Ireland. That the epidemic did not exert a material effect on the number of children born is perhaps reflective of what had come by 1914 to be the lowest birth rate in the British Isles. (Ireland could also lay claim to the lowest marriage rate – almost 30 per cent lower than the UK average.[5]) In Ireland's case, the demographic effects of the influenza epidemic were less far-reaching than those of countries with the highest death rates where birth rates plummeted and population profiles were affected for the next generation or more.[6]

With the effects of the virus sometimes lingering long after the initial bout of flu, this flu strain often left patients' bodies physically diminished for long periods. Dr Russell McNabb, writing from Birmingham Prison to his wife, hinted at the unusually debilitating effects of this form of influenza as it had affected one of his comrades: 'we are somewhat anxious as to Cusack's health, he had a bad cold, probably an attack of flu, last October, and has been poorly since; he has a hacking cough and an unaccountable lack of energy and is very easily exhausted'. Dr Kathleen Lynn contracted the infection in December 1918, but in July 1919, after finding the climb up Bray Head particularly draining, she attributed her exhaustion to her bout of the infection, chronicling in her journal, 'not over 'Flu yet'. Almost seventy years after the flu had struck, many on the Aran Islands blamed the flu epidemic for 'the fact that people no longer live as long on Aran as they used to'. One of the residues of the epidemic was the way in which it left healthy, strong individuals weakened and frail for months, and sometimes even years after their flu attack.[7]

When it came to politics, the epidemic affected the revolution in a number of unforeseen ways. In various parts of the country, it inconvenienced the election campaigns of nationalists and unionists alike as rallies had to be cancelled and marches called off owing to the flu's arrival, with anxiety over potential election turnout mounting as the outbreak wore on into December. Volunteers were among the many around the country who fell ill, and in the worst hit counties like Kildare, sickness was so rampant that even the police noticed the scaled back activity levels. RIC reports and newspapers meanwhile document the sudden increase in military funerals caused by flu deaths in republican ranks.

The Great Flu was yet another headache for an administration struggling to deal effectively with political prisoners. Eruption of the disease in Belfast Jail, the intended destination for internees, meant that policy had to be hurriedly revised and prisoners kept in their local jails where many 'became insubordinate' and fasting was 'resorted to' in a number of cases.[8] The deaths of Coleman and McCann added two more names to the list of Irish political martyrs, as the flu intensified the pressure on the British government to reach a decision about when and how to release the men and women interned for their part in the alleged 'German Plot'. For those in charge of the jails, the flu was a further strain on a system swaying under the stresses of hunger strikes, riots, and inmates' incessant demands.

In his study of political imprisonment in Ireland in the early twentieth century, William Murphy described some of the flu's sundry effects on the prison experiences of the various men and women who had been dispatched to British and Irish jails for political activity at this time. The flu's arrival introduced the real prospect of death to the internees as it left young, strong men fevered, bleeding, and delirious. The letters that passed through the censors' hands reveal the genuine concern and trepidation felt by prisoners both for the health of their fellow inmates and for those they had left at home. Even as the flu swept through the prison system, though, it had surprising repercussions: parole became easier to secure due to sickness both in the jails and among prisoners' families, and with regulations often relaxed as infection raced through the prisons, escapes were sometimes easier to ensure.[9]

Some of the most serious economic consequences of the epidemic were unsurprisingly felt in a number of Ireland's health institutions. Treating the huge volume of flu patients plunged St Michael's Hospital, Kingstown, 'heavily into debt'. The Royal City of Dublin Hospital in Baggot Street suffered due to its policy of refusing to turn away flu victims – despite being full, room was made for patients on the floor. By 1919, though, the institution owed more than £12,000, almost equivalent to a year's worth of running costs. The hospital eventually had to shut a number of its wards, and it was several years before any headway into the debt was made.[10]

The Great Flu also left its mark on the economies of charitable and insurance organisations. Attempts by the St Vincent de Paul Society to help the stricken cope with the epidemic 'made serious inroads' on its funds, with total net expenditure rising by £3,360 from 1917 to 1918, an increase of almost 10 per cent of its total outlay. In terms of some of the commercial organisations worst affected, the Galway Insurance Society saw benefits paid during the year rise by almost 10 per cent.[11]

One of the epidemic's clearest effects was to expose the flawed structure of the public health system in Ireland. It also demonstrated the way in which the sickness experience was class inflected, yet despite the repeated mentions in the press of the distress of the lower classes during the epidemic, there is little evidence that the flu outbreak spurred any attempts to deal with the root causes of the deep poverty that existed in corners of Irish cities and countryside. Although the sufferings of the destitute during the epidemic served as another reminder of 'how poor Ireland was' at this time, no effort was made to assess how best to deal with such sudden crises in public health or to evaluate how the disproportionate distress of the poverty-stricken could be prevented in the future. And as was the case in Britain, there was no review of preventive policies or emergency services in order to mitigate future outbreaks of epidemic disease. Though it highlighted such issues, the epidemic failed to generate the political interest or energy necessary to enact social reform.[12]

In terms of the Great Flu's socio-cultural significance, at the time, it sparked a search for meaning and significance – as demonstrated by the multitude of suggestions made as to its possible origins – which was often channelled by the church in the direction of religion, with prayers for an end to the sickness offered in masses around the country. The Archbishop of Dublin, for instance, wrote to the clergy in the diocese: 'in view of the present prevalence of serious illness...it is our duty to have recourse to the Throne of Mercy in earnest prayer that God in his infinite goodness may be pleased to deliver us from the dangers that threaten us'.[13] The flu highlighted the popular belief in the relationship between religious devotion and physical health, as reflected in the recourse to faith through prayers and mass offerings nationwide during the outbreak. Religion offered solace and comfort and provided a means of channelling anxieties and coping with grief. It was also used as an explanatory device, helping to give meaning to the deaths caused by a disease that was little understood: religion allowed the epidemic to be seen as part of a greater plan, as each death became a homecoming, a return to God.

The profusion of funerals during the Great Flu illustrated the continuation into the twentieth century of the funerary culture which had developed over the course of the nineteenth century. French historian Phillippe Ariés has written of the declining visibility of death in western Europe at this time, but the flu epidemic demonstrated that in Ireland at least, the ending of life continued to be treated with open and communal displays of mourning. While elsewhere, death was becoming increasingly confined to the private sphere, with funerals undergoing abbreviation and simplification and mourning frowned upon, in Ireland, public ceremony continued to mark the loss of life. Irish funerals were distinguished by their communal and highly visible nature, with processions through towns taking place and turnout corresponding with position held in the community – the larger the attendance, the more respected and esteemed the deceased had been in the area. Cremation may have been growing in popularity abroad, but in Ireland it was still crucial to mark loss publicly, with the ceremonies of death remaining very much in the public domain. Historian Linda Bryder has asked what the epidemic can tell us about attitudes towards death at this time; the months of the Great Flu in 1918/19 in Ireland would suggest strong continuity in terms of how Irish society acknowledged and responded to death and grief, underlining the emphasis placed on respect for the dead.[14]

There were elements of continuity too in the social response to disease, especially in the enduring importance of spatial themes when

it came to how communities reacted to the arrival of infection. Much
has been written on the emerging significance of space as a conceptual
category in recent years. Mike Crang refers to 'a reassertion of space
in social theory', while Doreen Massey has observed that 'if once it
was "time" that framed the privileged angle of vision, today, so it is
often said, that role has been taken over by space'. Stuart Elden, meanwhile, has called explicitly for the incorporation of ideas of space into
historiographical approaches, pointing to a need for the 'spatializa-
tion' of history and for the recognition that 'space, place and location
are crucial determining factors in any historical study'.[15]

An examination of the history of public health over the past two
centuries shows space to be a recurring theme, as patterns of interaction
and themes of separation and boundaries entered into experiences of
disease. In the nineteenth century, disease in Ireland was frequently
articulated in the language of place. Fevers and infections were
thought to originate from particular localities, and even from certain
houses and laneways. In Dublin, doctors could trace the cartography
of sickness in the city's neighbourhoods, and infection had an address,
situating itself in specific streets and buildings. Darby-square, for
instance, was 'a well-known hot-bed for contagion', with William's
Place, Long Lane, 'also worthy of note...we have frequently cases of
fever from this place'. There were many houses in the congested city
centre which were 'known fever nests' and noted 'fever houses'.
Disease may have been carried and spread by people, but at this time
its point of origin was conceived of in terms of place and locale rather
than from within the body.[16]

Folk memory of the Great Famine shows how themes of confinement, distance, and division informed social responses to disease, with
many tales of the exclusion of the sick from the community. The
Famine was thought to have marked the point at which the home first
became closed to strangers due to the need to keep the domestic
sphere safe from sickness: 'for the first time the doors were locked. A
sabh or long stick was drawn as a bolt inside the doors to keep out
strangers or people having the sickness.' Isolation and avoidance of
those suffering from infection was one of the most immediate
impulses: 'the people, when they got a fever, were moved out to the
barn, and a person put to mind them'. Families with fever victims were
left to themselves, and people 'were afraid to go near each other's
houses'.[17]

The compelling image of the 'scalpt' recurred frequently in
descriptions of how the diseased were treated during the 'Drochshaol',

indicating the stinging resonance in social memory of the way in which the sick were excluded from the community: 'they built up huts against a sheltered ditch, poles were stood on the outside and a roof thrown across them to the ditch and they were thatched with brambles, briars and rushes. Here in the huts or 'scalpts' the afflicted people had to live, their own people or family shunning them.' In some villages, 'they put up a sod-house', and 'anyone with fever was put into it to die. There was (*sic*) no doctors or attendants and no one was allowed in.' In other parts of the country, 'fever patients were not brought to any hospital but a sod shelter was built up around them wherever they might be found on the roadside'.[18]

Fear of these places of exclusion and sites of disease could last for decades, burned into community memory, and defining the contours of safety in the local landscape. One woman in Kerry told of the refusal to build on sites known to have had people with cholera in them, and also recalled being cautioned by her mother not to pick berries from the shell of a nearby ruined house for fear of infection. Elsewhere, children were warned to stay away from the remains of the 'burnt houses' in the locality – places where 'fear of infection' had been 'so great that the houses would not be entered at all, but would be fired, or their roofs and walls broken in, the bodies of fever victims left inside'.[19]

In 1918, ideas about space and place continued to influence and shape how society responded to disease. Influenza was thought of as a disease of contacts and relationships, transmitted in places where space was scarce and where bodies thronged together. It was popularly viewed as spread by 'human mixings', particularly in places such as theatres, schools, and any sort of crowded or enclosed area which minimised distance between individuals.[20]

The flu outbreak in Ireland also had a considerable impact on the 'space of everyday experience' and specifically on lived space and patterns of interaction. The sickness of whole families at the same time and the closure of schools and recreation outlets resulted in the greater concentration of life around the house, reducing the radius of daily living and pulling people in closer to the security of home. Fears of catching the disease influenced how close to one another people were willing to venture, with movement reduced, and social contact curbed in many areas. Some municipalities became markedly quieter, with people preferring to stay indoors, while there were also instances of villagers' reluctance to risk going into towns known to be witnessing outbreaks.[21]

Shades of topophobia – the fear of certain places – were discernible in popular perceptions of schools, offices, and theatres, as such sites came to be imagined as replete with threat and risk, believed to harbour potential for disseminating infection and death. The Great Flu thus illustrated some of the ways in which space and place 'entered into human lives and social arrangements' in times of epidemic disease with danger seen as greatest where bodies were closest together.[22]

While the Great Flu showed elements of continuity in terms of the behaviours elicited by the arrival of mass sickness, the urge to circumscribe the space between the healthy and the sick did not take as conspicuous or powerful a form as the bolting of houses or erection of scalpts in the nineteenth century. The epidemic also does not seem to have left any comparably lasting or loaded symbols as the 'burnt houses' or fever huts such as had been bequeathed by the last outbreaks of disease which the Registrar-General thought comparable to the flu outbreak.[23] Likewise, there do not appear to have been any episodes of violence provoked by the outbreak with communities forcefully rejecting the sick. The measures taken to establish boundaries between sick and healthy in 1918/19 were not as extreme or radical as in the nineteenth century, when whole towns could be isolated, in some cases their borders policed to prevent the entry of potential carriers of disease. Although the Great Flu rang with echoes of the past at times – for example, the rumoured isolation of Ballinasloe in the early stages of the epidemic – by 1918, the use of boundaries to demarcate sickness and health had diminished both in scale and vigour.[24]

While the social response to flu was not as dramatic or intense as in previous years when disease could cause waves of panic to sweep the country and prompt people to flee wholesale from villages and towns, the Great Flu nonetheless elicited distinct levels of fear and apprehension around Ireland. Although science was gradually allowing the causes of disease to be understood in terms of germs and microbes rather than fairies, curses, and other forms of the supernatural, thereby removing some of the most frightening aspects of illness, this strain of flu still managed to evoke dread and concern. This was most plainly manifest in the quieter streets and markets, the lowered attendance at wakes and funerals, and in the common wariness of the sick and the dead. In the face of a disease that overturned previous expectations of what it meant to suffer an episode of flu, fear was understandable and logical, especially in the context of the flu's altered demography; the way in which thousands of young, strong, healthy people could die within days, and sometimes even hours, flew in the face of human understanding.

Although many people at the time interpreted the Great Flu as a unique event, with both doctors and the laity even wondering if they were witnessing a completely new disease, the outbreak was characterised by a considerable degree of continuity with previous experiences of, and ideas about, disease. When it came to how Irish society reacted to and perceived disease in 1918, to a large extent the past endured. These strong elements of continuity in turn bring us back to the question as to whether the epidemic really 'made any difference' or not.

In the short term, the flu's intrusion on Irish society was sharp and far-reaching, causing disruption across virtually all facets of daily life. Politics, religion, economics, education, agriculture, law and order, were all subject to its troublesome effects. For the most part, though, the flu's impact was temporary, with normal practices and routines resuming after the waves of sickness had passed, leaving no long-term structural damage. At the same time, however, there were pockets of exception – hospitals which took years to climb out of the debt incurred, towns where the Irish language movement never recovered, men and women whose bodies were never the same again – which meant that the flu's effects sometimes persisted for years after the waves of disease had abated.

Nowhere were the long-term implications of the epidemic more pronounced than in the homes of those who lost a relative to the epidemic. Here it became 'a shaping episode in the lives of forgotten people', leaving a residue of 'suffering and illness, the widowed and the orphaned'. Mr J. O'Loughlin, a town commissioner from Loughrea, spoke of the 'awful scourge which had brought grief and misery to so many houses in the country', as the flu resulted in permanent absences in households around Ireland, with families doing their best to put themselves back together in the wake of the losses sustained. The Great Flu changed the lives of children who were left without parents and were consigned to industrial schools, where, according to officials, they would be 'saved from becoming useless'. In those households in which the wage-earner was struck, poverty became an immediate possibility, leading to the exhortation that magistrates at the police courts should 'spare the sick and dying, and, as had been done in England, refuse all decrees for eviction'. The impact of the epidemic on countless parents who witnessed the trauma of seeing their child die before them was no less significant than the tragedy of infants suddenly left without father or mother (or both), as the bereaved were left to grapple with new identities as husbands and wives became widows and widowers, and children became orphans. In Ireland, the flu of 1918/19 made the biggest difference at the level of family and community, reshaping and transforming the lives of those left behind.[25]

A 'tale of disaster'?

Michael O'Suilleabhain was still a schoolboy when the flu arrived in Ireland. Reflecting decades later on the distress it caused in west Cork, his assessment of the epidemic was that it was a 'tale of disaster'. And for certain parts of the country like Inishowen, or towns like Naas or Wexford, the disease was penetrating in its reach and disastrous in its effects. The Governor of Clonmel borstal hurried to explain to the Chairman of the General Prisons Board in Dublin why he had allowed the institution to be used as an aid centre during the epidemic, detailing the flu's impact on the town: 'upwards of 2,000 inhabitants…were incapacitated by the Influenza Epidemic…in many instances amongst the poorer classes whole families were laid low, many from want of nourishment and fuel…The Medical Men cannot get round all the cases. Every nurse available is at work, and the deaths have been considerable.' He felt that local relief efforts had 'saved the lives of several – who had neither food or coal (*sic*) – or the ability to wait upon themselves'. At the same time, though, a survey of its impact nationwide illustrates that the epidemic varied considerably in intensity and significance across social, demographic, and geographic lines. In certain parts, things continued as usual – Mitchelstown, for example, was deemed to have maintained its 'normal condition' throughout the three waves of infection – while in others, sickness brought disorder and tested social cohesion.[1]

Unsurprisingly, the health sector was one of the areas of society worst hit in 1918. The intensity of the pressure is betrayed by the frequent absence of the epidemic from hospital records. There is virtually no mention of it in the government's annual hospital report for that year, and sources from several individual hospitals contain only scattered references to the influenza outbreak, suggesting that doctors and nurses were left with no time to fully detail the scale of the flu's effects. Similarly, there is no record of the weakened bodies of those who endured bad bouts of the disease but managed to survive. Recovery from this flu could be a long and frustrating process, lasting months or even years. Some never regained their full strength or vitality.[2]

Grinding on for almost a year, the epidemic exposed the weight of responsibility shouldered by the ordinary practitioners (Medical Officers) in the provision of state healthcare, as they toiled 'night and day' to cope with caseloads that could number in the hundreds. The real extent of the work done by nurses is more difficult to ascertain as their voices are less audible in public discourse on the epidemic. This is consistent with the way in which nurses have often remained unseen in both public debate and in the expression of health and social policy in the past. Their labours during the outbreaks received little coverage in newspapers, and they did not have the same degree of public prominence as doctors who frequently sat in on, and contributed to, the meetings of local authorities.[3]

The inability of the state to cope alone with the health chaos was mitigated somewhat by a vigorous response from civil society, as compassion manifested itself in localities around the country – philanthropy proved to be one of the most effective dynamics within the emergency social system that sprang up to cope with the immediate needs precipitated by the epidemic. The reaction of the voluntary sector to the flu outbreak may help to explain why Ireland did not experience a higher casualty rate at the hands of the Great Flu, as its mortality levels approximated to the European average. Research in Japan has demonstrated that the standard and swiftness of local reactions were even more decisive than expected factors such as the ratio of doctors to population, or levels of income per household. The responsibility assumed by civil society for the physical well-being of the community was consistent with the nineteenth century, when for much of the early decades health had not been a government priority, but was left largely in the hands of voluntary initiatives.[4]

Also helping to prevent escalation of the epidemic from disaster into catastrophe, priests provided leadership and guidance in their communities at this time of sickness. They visited the sick themselves, and in some communities were observed to be as busy as the local doctors, helping families to negotiate the epidemic experience. Nuns too played a valuable part by helping to nurse flu victims, filling in for the bedridden staff of hospitals and workhouses, and even setting up emergency healthcare facilities in some areas. Although recent images of the Catholic Church have portrayed its insidiousness and stifling authority in Ireland – John McGahern has written of how 'the Catholic Church was dominant and in control of almost everything, directly or indirectly' – episodes such as the flu epidemic demonstrate some of the positive contributions of the church to community life, and are consistent with Diarmaid Ferriter's observation of clerical responsiveness to social issues in the twentieth century.[5]

When it came to the routines of daily life, oftentimes the Great Flu caused disturbance rather than outright disaster. Household routines were upset to some extent at least, with children kept home from school, sometimes for a period of several weeks at a time. Many of the businesses in local towns also suffered disruptions due to the illness of staff. Leisure activities and opportunities frequently had to be postponed or forsaken, while the trappings and traditional customs of death were sacrificed or modified in the worst hit places due to the high morbidity and people's fear of infection.

Though the consequences of the flu for the individual and the family unit could be profound and far-reaching, at the same time, life moved on, and it would seem that for the most part, Irish society coped relatively well with the Great Flu. Panic was largely avoided, although a distinct level of anxiety and fear was manifest. This sometimes combined with extensive morbidity levels to result in reduced social contact in parts of the country, and in the avoidance or abandonment of stricken families. In this way, the Great Flu recalled responses characteristic of the nineteenth century, when social bonds could be severed by the arrival of epidemic disease.

Almost 20,000 families in Ireland were irrevocably changed by the epidemic experience, and in these households, the outbreak constituted that critical moment when simply everything changed. For the rest of society, though, the Great Flu's effects appear to have been largely tempered by its transience; it hit hard but was relatively brief – especially in comparison with the protracted years of suffering in the 1840s. The Great Flu may have been a 'tale of disaster', but was by no means one of catastrophe. Though sharp and intense, the epidemic's impact was not comparable in depth or length to the sustained trauma of the Famine, after which Ireland 'was never the same again'. While people in 1918 may have occasionally used the Famine as a frame of reference, the epidemic could not inflict the levels of distress endured in the mid-nineteenth century.[6]

Any attempt to characterise or define the way in which Ireland witnessed the Great Flu raises the issue of the pandemic's universality, and the degree to which it was a shared experience. Niall Johnson has written that one of the pandemic's 'most compelling aspects' was 'how universal the experience was' as it displayed a 'marked universality, a universality in reach and universality in impact'. K. David Patterson concluded that the pandemic illustrated how the world had become 'a single epidemiological unit', and historian Sandra Tomkins noted the 'global trail of misery and death' left by this new strain of influenza.[7]

To an extent, Ireland shared in what seemed at first glance to be a worldwide ordeal, as countless Irish families joined the millions that were embarking on the work of mourning, beginning to come to terms with the violence of sudden loss. The years 1918 and 1919 saw an almost unquantifiable number of people worldwide thrust into grief simultaneously, left to confront the problem of how to go back to a life that was starkly different from before. The sudden burdens of death and the difficulties posed by widespread sickness across society were problems witnessed in all parts of the world, and in Ireland too there were shortages of coffins and hearses, leaving bodies to mount in morgues and funeral homes. Officials recorded similar problems in places as far apart as Montreal and Spain, Rio de Janeiro and Reykjavik. Few social systems were prepared for or able to cope with the levels of death that accompanied the Great Flu.[8]

The disruptive social effects of the disease and the suffering of the lower classes were further features which were typical of the pandemic. Although some historians judged that the disease displayed an indiscriminate quality, research now suggests that class was an important factor in explaining the wide variations in mortality which showed up internationally. While rich and poor alike got sick, mortality was more concentrated at the lower end of the social scale, as the Great Flu accentuated existing patterns of inequality.[9]

Another shared feature was the jarring irony that the disease claimed most of its victims from the group that usually enjoyed the most robust health – the young adult population. The flu stole the most active and able members of society so that the totality of its effects are difficult to quantify; not only did it take lives, but the pandemic checked the potential contribution these young men and women could have made to their respective communities and societies.

On an epidemiological level, the symptoms of the disease and its sometimes alarming physicality were felt across oceans and borders, while the conflation of the disease with plague took place both in Ireland and elsewhere in the West. The association was understandable as the symptoms of this flu shared several features with pneumonic plague, including fever, weakness, chest pain, bloody sputum, person-to-person transmission via droplets from the mouth, and the real possibility of swift death. The murmurs of plague were a powerful reason why fear was a common social response to this influenza. At the same time, however, the compassion evoked by the pandemic was also clear and the spirit of voluntarism was manifest in Ireland and around the world from Bombay to Japan, to New Zealand and Paraguay, Fiji and Copenhagen, as volunteers offered their services to assist the sick.[10]

The universality of the pandemic also ran parallel with a specificity of experience, as each country, if not each city, town, and village, had its own distinct encounter with the Great Flu, leading historians more recently to caution against accepting that the pandemic was the same the world over.[11]

In Ireland, the way in which the disease arrived and spread over the country corresponded with its geography in places such as Russia, North America, India, and Africa, as troop movements and transport networks – particularly the railway system – proved crucial in facilitating the entry and progress of the disease. And as has been found in Japan, in rural Ireland too, immunity was a key element in determining patterns of severity. If a town or village was hit by the first wave, the second wave tended to be relatively mild by comparison with places which had been bypassed by the first flu visitation. Areas which had been lucky enough not to be severely hit by the virulent second wave, however, tended to be badly stricken by the third. Immunity was a less important factor for cities, with urban areas such as Dublin, Cork, Belfast, and Galway affected by all three waves. The epidemic was felt most deeply in places at either end of the urban–rural continuum: closely packed cities and isolated settlements both seemed to foster the flu's potential for damage. When it comes to the structure of the epidemic, though, it is harder to apply standard frameworks to Ireland, as the second and third waves overlapped to a large extent, making it hard to clearly distinguish the latter incursions of disease.[12]

State response was another aspect which militated against a completely universal experience of the Great Flu as governments and authorities reacted to the threat in very different ways. The minimal role played by the LGB in Ireland contrasted with the promptness and vigour evident in state responses in Canada and Switzerland for instance, where churches were swiftly closed to prevent the spread of the disease and money was poured into the coffers of local authorities to fuel relief work.[13]

In Ireland, responsibility for prevention and aid was left to local authorities, whose quality of response in turn varied from county to county and from town to town. The improvisational, decentralised response to the epidemic was characteristic of the British colonial system, not only on its peripheries but also domestically, with the onus on rural and urban district councils to deal with the outbreak. Few modern states coped well with the flu but the reasons for this inability to effectively address its effects were particular to each location. In Britain, there was a need to carry on in the face of war, whereas in Ireland, dealing with the flu was made more problematic by a complicated, outdated health system which militated against formulation of a coherent response or effective distribution of aid and resources.

In terms of the medical reaction, there was evidence of both similarity with their counterparts abroad, as well as particularity, when it came to the reaction of doctors and nurses in Ireland. With regard to understanding and treating the disease, Irish doctors had much in common with their international counterparts. The strong investment in bacteria as a primary cause, and in the virtue of the vaccination approach; the persistence of miasmatic and sanitarian ideas; the types of treatments and preventives advocated – bed rest, alcohol, cleanliness, nourishing food, quinine, and aspirin – all featured in the advice given by doctors in Ireland and in places such as the US, France, and Britain.[14] The flu's arrival also showed how the reluctant acceptance of bacteriology had developed into reliance as physicians increasingly looked to the laboratory to provide them with the explanations for and answers to disease. The physical and emotional challenges of the crisis, the theoretical uncertainties over the origins and causes of the disease, and the confusing array of symptoms presented by patients were further elements that gave the appearance of a common medical experience of 'this strange malady'.[15]

While many historians point to the shame witnessed by doctors at their helplessness, and their consequent desire to bury the memory of the event, many Irish practitioners seem to have felt that they had done their best in the face of limited resources and knowledge. There was a sense that 'they could not do better than they had done', and that all the doctors had given 'everything they could', working '20 out of 24 hours, travelling the length and breadth' of their 'vast district(s), in bleak winter weather', in an effort 'to cope with the recent epidemic of influenza'.[16] Although the pride of some doctors may indeed have been undermined by their powerlessness to cure or prevent the disease, others believed that they had performed to the best of their ability. Though affected by its memory, Irish doctors were not ashamed at how they had reacted to the epidemic.

The uniqueness of local experience and the need to question established trends in the historiography of the pandemic, meanwhile, are suggested by an examination of its cultural dimensions. For instance, when it came to naming and explaining the disease in Ireland, it was rarely called 'Spanish flu'. This corresponds with Eugenia Tognotti's observation that Italians also found this name inappropriate, while Niall Johnson has illustrated that a huge variety of names were used in countries around the world, often deriving from local conditions and traditional under-standings of disease. The way in which the event came to be accepted as the 'Spanish flu' pandemic would seem thus to warrant closer examination.[17]

The question of blame also depended largely on the socio-political environment of the respective society (at times even each community), as the epidemic had the potential to bring underlying social tensions into sharp relief. In Ireland, although blame never led to widespread social antagonisms, a certain amount of responsibility for the outbreak was foisted on soldiers. Objects of blame varied from country to country, however, and depended largely on people's immediate circumstances: to British troops, the disease was 'Flanders Grippe', while the Japanese dubbed it 'American influenza' and Russians christened it 'Chinese Disease'. The assorted objects of blame were among the obstacles preventing a complete 'unification of the globe by disease'.[18]

Explanations for the flu were also particular to locality and culture. In Ireland, popular understanding frequently carried religious and moral undertones, with the epidemic explained variously as the will of God and as a repercussion of the carnage sustained in the Great War. People also looked to the past to help them understand what was hap-pening, but had trouble finding historical precedents for an outbreak of disease which had opened a gap between expectation and experience as a 'homely malady' challenged medical certainties. The absence of the Great Flu from narratives of the twentieth century could be seen as reflective of the 'unintelligibility of mass death' and of the problems witnessed in reconciling the significance of the individual death with the meaning of millions of losses. That many flu studies are concerned with counting the death toll is perhaps partly explained by the 'illusion of certitude and control' that can be provided by quantification. Compiling the numbers of the pandemic allows for the imposing of some kind of sense and order on a tragedy whose scale – as many as 80–100 million dead – is almost unfathomable.[19]

An examination of memory of the epidemic in Ireland points to the need to query and qualify the frequent references to the 'forgotten' pandemic.[20] Even years after the flu outbreak had occurred, its Irish witnesses could still recall it in typically vivid terms, and it was remembered as a salient event in many family and community histories. Autobiographies, biographies, local and oral histories indicate that those who lived through it and saw its effects first hand did not forget the flu's visit. However, it was an almost universally upsetting or uncomfortable memory – for the families who lost parents, children, siblings; for governments and officials who were unprepared and unable to deal with such a public health crisis; and for the vastly over-stretched doctors and nurses who could only do their best against a disease that was still a mystery.

The troubling memories which were left by the pandemic meant that there was little will to talk about or remember these months of disease and death, ensuring a tacit agreement not to memorialise what was a tragic period of social history. This in turn was facilitated by the way in which the event did not come under the historical lens until decades afterwards, helping to make it seem as if a collective 'forgetting' had taken place; the result was that any memory of the epidemic was more likely to endure in societies with strong oral history traditions. The flu outbreak moreover was felt to stand apart from other incursions of disease, and perceptions of its unique and unprecedented nature made it difficult to integrate the Great Flu into wider political or social narratives, creating further problems for perpetuation of its memory. Many of those who lived through the Great Flu did not forget it, but at the same time, there was no especial eagerness to preserve the memory of what was one of the most virulent and devastating outbreaks of disease in history: as Kathleen Lynn put it, 'there is no one who would not be thankful to have seen the last of the 'Flu'. Silence offered refuge from difficult, unsettling memories.[21]

Notes

INTRODUCTION: THE STORY OF A NEW DISEASE

1. *Medical Press*, 157, 8 (30 October 1918), p.329.
2. *Irish Times*, 25–26 February 1919; *Cork Examiner*, 26 February 1919.
3. I.D. Mills, 'The 1918–1919 Influenza Pandemic – The Indian Experience', *The Indian Economic and Social History Review*, 23, 1 (1986), pp.35–6; W.I.B. Beveridge, *Influenza* (London, 1977), p.31; *Ireland's Own*, 33, 848 (5 March 1919), p.159; Ministry of Health, *Report on the Pandemic of Influenza, 1918–19* (London, 1920), pp.280–1, 260, 272.
4. David Hogan, *The Four Glorious Years* (London, 1971), p.47; *Farmer's Gazette*, 77, 43 (1918), p.949; John M. Barry, *The Great Influenza* (London, 2005), p.4.
5. Alfred Crosby, *America's Forgotten Pandemic* (Cambridge, 2003), p.311; Barry, *The Great Influenza*, p.5; Kevin Danaher, 'The Plague!', *Biatas*, 18, 9 (1954), p.344; Cornelia Henley, 'The Toxic Second Period of the 1918–1919 Influenza Pandemic in Hungary', *The Medical Journal of Australia*, 1, 18 (1975), p.571.
6. *Derry Journal*, 28 October 1918; Ministry of Health, *Report on the Pandemic of Influenza*, pp.267, 202.
7. Fred van Hartesveldt, 'Introduction', in Fred van Hartesveldt (ed.), *The 1918–1919 Pandemic of Influenza: The Urban Impact in the Western World* (New York, 1992), p.2; Sam Adamo, 'Rio de Janeiro', in van Hartesveldt (ed.), *The 1918–1919 Pandemic of Influenza*, p.186; *British Medical Journal*, 4 April 1919, p.417; Ministry of Health, *Report on the Pandemic*, p.vi.
8. Ministry of Health, *Report on the Pandemic*, p.54; Niall P.A.S. Johnson and Juergen Mueller, 'Updating the Accounts: Global Mortality of the 1918–1920 "Spanish" Influenza Pandemic', *Bulletin of the History of Medicine*, 76, 1 (2002), p.113.
9. *British Medical Journal*, 23 November 1918, p.567; 26 October 1918, p.465; D.W. Macnamara, 'Memories of 1918 and "the 'Flu"', *Journal of the Irish Medical Association*, 35, 208 (1954), p.305.
10. Ministry of Health, *Report on the Pandemic*, pp.101–2; S.W. Patterson, 'The Pathology of Influenza in France' (http://www.vlib.us/medical/mja.htm (Accessed 26 June 2010)).
11. *The Lancet*, 28 December 1918, p.884; 13 July 1918, p.34.
12. Michael Gale Jr and Yueh-Ming Loo, 'Fatal Immunity and the 1918 Virus', *Nature*, 445, 7125 (18 January 2007), p.267; Andreas von Bubnoff, 'The 1918 Flu Virus is Resurrected', *Nature*, 437, 7060 (6 October 2005), p.794; Chief of the molecular pathology department at the Armed Forces Institute of Pathology in Washington, Jeffrey Taubenberger has been working on the 1918 flu virus since 1995 (William McNeill, 'The Flu of Flus', *The New York Review of Books*, 47, 2 (2000), p.30).
13. Ministry of Health, *Report on the Pandemic*, pp.40, xiv, 90–1.
14. *Cork Examiner*, 12 November 1918; in Tralee, 'nearly all the victims' were 'bread-winners and the mortality amongst youngsters' was also 'very heavy' (*Kerryman*, 16 November 1918); Bureau of Military History Witness Statement (BMH WS) 1650; Clifden Poor Law Minutes, 18 September 1918–26 November 1919, pp.176–7; *Connacht Tribune*, 8 March 1919.
15. Magnus Gottfredsson, 'Lessons from the Past: Familial Aggregation Analysis of Fatal Pandemic Influenza (Spanish Flu) in Iceland in 1918', *Proceedings of the National Academy of Sciences*, 105, 4 (2008), p.1306; Gale, Jr and Loo, 'Fatal Immunity and the 1918 virus', p.267.

16. Robert Brown, 'Revisiting Spanish Flu', *Wellcome Science,* 1 (2005), p.43; Gina Kolata, *Flu: The Story of the Great Influenza Pandemic of 1918 and the Search for the Virus that Caused it* (London, 1999), p.15; Howard Phillips and David Killingray, 'Introduction', in Howard Phillips and David Killingray (eds), *The Spanish Influenza Pandemic of 1918–19: New Perspectives* (London, 2003), pp.11–12.
17. Phillips and Killingray, 'Introduction', pp.2, 18–19; Howard Phillips, *'Black October': The Impact of the Spanish Influenza Epidemic of 1918 on South Africa* (Pretoria, 1990); Geoffrey W. Rice, *Black November: The 1918 Influenza Pandemic in New Zealand* (Christchurch, 1998); Niall Johnson, *Britain and the 1918–19 Influenza Pandemic: A Dark Epilogue* (New York, 2006).
18. J.S. Oxford, 'The so-called Great Spanish Influenza Pandemic of 1918 may have originated in France in 1916', *Philosophical Transactions of the Royal Society of London,* 356, 1416 (2001), pp.1857, 1859; J.S. Oxford, A. Sefton, R. Jackson, N.P.A.S. Johnson, and R.S. Daniels, 'Who's That Lady?', *Nature Medicine,* 5, 12 (1999), p.1352.
19. Donald R. Olson, Lone Simonsen, Paul J. Edelson, and Stephen S. Morse, 'Epidemiological Evidence of an Early Wave of the 1918 Influenza Pandemic in New York City', *Proceedings of the National Academy of Sciences of The United States of America,* 102, 31 (2 August 2005), pp.11062–3; Crosby, *America's Forgotten Pandemic,* p.21.
20. Crosby, *America's Forgotten Pandemic,* pp.28, 172, 190; Harry R. Rudin, *Armistice 1918* (New Haven, CT, 1967), pp.110, 197–9, 398.
21. *Wicklow People,* 1 June 1918; *Cork Examiner,* 12 July 1918; *Mayo News,* 5 October 1918; Michael Hopkinson, *The Irish War of Independence* (Dublin, 2002), p.26.
22. *Roscommon Herald,* 11 January 1919; BMH WS/1692, p.4. Sincerest thanks to Eve Morrison for being so kind as to provide me with the references to the epidemic contained in the Bureau of Military History Witness Statements; *Cork Examiner,* 29 October 1918; Michael Brennan, *The War in Clare, 1911–1921: Personal Memoirs of the War of Independence* (Dublin, 1980), p.37.
23. Ruth Barrington, *Health, Medicine and Politics in Ireland 1900–1970* (Dublin, 1987), p.87.
24. Ministry of Health, *Report on the Pandemic,* pp.51–4; Diarmaid Ferriter, *The Transformation of Ireland* (London, 2004), p.185; Sir William J. Thompson, 'Mortality from Influenza in Ireland', *Journal of the Statistical and Social Inquiry Society of Ireland,* 14 (1920), p.1.
25. Ferriter, *The Transformation of Ireland,* p.22; Roy Porter, 'The Patient's View: Doing Medical History from Below', *Theory and Society,* 14, 2 (1989), p.194.
26. Catherine Rollet, 'The "Other War" II: Setbacks in Public Health', in Winter and Robert (eds), *Capital Cities at War* (Cambridge, 1997), p.482; Jay Winter, 'Surviving the War: Life Expectation, Illness, and Mortality Rates in Paris, London, and Berlin, 1914–1919', in Jay Winter and Jean-Louis Robert (eds), *Capital Cities at War,* p.520; Svenn-Erik Mamelund, 'A Socially Neutral Disease? Individual Social Class, Household Wealth and Mortality from Spanish Influenza in Two Socially Contrasting Parishes in Kristiania in 1918–19', *Social Science and Medicine* 62, 4 (2006).
27. D. Ann Herring and Lisa Sattenspiel, 'Death in Winter: Spanish Flu in the Canadian Subarctic', in Howard Phillips and David Killingray (eds), *The Spanish Influenza Pandemic of 1918–19: New Perspectives* (London, 2003), p.170.
28. Danaher, 'The Plague!'
29. See for instance, Sandra M. Tomkins, 'The Failure of Expertise: Public Health Policy in Britain during the 1918–19 Influenza Epidemic', *Social History of Medicine,* 5, 3 (1992); Mridula Ramanna, 'Coping with the Influenza Pandemic: The Bombay Experience', in Phillips and Killingray (eds), *The Spanish Influenza Pandemic of 1918–19; Clare Champion,* 16 November 1918.
30. Phillips and Killingray, 'Introduction', p.20. Among the exceptions to this neglect is Terence Ranger's inquiry into the challenges posed by the epidemic to 'existing explanations of affliction' in South Rhodesia (modern Zimbabwe): Terence Ranger, 'The Influenza Pandemic in Southern Rhodesia: A Crisis of Comprehension', in David Arnold (ed.), *Imperial Medicine and Indigenous Societies* (Manchester, 1988), p.172; Guy Beiner, 'Out in the Cold and Back: New-Found Interest in the Great Flu', *Cultural and Social History,* 3, 4 (2006), p.503.
31. George Lichteim, *Europe in the Twentieth Century* (London, 1972), p.544.
32. Anne Dolan, *Commemorating the Irish Civil War: History and Memory, 1923–2000* (Cambridge, 2003), p.2.
33. Richard J. Evans, *Death in Hamburg: Society and Politics in the Cholera Years, 1830–1910* (Oxford, 1987), p.viii.

34. Martin Bootsma and Neil Ferguson, 'The Effect of Public Health Measures on the 1918 Influenza Pandemic in US Cities', *Proceedings of the National Academy of Sciences of the United States of America*, 104, 18 (2007), p.7588; C.J. Murray, Alan D. Lopez, Brian Chin, Dennis Feehan and Kenneth H. Hill, 'Estimation of Potential Global Pandemic Influenza Mortality on the Basis of Vital Registry Data from the 1918–20 Pandemic: a Quantitative Analysis', *The Lancet*, 368, 9554 (2006), p.2211; S.A. Richard, N. Sugaya, L. Simonsen, M.A. Miller, and C. Viboud, 'A Comparative Study of the 1918–1920 Influenza Pandemic in Japan, USA and UK', *Epidemiology and Infection*, 137, 8 (2009), p.1063.

35. *Farmer's Gazette*, 77, 45 (1918), p.1001; 'Influenza: The Changing Virus', *The Medical Journal of Australia*, 1, 18 (1975), p.547.

CHAPTER ONE: THE GEOGRAPHY OF THE NEW INFLUENZA

1. *Tipperary Star*, 9 November 1918.
2. Stephen Kern, *The Culture of Time and Space, 1880–1918* (Cambridge, MA, 2003), pp.213–42.
3. Ibid., p.230.
4. Niall P.A.S. Johnson and Juergen Mueller, 'Updating the Accounts: Global Mortality of the 1918–1920 "Spanish" Influenza Pandemic', *Bulletin of the History of Medicine*, 76, 1 (2002), p.114.
5. *Mayo News*, 21 December 1918; 4 January 1919; CSO RP 1919/175; Beatriz Echeverri, 'Spanish Influenza Seen from Spain', in Howard Phillips and David Killingray (eds), *The Spanish Influenza Pandemic of 1918–19: New Perspectives* (London, 2003), p.181; for the difficulty in definitively separating the second and third waves, see for instance the *Mayo News*, December 1918 – January/February 1919, during which period influenza was rarely absent from the county.
6. *Belfast Telegraph*, 11 June 1918; *The Lancet*, 13 July 1918, p.51; Matthew Smallman-Raynor, Niall Johnson and Andrew D. Cliff, 'The Spatial Anatomy of an Epidemic: Influenza in London and the County Boroughs of England and Wales, 1918–1919', *Transactions of the Institute of British Geographers*, 27, 4 (2002), p.457; Niall A.S. Johnson, 'The Overshadowed Killer: Influenza in Britain in 1918', in Phillips and Killingray (eds), *The Spanish Influenza Pandemic of 1918–19*, p.145; D. Ann Herring, '"There Were Young People and Old People and Babies Dying Every Week": The 1918–1919 Influenza Pandemic at Norway House', *Ethnohistory*, 41, 1 (1994), p.83; Amir Afkhami, 'The 1918 Influenza Pandemic in Iran', *Bulletin of the History of Medicine*, 76, 22 (2003), p.373; *Western News*, 22 June 1918; *Sligo Champion*, 29 June 1918; Cork Poor Law Union, Board of Guardians Minute Books, BG 69 A 149, pp.315, 321.
7. *Tipperary Star*, 29 June 1918; Echeverri, 'Spanish Influenza Seen from Spain', p.176.
8. Royal Irish Constabulary (RIC) Reports, CO 904/107, p.311; *Irish Times*, 10 October 1918.
9. Sir John Moore, 'Influenza from a Clinical Standpoint', *The Practitioner*, 102, 1 (January 1919), pp.27–8; Ministry of Health, *Report on the Pandemic of Influenza, 1918–19* (London, 1920), p.203; Echeverri, 'Spanish Influenza Seen from Spain', p.178.
10. Smallman-Raynor, Johnson, and Cliff, 'The Spatial Anatomy of an Epidemic', pp.462–4.
11. *King's County Chronicle*, 10 October 1918; *Irish Times*, 10 October 1918; *Mayo News*, 19 October 1918; Ballyshannon Union, Board of Guardians Minutes, BG/38/1/84, p.79.
12. BMH WS/1692, p.4; Ministry of Health, *Report on the Pandemic*, pp.53–4, *Roscommon Herald*, 4 January 1919; *Mayo News*, 26 October 1918; *Belfast Telegraph*, 24 February 1919; CSO RP 1918/30353; *The People* (Wexford), 1 March 1919; BMH WS/1313, pp.3–4.
13. K. David Patterson and Gerald F. Pyle, 'The Geography and Mortality of the 1918 Influenza Pandemic', *Bulletin of the History of Medicine*, 65,1 (1991), p.10; *Cork Examiner*, 9 October 1918 and 19 October 1918; *Fifty-fifth Detailed Annual Report of the Registrar-General for Ireland* [Cmd. 450], H.C. 1919, x, pp.50, 52; *Sligo Champion*, 28 December 1918.
14. *Freeman's Journal*, 13 November 1918; *Tipperary Star*, 19 October 1918; *Connacht Tribune*, 23 November 1918; *Down Recorder*, 14 December 1918.
15. See *Connacht Tribune*, May–July and November–December 1918; Minutes of Board of Guardians Meetings Gort, GOI/12/100, p.358; *Western News*, 22 June 1918; *Tuam Herald*, 2 November 1918; Galway Rural District Council Collection, 1904–1925, GOI/9/3, p.1159; Clifden Poor Law Minutes, 18 September 1918–26 November 1919, p.109; *Galway Observer*, 28 December 1918.
16. See *Sligo Champion*, November 1918, 25 January 1919, 28 December 1918, and 7 September 1918.

17. *Tipperary Star*, 11 January 1919; *The Kerryman*, 18 January 1919; Reports of influenza came from Mayo in the third week of January, following signs of outbreaks in Sligo (*Mayo News*, 18 January 1919; *Sligo Champion*, 11 January 1919); *Fermanagh Times*, 23 January 1919; *The People* (Wexford), 22 January 1919; *Freeman's Journal*, 6 February 1919; Minute Books of Rathdown Union, BG 137 A 152, pp.388–9; Rathdrum Minute Books 1919, PLUR/WR/137, p.67; Balrothery Union Minute Books, MFGS 49 BG A 144, p.294; *Meath Chronicle*, 8 February 1919; Echeverri, 'Spanish Influenza Seen from Spain', p.181.

18. See *The People* (Wexford), October–November 1918, and January–February 1919.

19. *Connacht Tribune*, March and April 1919; Clifden Poor Law Minutes, 18 September 1918–26 November 1918, pp.176–7.

20. Ciara Breathnach, *The Congested Districts Board of Ireland, 1891–1923* (Dublin, 2005), p.11; Johnson, 'The overshadowed killer', p.148; Johnson and Mueller, 'Updating the Accounts', p.106; Geoffrey W. Rice and Edwina Palmer, 'Pandemic Influenza in Japan, 1918–19: Mortality Patterns and Official Responses', *Journal of Japanese Studies*, 19, 2 (1993), p.415.

21. Rice and Palmer, 'Pandemic Influenza in Japan', p.415; *The People* (Wexford), 26 October 1918; *Fifty-fifth Detailed Annual Report of the Registrar-General for Ireland*, pp.50–7; *Irish Times*, 7 November 1918; *Kilkenny People*, 13 July 1918.

22. *The Lancet*, 5 April 1919, p.583.

23. Patterson and Pyle, 'The Geography and Mortality of the 1918 Influenza Pandemic', p.4; Gerardo Chowell, L.M.A. Bettencourt, N. Johnson, W.J. Alonso, and C.V. Viboud, 'The 1918–1919 Influenza Pandemic in England and Wales: Spatial Patterns in Transmissibility and Mortality Impact', *Proceedings of the Royal Society B*, 275 (2008), p.508.

24. Doreen Massey, *For Space* (London, 2005), p.193; Rice and Palmer, 'Pandemic Influenza in Japan', p.400; *Kilkenny People*, 9 November 1918.

25. *The People* (Wexford), 20 November 1918; *Fifty-fifth Detailed Annual Report of the Registrar-General for Ireland*, pp.50–7.

26. *Roscommon Herald*, 30 November 1918; *Fifty-fifth Detailed Annual Report of the Registrar-General for Ireland*, pp.50–7. For aid efforts in Thurles, see the *Tipperary Star*, 26 October 1918, and 16 November 1918, and for relief work in Limerick and Clonmel see the *Limerick Chronicle*, 31 October 1918, and General Prisons Board Files (GPB) 1918/7063.

27. *Fifty-fifth Detailed Annual Report of the Registrar-General*, p.xvia; *Fifty-sixth Detailed Annual Report of the Registrar-General for Ireland* [Cmd. 997], H.C. 1920, xi, p.xvii.

28. Niall Johnson, *Britain and the 1918–1919 Influenza Pandemic: A Dark Epilogue* (London, 2006), p.63.

29. Keith Jeffery, *Ireland and the Great War* (Cambridge, 2000), p.6; *Fifty-fifth Detailed Annual Report of the Registrar-General for Ireland*, pp.xvia, 54–5, 50; David Fitzpatrick, 'Militarism in Ireland, 1900–1922', in Keith Jeffery and Thomas Bartlett (eds), *A Military History of Ireland* (Cambridge, 1996), p.389.

30. *Freeman's Journal*, 24 June 1919; Ministry of Health, *Report on the Pandemic*, p.229.

31. Alfred Crosby, *America's Forgotten Pandemic* (Cambridge, 2003), p.56; Echeverri, 'Spanish Influenza Seen from Spain', p.177; Richard Collier, *The Plague of the Spanish Lady* (London, 1974), p.84; *Irish Independent*, 21 November 1918.

32. *Irish Times*, 12 and 17 February 1919; *Sixty-second Annual Report of the Board of Superintendence of the Dublin Hospitals, with Appendices. For the Year 1919–1920* [Cmd. 1260], H.C. 1920, xiii, p.862.

33. Esyllt W. Jones, '"Co-operation in All Human Endeavour": Quarantine and Immigrant Disease Vectors in the 1918–1919 Influenza Pandemic in Winnipeg', *Canadian Bulletin of Medical History*, 22, 1 (2005), p.62; Joanna Bourke, *Dismembering the Male: Men's Bodies, Britain and the Great War* (London, 1996), p.70.

34. Johnson, 'The Overshadowed Killer', p.146; Crosby, *America's Forgotten Pandemic*, p.56; Echeverri, 'Spanish Influenza Seen from Spain', p.177; Jones, '"Co-operation in All Human Endeavour"', p.62; Patterson and Pyle, 'The Geography and Mortality of the 1918 Influenza Pandemic', p.10; Robert Brown, 'The Great War and the Great Flu Pandemic of 1918', *Wellcome History*, 24 (October 2003), p.6.

35. Echeverri, 'Influenza Seen from Spain', p.177; Geoffrey W. Rice, 'Japan and New Zealand in the 1918 Influenza Pandemic', in Howard Phillips and David Killingray (eds), *The Spanish Influenza Pandemic of 1918–19: New Perspectives* (London, 2003), pp.73–4; Johnson, 'The Overshadowed Killer', p.146; Johnson, *Britain and the 1918–19 Influenza Pandemic*, p.57.

36. Cliff, Johnson, and Smallman-Raynor 'Spatial Anatomy of an Epidemic', p.460; Johnson, *Britain and the 1918–19 Influenza Pandemic*, p.58; A.D. Cliff, P. Haggett, J.K. Ord, and G.R.

Versey, *Spatial Diffusion: An Historical Geography of Epidemics in an Island Community* (Cambridge, 1981), p.90; Johnson, 'The Overshadowed Killer', p.146.
37. Echeverri, 'Spanish Flu Seen from Spain', p.188.
38. *Connacht Tribune*, 28 December 1918; *Fermanagh Times*, 20 February 1919; *Sligo Champion*, 30 November 1918; *Derry Journal*, 2 December 1918; *The Kerryman*, 7 December 1918.
39. Johnson, *Britain and the 1918–19 Influenza Pandemic*, p.59; Johnson and Mueller, 'Updating the Accounts', p.106; *British Medical Journal*, 3 April 1920, p.465.
40. Ministry of Health, *Report on the Pandemic*, pp.280–1; Johnson, *Britain and the 1918–19 Influenza Pandemic*, pp.82–3.
41. *Fifty-fifth Detailed Annual Report of the Registrar-General for Ireland*, p.52.

CHAPTER TWO: THE DEMOGRAPHY OF THE EPIDEMIC

1. *Freeman's Journal*, 5 November 1918.
2. Gearóid Ó Crualaoich, 'The "Merry Wake"', in James S. Donnelly Jr and Kerby A. Miller (eds), *Irish Popular Culture, 1650–1850* (Dublin, 1998), p.195; Michael O'Suilleabhain, *Where Mountainy Men have Sown* (Tralee, 1965), p.48; Royal Irish Constabulary (RIC) Reports, CO 904/107, p.280; *Freeman's Journal*, 25 October 1918; *Mayo News*, 1 March 1919; *Church of Ireland Gazette*, 21 March 1919, p.187; *Fifty-sixth Detailed Annual Report of the Registrar-General for Ireland* [Cd 997], H.C. 1920, xi, pp.xiv–xv; N.P.A.S. Johnson and Juergen Mueller, 'Updating the Accounts: Global Mortality of the 1918–1920 "Spanish" Influenza Pandemic', *Bulletin of the History of Medicine*, 76, 1 (2002), p.113; William J. Thompson, 'Mortality from Influenza in Ireland', *Dublin Journal of Medical Science*, 4, Fourth Series (June 1920), p.174.
3. Alice Reid, 'The Effects of the 1918–1919 Influenza Pandemic on Infant and Child Health in Derbyshire', *Medical History*, 44, 1 (2005), p.29; Sandra Tomkins, 'The Failure of Expertise: Public Health Policy in Britain during the 1918–19 Influenza Epidemic', *Social History of Medicine*, 5, 3 (1992), p.446; Catherine Rollet, 'The "Other War": Setbacks in Public Health', in Jay Winter and Jean-Louis Robert (eds), *Capital Cities at War* (Cambridge, 1997), pp.481–2.
4. Howard Phillips and David Killingray, 'Introduction', in Phillips and Killingray (eds), *The Spanish Influenza Pandemic of 1918–19*, p.8; Reid, 'The Effects of the 1918–1919 Influenza Pandemic', p.29; *Twenty-ninth Annual Report of the Registrar-General (Ireland)* [C. 7255], H.C. 1893-4, xxi, pp.8, 14.
5. *Forty-seventh Annual Report of the Local Government Board for Ireland* [Cmd. 578], H.C. 1920, xxi, p.39; Thompson, 'Mortality from Influenza in Ireland', p.184 ; 'Section of State Medicine', *Dublin Journal of Medical Science*, 7, Fourth Series (1920), p.353.
6. Ministry of Health, *Report on the Pandemic of Influenza, 1918–19* (London, 1920), pp.90–1.
7. 'Ninetieth Annual Report of the Protestant Orphan Society for the period ending 31st January 1919' (1045/1/90), pp.10–11; *Forty-seventh Annual Report of the Local Government Board for Ireland*, p.36.
8. *Society of St Vincent de Paul, Ireland. Report of the Council for the Year 1918* (Dublin, 1919), p.20; *Cork Examiner*, 19 October 1918, 8 November 1918; *Irish Independent*, 2 November 1918; *Freeman's Journal*, 7 November 1918; *Connacht Tribune*, 8 March 1919; Ministry of Health, *Report on the Pandemic*, p.52; *Cork Examiner*, 12 November 1918; Turtle Bunbury and James Fennell, *Vanishing Ireland* (Dublin, 2006), p.113.
9. The Kathleen Lynn Diaries, Royal College of Physicians of Ireland, Volume I, p.29; Captain John Speares, 'Influenza', *Transactions of the Royal Academy of Medicine in Ireland*, 37 (1919), p.397; *Connacht Tribune*, 8 March 1919; *Freeman's Journal*, 5 November 1918, 9 November 1918; *Irish Independent*, 4 November 1918; Ministry of Health, *Report on the Pandemic*, p.viii.
10. Terry Devitt, 'Study uncovers a lethal secret of the 1918 influenza virus' (http://www.news.wisc. edu/13360.html (Accessed 27 April 2007)).
11. Patrick Zylberman, 'A Holocaust in a Holocaust: The Great War and the Influenza Pandemic of 1918 in France', in Phillips and Killingray (eds), *The Spanish Influenza Pandemic of 1918–19*, p.197; Thompson, 'Mortality from Influenza', p.179; *Twenty-ninth Detailed Annual Report of the Registrar-General (Ireland)*, pp.154–5; *Fifty-fourth Annual Report of the Registrar-General for Ireland* [Cd. 9123], H.C. 1918, vi, p.xvi.
12. *Cork Examiner*, 18 November 1918; *Connacht Tribune*, 16 November 1918; Rollet, 'The "Other War" II', pp.482–3; Kevin McCracken and Peter Curson, 'Flu Downunder. A Demographic and

Geographic Analysis of the 1919 Epidemic in Sydney, Australia', in Phillips and Killingray (eds), *The Spanish Influenza Pandemic of 1918–19*, p.121.

13. Phillips and Killingray, 'Introduction', p.23; Rollet, 'The "Other War" II', p.482; *The Lancet*, 18 October 1919, p.699; *Fifty-fourth Detailed Annual Report of the Registrar-General for Ireland*, p.xxv; *Fifty-fifth Detailed Annual Report of the Registrar-General for Ireland* [Cmd. 450], H.C. 1919, x, p.xxv; *Fifty-sixth Detailed Annual Report of the Registrar-General for Ireland*, p.xxvi.

14. Reid, 'The Effects of the 1918–1919 Influenza Pandemic'.

15. Dr Kathleen Lynn, witness statement (BMH/WS 357, part 2, p.11).

16. The Kathleen Lynn Diaries. Volume 1, pp.16, 17, 41.

17. Marilyn Cohen and Joan Vincent, 'Anthropological and Sociological Studies', in Laurence M. Geary and Margaret Kelleher (eds), *Nineteenth Century Ireland: A Guide to Recent Research* (Dublin, 2005), p.113.

18. Minute Books, Board of Guardians, South Dublin Poor Law Union: BG 79/A80-A82, pp.303–4, 330, 728, 759, 761, 764, 765, 839, 840; *Freeman's Journal*, 8 July 1918; *Meath Chronicle*, 13 July 1918, 9 November 1918; *Connacht Tribune*, 23 November 1918, 7 December 1918; *Derry People and Donegal News*, 23 November 1918. Flu also hit workhouses in Limerick, Ennis, Carrick-on-Shannon, Castlerea, Enniskillen, Macroom, Letterkenny, and Derry (*Limerick Chronicle*, 31 October 1918, 7 November 1918; *Roscommon Herald*, 2 and 9 November 1918; *Fermanagh Times*, 20 February 1919; *Cork Examiner*, 12 November 1918; *Derry Journal*, 18 November 1918); *Meath Chronicle*, 26 October 1918, 9 November 1918; *Belfast Telegraph*, 11 November 1918.

19. *Wicklow People*, 1 March 1919.

20. *Limerick Chronicle*, 25 February 1919; Shillelagh Board of Guardians Minutes 1918, PLUS/WR/76, p.378; *Fermanagh Times*, 24 December 1918.

21. *Roscommon Herald*, 16 November 1918.

22. *Westmeath Examiner*, 10 August 1918; *Limerick Chronicle*, 14 November 1918, 13 March 1919; *Sligo Champion*, 7 September 1918, 15 February 1919; Richmond District Asylum, Dublin, *Annual Report of the Medical Superintendent to the Joint Committee of Management for the Years 1918 and 1919* (Dublin, 1921), p.58; *Fermanagh Times*, 19 December 1918; *Mayo News*, 28 December 1918.

23. In 1917, influenza caused just twenty-nine deaths of all the patients who died in the District and Auxiliary Asylums (*Sixty-seventh Annual Report of the Inspectors of Lunatics (Ireland)* [Cmd. 32], H.C. 1919, xxv, pp.19–20, 16–17, 42–3); *Sixty-eighth Annual Report of the Inspector of Lunatics Ireland, Being for the Year Ending 31st December, 1918* [Cmd. 579], H.C. 1920, xxi, pp.384–6, 408–9; K. David Patterson, 'The Influenza Epidemic of 1918–19 in the Gold Coast', *The Journal of African History*, 24, 4 (1983), p.495; David Killingray, 'The Influenza Pandemic of 1918–19 in the British Caribbean', *Social History of Medicine*, 7, 1 (1994), p.66; Gina Kolata, *Flu: The Story of the Great Influenza Pandemic of 1918 and the Search for the Virus that Caused it* (London, 1999), p.141.

24. John Speares, 'Influenza', *Transactions of the Royal Academy of Medicine in Ireland*, 37 (1919), p.404; *The Lancet*, 4 January 1919, p.5; Bunbury and Fennell, *Vanishing Ireland*, p.140; *Meath Chronicle*, 9 April 1919; Speares, 'Influenza', p.406.

25. *Fifty-seventh Report of the Inspector Appointed to Visit the Reformatory and Industrial Schools of Ireland* [Cmd.571], H.C. 1920, xxv, pp.14–15; *King's County Chronicle*, 20 March 1919; *Fifty-eighth Report of the Inspector Appointed to Visit the Reformatory and Industrial Schools of Ireland* [Cmd. 1128], H.C. 1921, xvii, p.8.

26. The epidemic caused few deaths though – of the four deaths in local and convict prisons for the year 1918, only one was due to influenza (*Forty-first Report of the General Prisons Board, Ireland, 1918–1919* [Cmd. 687], H.C. 1920, xxiii, p.73); General Prisons Board (GPB) Files 1918/6971. Sincerest thanks to Dr William Murphy who pointed me towards several of the references to the epidemic in the GPB Files.

27. GPB 1919/3261; GPB 1919/1862;GPB 1919/1977; GPB 1919/2215; GPB 1919/1991.

28. GPB 1919/3510; GPB 1919/5126.

29. Sir C.A. Cameron, *Report Upon the State of Public Health in the City of Dublin for the Year 1917* (Dublin, 1918), pp.75–8; Sir C.A. Cameron, *Report Upon the State of Public Health in the City of Dublin for the Year 1918* (Dublin, 1919), pp.79–82; Ministry of Health, *Report on the Pandemic*, p.237.

30. *Church of Ireland Gazette*, 8 November 1918, p.747; 27 December 1918, p.866; 7 March

1919, p.156; *Meath Chronicle*, 16 November 1918; *Freeman's Journal*, 28 October 1918; *Wicklow People*, 26 October 1918; *Irish Catholic*, 7 December 1918; *Wicklow People*, 19 October 1918; *Meath Chronicle*, 2 November 1918, 9 November 1918; *Freeman's Journal*, 6 November 1918, 9 November 1918; *Connacht Tribune*, 27 July 1918; *Church of Ireland Gazette*, 7 March 1919; Mridula Ramanna, 'Coping with the Influenza Pandemic. The Bombay Experience', in Phillips and Killingray (eds), *The Spanish Influenza Pandemic of 1918–19* (London, 2003), p.88; *Meath Chronicle*, 12 October 1918.

31. *Irish Independent*, 4 November 1918; *King's County Chronicle*, 7 November 1918; *Freeman's Journal*, 11 July 1918; *Cork Examiner*, 9 July 1918; *Connacht Tribune*, 2 November 1918.
32. *King's County Chronicle*, 24 October 1918; *Cork Examiner*, 18 July 1918; *Wicklow People*, 26 October 1918, 23 November 1918; *Roscommon Herald*, 9 November 1918; *Sligo Champion*, 23 November 1918.
33. Peter Somerville-Large, *Cappaghglass* (London, 1985), p.76; *Cork Examiner*, 23 October 1918.
34. Rudyard Kipling, *The Irish Guards in the Great War: The Second Battalion* (Kent, 1997), p.181.
35. Kipling, *The Irish Guards in the Great War: the First Battalion* (Kent, 1997), pp.245–6, 23, 246.
36. Ibid., p.288.
37. *The People* (Wexford), 18 January 1919, 11 January 1919; *Irish Opinion*, 4 January 1919, p.548.
38. *Meath Chronicle*, 16 November 1918, 23 November 1918; *Freeman's Journal*, 31 October 1918, and *Wicklow People*, 2 November 1918. For sickness among politicians, see for instance *Freeman's Journal*, 28 October 1918, 6 November 1918 and *Connacht Tribune*, 15 March 1919. For stricken solicitors and barristers, see *Freeman's Journal*, 28 October 1918 and 5 November 1918; *Connacht Tribune*, 1 March 1919; *Irish Catholic*, 15 June 1918, p.2; *Irish Times*, 1 November 1918; Note dated 18 November 1919 in CSO RP 1918/30487; *Kilkenny People*, 2 November 1918; *Sligo Champion*, 30 November 1918; *Connacht Tribune*, 8 March 1919, 22 February 1919; *Irish Independent*, 2 November 1918; *Meath Chronicle*, 9 November 1918; Norbert Elias and J.L. Scotson, 'Cohesion, Conflict and Community Character', in Colin Bell (ed.), *The Sociology of Community* (London, 1974), p.31.
39. Cohen and Vincent, 'Anthropological and Sociological Studies', p.115; *Irish Independent*, 2 November 1918; *Meath Chronicle*, 5 April 1919; *Mayo News*, 16 November 1918; *Wicklow People*, 9 November 1918, 16 November 1918.
40. Bunbury and Fennell, *Vanishing Ireland*, p.99; Niall MacFhionnghaile, *Dr McGinley and His Times: Donegal 1900–1950* (Letterkenny, 1985), p.110 ; 'Section of State Medicine', *Dublin Journal of Medical Science*, 7, Fourth Series (1920), p.353.
41. Ruth Barrington, *Health, Medicine and Politics in Ireland 1900–1970* (Dublin, 1987), pp.3–23.
42. *Connacht Tribune*, 12 April 1919; CO 904/107, p.511; *Connacht Tribune*, 16 November 1918; CSO RP 1919/175; *Derry Journal*, 29 November 1918.
43. *Cork Examiner*, 10 July 1918; *Irish Times*, 3 March 1919; *Kilkenny People*, 1 March 1919; *The People* (Wexford), 9 November 1918; *King's County Chronicle*, 19 December 1918; *Forty-seventh Annual Report of the Local Government Board for Ireland*, p.25; *Fifty-sixth Detailed Annual Report of the Registrar-General for Ireland*, pp.xiv–xv.
44. *Irish Independent*, 2 November 1918; *Freeman's Journal*, 21 October 1918.
45. *Forty-seventh Annual Report of the Local Government Board for Ireland*, p.25; Cameron, *Report Upon the State of Public Health in the City of Dublin for the Year 1917*, pp.75–8; *Report Upon the State of Public Health in the City of Dublin for the Year 1918*, pp.79–82.
46. Svenn Erik Mamelund, 'A Socially Neutral Disease? Individual Social Class, Household Wealth and Mortality from Spanish Influenza in Two Socially Contrasting Parishes in Kristiania in 1918–19', *Social Science and Medicine*, 62, 4 (2006).
47. Michel Foucault, *Madness and Civilisation* (London, 1993), pp.38–9; Colin Brown, 'The Influenza Pandemic of 1918 in Indonesia', in Norman G. Owen (ed.), *Death and Disease in Southeast Asia: Explorations in Social, Medical and Demographic History* (Oxford, 1987), p.241; McCracken and Curson, 'Flu Downunder', pp.123–5.
48. *Derry People and Donegal News*, 9 November 1918; *Irish Independent*, 2 November 1918; *Society of St Vincent de Paul. Report of the Council of Ireland for the Year 1919* (Dublin, 1920), p.56.
49. *Society of St Vincent de Paul. Report of the Council of Ireland for the Year 1918* (Dublin,

1919), p.20; *Derry People and Donegal News*, 9 November 1918; *Irish Times*, 2 July 1918; *Wicklow People*, 26 October 1918.

50. *Wicklow People*, 26 October 1918, 2 November 1918, 26 October 1918; *Irish Times*, 8 November 1918; *Cork Examiner*, 9 November 1918; Niall Johnson, *Britain and the 1918–1919 Influenza Pandemic: A Dark Epilogue* (London, 2006), p.196.

51. Mary E. Fissell, 'Making Meaning from the Margins: The New Cultural History of Medicine', in Frank Huisman and John Harley Warner (eds), *Locating Medical History* (London, 2004), p.384; Pierre Bourdieu, *In Other Words: Essays towards a Reflexive Sociology* (Oxford, 1990), p.135.

52. Thomas Wrigley Grimshaw, *Report on the Smallpox Epidemic, 1871–73, as Observed in Cork Street Fever Hospital* (Dublin, 1873), p.6; *Irish Builder*, 17, 369 (15 May 1875), p.117; *Society of St Vincent de Paul. Report of the Council of Ireland for the Year 1918*, p.15.

CHAPTER THREE: THE SOCIAL IMPACT OF THE GREAT FLU

1. *King's County Chronicle*, 7 November 1918.

2. Niall Johnson, *Britain and the 1918–19 Influenza Pandemic: A Dark Epilogue* (London, 2006), p.119; Fred van Hartesveldt, 'Introduction', in Fred van Hartesveldt (ed.), *The 1918–19 Pandemic of Influenza: The Urban Impact in the Western World* (New York, 1992). p.11.

3. *Freeman's Journal*, 6 November 1918; *Mayo News*, 9 November 1918.

4. The Kathleen Lynn Diaries, Volume I, pp.27, 14; *Irish Independent*, 2 November 1918; *Freeman's Journal*, 9 July 1918, 17 October 1918; *Cork Examiner*, 11 November 1918.

5. Pierre Bourdieu, *In Other Words: Essays towards a Reflexive Sociology* (Oxford, 1990), p.136.

6. *Forty-first Report of the General Prisons Board, Ireland, 1918–19, with an Appendix* [Cmd. 687], H.C. 1920, xxiii, pp.57–8; *Forty-seventh Annual Report of the Local Government Board for Ireland* [Cmd. 578], H.C. 1920, xxi, p.28; *Annual Report of the Commissioners of Education in Ireland. For the Year 1919* [Cmd. 884], H.C. 1920, xv, p.727; *Eighty-fifth Report of the Commissioners of National Education in Ireland, School Year 1918–19* [Cmd. 1048], H.C. 1920, xv, p.825; Sir William Thompson, 'Mortality from Influenza in Ireland', *Dublin Journal of Medical Science*, 4, Fourth Series (1920), p. 174; *Fifty-seventh Report of the Inspector Appointed to Visit the Reformatory and Industrial Schools of Ireland* [Cmd. 571], H.C. 1920, xxv, pp.14–15; Bourdieu, *In Other Words*, p.136.

7. Thompson, 'Mortality from Influenza in Ireland', p.180; RIC Reports, CO 904/107, p.311.

8. Peter Gatenby, *Dublin's Meath Hospital* (Dublin, 1996), p.95; *Connacht Tribune*, 27 July 1918; *Irish Independent*, 2 November 1918.

9. *Cork Examiner*, 16 July 1918, 28 October 1918, 12 November 1918; *Meath Chronicle*, 26 October 1918; *Connacht Tribune*, 8 March 1919, 1 March 1919; *Down Recorder*, 18 January 1919, 29 March 1919; *Westmeath Examiner*, 30 November 1918; *Limerick Chronicle*, 16 November 1918; *Tipperary Star*, 26 October 1918; *Kilkenny People*, 2 November 1918; *King's County Chronicle*, 31 October 1918; *The People* (Wexford), 26 October 1918; *Irish Times*, 9 November 1918.

10. *Irish Times*, 12 November 1918; Sir Charles A. Cameron, *Report Upon the State of Public Health in the City of Dublin for the Year 1919* (Dublin, 1920), p.36; *Sixty-first Annual Report of the Board of Superintendence of the Dublin Hospitals, with Appendices for the Year 1918–19* [Cmd. 480], H.C. 1919, xiii (part 1).

11. *Forty-seventh Annual Report of the Local Government Board for Ireland*, p.34; *Irish Independent*, 4 November 1918; CO 904/107, p.304; *Wicklow People*, 9 November 1918.

12. *The Kerryman*, 2 November 1918; *Freeman's Journal*, 15 October 1918, 17 October 1918, 29 October 1918, 9 November 1918; *King's County Chronicle*, 31 October 1918, 28 November 1918; Chief Secretary's Office Registered Papers (CSO RP) 1920/15756; *Connacht Tribune*, 1 March 1919.

13. *Eighty-fifth Report of the Commissioners of National Education in Ireland*, p.825; *Sligo Champion*, 7 December 1918; *Freeman's Journal*, 15 October 1918; *Eighty-Fifth Report of the Commissioners of National Education in Ireland*, p.826.

14. *Annual Report of the Commissioners of Education in Ireland. For the Year 1919*, pp.727–8; *Freeman's Journal*, 8 March 1919; John Cowell, *'A Noontide Blazing': Brigid Lyons Thornton – Rebel, Soldier, Doctor* (Dublin, 2005), p.145.

15. *Freeman's Journal*, 23 October 1918, 19 February 1919; CSO RP 1920/15756.

16. *Irish Catholic*, 2 November 1918; *Cork Examiner*, 27 February 1919, 30 October 1918;

Connacht Tribune, 29 March 1919; Beatriz Echeverri, 'Spanish Influenza Seen from Spain', in Howard Phillips and David Killingray (eds), *The Spanish Influenza Pandemic of 1918–19: New Perspectives* (London, 2003) p.180; Isaac Starr, 'Influenza in 1918: Recollections of the Epidemic in Philadelphia', *Annals of Internal Medicine*, 85, 4 (1976), p.517; Richard Collier, *The Plague of the Spanish Lady* (London, 1974), p.148; Kevin McCracken and Peter Curson, 'Flu Downunder. A Demographic and Geographic Analysis of the 1919 Epidemic in Sydney, Australia', in Phillips and Killingray (eds), *The Spanish Influenza Pandemic of 1918–19*, p.116.

17. *Derry People and Donegal News*, 9 November 1918; *Irish Independent*, 4 November 1918; *Church of Ireland Gazette*, 15 November 1918, p.765; *Cork Examiner*, 16 October 1918; *Meath Chronicle*, 16 November 1918; *Freeman's Journal*, 16 November 1918.

18. *Cork Examiner*, 8 November 1918; *Mayo News*, 30 November 1918; *Freeman's Journal*, 30 October 1918; *Wicklow People*, 19 October 1918.

19. Niall MacFhionnghaile, *Dr McGinley and his Times: Donegal 1900–1950* (Letterkenny, 1985), p.110; *Cork Examiner*, 12 November 1918; *Mayo News*, 14 December 1918; *The Kerryman*, 9 November 1918; *Mayo News*, 16 November 1918.

20. *Freeman's Journal*, 29 June 1918, 25 October 1918, 31 October, 31 November 1918; *Cork Examiner*, 19 July 1918, 9 July 1918, 8 November 1918, 9 November 1918; CO 904/107, p.311; *Down Recorder*, 30 November 1918; *Kilkenny People*, 2 November 1918; *King's County Chronicle*, 7 November 1918, 27 February 1919; *Derry Journal*, 2 December 1918; *Mayo News*, 16 November 1918; *Down Recorder*, 30 November 1918; *Ulster Guardian*, 15 June 1918, 8 March 1919; *The People* (Wexford), 26 October 1918; *Irish Times*, 4 November 1918.

21. CO 904/108, p.707; *Down Recorder*, 29 June 1918; *Freeman's Journal*, 5 November 1918; *Connacht Tribune*, 29 March 1919; Jeremiah Clarke, *When Youth Was Mine: A Memoir of Kerry 1902–1925* (Dublin, 1998), p.60; Thomas Johnson Westropp, 'A Study of the Folklore on the Coast of Connacht, Ireland', *Folklore*, 29, 4 (1918), p.305.

22. *Irish Independent*, 2 November 1918; *Cork Examiner*, 14 November 1918; *Connacht Tribune*, 23 November 1918, 8 March 1919; *Freeman's Journal*, 25–29 October 1918, 5–7 November 1918; *Wicklow People*, 16 November 1918; CSO RP 1918/30353.

23. CO 904/108, pp.408, 646, 887, 531; CSO RP 1919/175; CSO RP 1919/9553.

24. *Freeman's Journal*, 5 November 1918; *Meath Chronicle*, 16 November 1918; CO 904/107, p.248; *Mayo News*, 14 December 1918; *Down Recorder*, 7 December 1918, 14 December 1918.

25. CO 904/164, p.888; *Freeman's Journal*, 30 October 1918; *Forty-first Report of the General Prisons Board, Ireland, 1918–19, with an Appendix* [Cmd. 687], H.C. 1920, xxiii, p.57; GPB 1918/8338; *Mayo News*, 2 November 1918.

26. GPB 1918/8338.

27. GPB 1918/ 8338; GPB 1918/6970; GPB 1918/6971.

28. *Irish Opinion*, 11 January 1919, p.558; CO 904/164, p.923.

29. Deaglan Bric, 'Pierce McCan, MP (1882–1919), Part II', *Tipperary Historical Journal* (1989), p.112.

30. CO 904/164, pp.904, 1005, 908.

31. Bric, 'Pierce McCan', p.114.

32. BMH WS/1322, pp.36–7; BMH WS/811, p.3; Bill Kelly, 'Escape of de Valera, McGarry and Milroy ("German Plot" Prisoners) from Lincoln Jail', in Florence O'Donoghue (ed.), *Sworn to be Free: The Complete Book of IRA Jailbreaks 1918–1921*(Tralee, 1971), p.45.

33. George Geraghty and Frank Shouldice, 'The Break-Out from Usk Jail in Wales by Four "German Plot" Prisoners', in O'Donoghue (ed.), *Sworn to be Free*, pp.26–32.

34. Piaras Béaslaí, 'Twenty Got Away in the Big Daylight Escape from Mountjoy Jail', in O'Donoghue (ed.), *Sworn to be Free*, pp.755, 856.

36. CO 904/107, pp.467, 540, 553, 617, 646, 652, 886; CO 904/108, pp.144, 385, 388, 487, 727, 769; for reports on the deaths of Volunteers from flu, see also: *Wicklow People*, 23 November 1918; *Mayo News*, 30 November 1918, 7 December 1918; *Roscommon Herald*, 19 October 1918; *Sligo Champion*, 1 March 1919.

37. *Irish Independent*, 24 November 1918; *Meath Chronicle*, 9 November 1918; *Mayo News*, 21 December 1918; *Wicklow People*, 16 November 191, 23 November 1918; Cowell, 'A Noontide Blazing', pp.9, 145; Sean Moylan for instance remained weak for many months after his bout of flu (Peter Hart, *The IRA and its Enemies* (Oxford, 1998), pp.249–50).

38. BMH WS/1650, p.9; BMH WS/1093, p.25. It is perhaps worth noting that both Meath and Kilkenny registered low levels of IRA activity during the War of Independence, recording only eight operations apiece in the period 1919–1921 (Charles Townshend, *Ireland: The 20th Century* (New York, 1998), p.95). The statements regarding the effects of the epidemic in these areas could thus be read either as providing an excuse for low activity levels or providing an explanation for same, which is possible considering the importance that local individuals could have in spurring on action during the revolutionary period; BMH WS/1195, p.8; BMH WS/905, p.1.

39. Michael Farry, *Sligo 1914–1921: A Chronicle of Conflict* (Trim, 1992), p.150; BMH WS/1176, p.5; BMH WS/1718, p.8.

40. CO 904/164, p.1040.

41. *King's County Chronicle*, 24 October 1918; Catherine Rollet, 'The "Other War" II: Setbacks in Public Health', in Jay Winter and Jean-Louis Robert (eds), *Capital Cities at War* (Cambridge, 1997), p.483; Turtle Bunbury and James Fennell, *Vanishing Ireland* (Dublin, 2006), p.99; *Freeman's Journal*, 31 October 1918; *Wicklow People*, 26 October 1918; *Cork Examiner*, 26 October 1918, 11 November 1918.

42. *Connacht Tribune*, 29 March 1919, 8 March 1919, 29 March 1919, 12 April 1919; *Wicklow People*, 26 October 1918; Galway Poor Law Union Minutes 1919, No 1, p.197; *Meath Chronicle*, 9 November 1918; *Tuam Herald*, 22 March 1919; *Belfast Telegraph*, 22 October 1918; *Tipperary Star*, 12 October 1918.

43. *Galway Observer*, 28 December 1918; *Connacht Tribune*, 23 November 1918, 28 December 1918; *Meath Chronicle*, 16 November 1918; *Wicklow People*, 23 November 1918; *Derry People and Donegal News*, 9 November 1918; Scott F. Dowell and Joseph S. Bresee, 'Pandemic Lessons from Iceland', *Proceedings of the National Academy of Sciences*, 105, 4 (2008), pp.1109–10.

44. Doreen Massey, *For Space* (London, 2005), pp.185–6; 11 November 1918, Minutes of Rathdrum Rural District Council, WLAA/RDCR/M/18, p.406.

45. *Cork Examiner*, 18 November 1918; *Freeman's Journal*, 7 November 1918; *Irish Times*, 12 November 1918; Conrad H. Arensburg, *The Irish Countryman* (Gloucester, MA., 1959), p.215; *Down Recorder*, 8 March 1919.

46. *Connacht Tribune*, 7 December 1918; Milford Union Board of Guardians Minutes, BG 119/86, p.34.

47. For cancellations of concerts and dances see the following: *Fermanagh Times*, 30 January 1919; *The People* (Wexford), 9 November 1918; *Mayo News*, 2 November 1918, *Donegal Vindicator*, 28 February 1919. For some of the disruptions to sporting activities, see *Tipperary Star*, 2 November 1918, *Roscommon Herald*, 1 March 1919.

48. *Sligo Champion*, 30 November 1918; *Freeman's Journal*, 29 October 1918; Daniel J. Murphy (ed.), *Lady Gregory Journals, Volume One* (Buckinghamshire, 1978), pp.31, 67; *Tipperary Star*, 2 November 1918; *Mayo News*, 7 December 1918.

49. *King's County Chronicle*, 31 October 1918, 14 November 1918; *Freeman's Journal*, 29 October 1918, 1 November 1918; *Mayo News*, 30 November 1918; *Sligo Champion*, 22 February 1919; *Limerick Chronicle*, 25 February 1919; *Roscommon Herald*, 23 November 1918; *Mayo News*, 2 November 1918, 23 November 1918; Edward O'Malley, *Memories of a Mayoman* (Dublin, 1981), p.19.

50. *Connacht Tribune*, 24 May 1919; *Freeman's Journal*, 29 October 1918 – 2 November 1918, 7 November 1918; *Down Recorder*, 14 December 1918.

51. Guy Beiner, 'Out in the Cold and Back: New-Found Interest in the Great Flu', *Cultural and Social History*, 3, 4 (2006), p.501; *Connacht Tribune*, 7 December 1918; *Wicklow People*, 23 November 1918.

52. *Connacht Tribune*, 28 December 1918, 29 March 1919, 19 April 1919; *Derry People and Donegal News*, 9 November 1918, 4 January 1919; *King's County Chronicle*, 28 November 1918, 5 December 1918, 19 December 1918; *Roscommon Herald*, 23 November 1918; *The Kerryman*, 29 March 1919; *Wicklow People*, 16 November 1918, 23 November 1919; *Freeman's Journal*, 29 June 1918, 22 October 1918, 25 October 1918, 14 February 1919, 14 November 1919; *Kilkenny People*, 15 March 1919.

53. Emmanuel Sivan, 'Private Pain and Public Remembrance in Israel', in Jay Winter and Emmanuel Sivan (eds), *War and Remembrance in the Twentieth Century* (New York, 1999), p.180; Bunbury and Fennell, *Vanishing Ireland*, p.113.

54. *Connacht Tribune*, 8 March 1919.

55. The Kathleen Lynn Diaries, Volume 1, p.13; Hilary Pyle, *Cesca's Diary 1913–1916* (Dublin, 2005), p.280; *Irish Catholic*, 2 November 1918; *Freeman's Journal*, 29 October 1918; *Society of St Vincent de Paul, Ireland. Report of the Council of Ireland for the Year 1918*, p.25; see also, *Freeman's Journal*, 4 November 1918.

56. *Society of St Vincent de Paul, Ireland. Report of the Council of Ireland for the Year 1918*, p.20; see also *Society of St Vincent de Paul. Report of the Council of Ireland for the Year 1919* (Dublin, 1920), p.43; *Freeman's Journal*, 6 November 1918; *Mayo News*, 14 December 1918.

57. Bunbury and Fennell, *Vanishing Ireland*, p.37; *Weekend Review, Irish Times*, 7 January 2006; Gina Kolata, *Flu: The Story of the Great Influenza Pandemic of 1918 and the Search for the Virus that Caused it* (London, 1999), p.106.

58. *Mayo News*, 1 February 1919; *Tipperary Star*, 26 October 1918, 14 December 1918; *Wicklow People*, 9 November 1918, 16 November 1918; *King's County Chronicle*, 28 November 1918; *Connacht Tribune*, 12 April 1919, 26 April 1919; *Society of St Vincent de Paul. Report of the Council of Ireland for the Year 1918*, p.20.

59. Rollet, 'The "Other War" II', p.485.

CHAPTER FOUR: FEAR IN THE EPIDEMIC

1. Ministry of Health, *Report on the Pandemic of Influenza, 1918–1919* (London, 1920), pp.259, 372; K. David Patterson, 'The Influenza Epidemic of 1918–19 in the Gold Coast', *Journal of African History*, 24, 4 (1983), p.491.

2. Gina Kolata, *Flu: The Story of the Great Influenza Pandemic and the Search for the Virus that Caused it* (London, 1999), pp.88, 94, 151–4; Ministry of Health, *Report on the Pandemic of Influenza*, pp.208, 259, 267; Patrick Zylberman, 'A Holocaust in a Holocaust: The Great War and the 1918 Influenza Epidemic in France', in Howard Phillips and David Killingray (eds), *The Spanish Influenza Pandemic of 1918–19: New Perspectives* (London, 2003) p.194.

3. Theodore Zeldin, 'Personal History and the History of the Emotions', *Journal of Social History*, 15, 3 (1982), pp.343–4; E. Anthony Rotundo, 'Review', *Journal of American History*, 85, 4 (1999), p.1567; Steven Gordon, 'Review', *Journal of Social History*, 33, 2 (1999), pp.469–71; 'Emotions in Russian History and Culture' (http://www.aatseel.org/100111/files/emotions_in_russian_histor.doc (Accessed 20 August 2008)).

4. Peter N. Stearns and Carol Z. Stearns, 'Emotionology: Clarifying the History of Emotions and Emotional Standards', *The American Historical Review*, 90, 4 (1985), p.830; A.T.Q. Stewart Interview, *History Ireland*, 1, 2 (1993), p.58; Kevin Danaher, 'The Plague!', *Biatas*, 18, 9 (1964), p.544.

5. Patrick Logan, *Making the Cure* (Dublin, 1972), p.27; Roger J. McHugh, 'The Famine in Irish Oral Tradition', in T. Desmond Williams and R. Dudley Edwards (eds), *The Great Famine* (New York, 1957), p.414.

6. George Peacocke, 'Influenza', *Transactions of the Royal Academy of Medicine in Ireland*, 37 (1919), p.393; Darrell Figgis, *A Second Chronicle of Jails* (Dublin, 1919), p.101; *Society of St Vincent de Paul. Report of the Council of Ireland for the Year 1918* (Dublin, 1919), p.15; *Irish Times*, 30 October 1918.

7. CO 904/164, pp.698, 797, 923–4; William Murphy, 'The Tower of Hunger: Political Imprisonment in Ireland, 1910–1921' (PhD Thesis, University College Dublin, 2006), pp.255–6.

8. CO 904/164, pp.888–9, 895; Piaras Béaslaí Papers, Ms 33,972(15).

9. Daniel J. Murphy (ed.), *Lady Gregory's Journals. Volume One* (Buckinghamshire, 1978), p.31.

10. CSO RP/15746.

11. Pierce McCann Papers, Ms 26,772 (4); GPB 1918/6971.

12. *Roscommon Herald*, 14 December 1918, 2 November 1918; *Kilkenny People*, 2 November 1918; *Tipperary Star*, 2 November 1918; *The Kerryman*, 9 November 1918.

13. *Tuam Herald*, 29 June 1918.

14. *Connacht Tribune*, 28 December 1918, 26 April 1919; *Cork Examiner*, 20 November 1918.

15. *Mayo News*, 26 October 1918; McHugh, 'The Famine in Irish Oral Tradition', p.419.

16. *Limerick Chronicle*, 31 October 1918; *Belfast Telegraph*, 4 December 1918. Eventually a doctor was sent for, who had the men removed to the Union hospital where they later died; *Meath Chronicle*, 16 November 1918; Rathdrum Union Minute Books, PLUR/WR/137, p.126; *The People* (Wexford), 23 November 1918, 16 November 1918, 30 November 1918.

17. Cathal Póirtéir, *Famine Echoes* (Dublin, 1995), p.103; *Freeman's Journal*, 8 November 1918; BMH WS/ 1650, p.9; Cork Poor Law Union, Board of Guardians Minute Books, BG A 150, p.460; Lupton, *The Imperative of Health*, p.62; *Wicklow People*, 29 March 1919.
18. *Sligo Champion*, 15 February 1919.
19. *Fermanagh Times*, 13 February 1919.
20. *King's County Chronicle*, 28 November 1918; McHugh, 'The Famine in Irish Oral Tradition', p.417; Cathal Póirtéir, *Glórtha ón Ghorta* (Dublin, 1996), p.134.
21. *Freeman's Journal*, 24, 15 and 19 October 1918; Niall Johnson, *Britain and the Influenza Pandemic of 1918–1919: A Dark Epilogue* (London, 2006), p.127; *Galway Observer*, 7 December 1918; *The People* (Wexford), 2 November 1918; *Irish Times*, 23 July 1918. See also *Limerick Chronicle*, 6 March 1919.
22. *Connacht Tribune*, 28 December 1918; *Derry Journal*, 6 December 1918; *Irish Times*, 22 February 1919.
23. *Down Recorder*, 7 December 1918; *The People* (Wexford), 9 November 1918 and 1 March 1919. For a sample of the advice regarding crowd avoidance, see the following: *Kilkenny People*, 2 November 1918; *Derry Journal*, 28 October 1918, 15 November 1918; *Freeman's Journal*, 25 October 1918, 29 October 1918, 11 November 1918; *Mayo News*, 14 December 1918; Stephen Kern, *The Culture of Time and Space, 1880–1913* (London, 2003), p.221.
24. *Freeman's Journal*, 28 and 29 June 1918.
25. *Belfast Telegraph*, 30 October 1918; *Cork Examiner*, 5 July 1918, 18 November 1918; *Connacht Tribune*, 7 December 1918; John Hassan, *The Seaside, Health and the Environment in England and Wales since 1800* (Aldershot, 2003), pp.2, 5; *Meath Chronicle*, 28 December 1918; T.P.C. Kirkpatrick, *Pulmonary Phthisis* (Dublin, 1898), p.6.
26. Bourke, *Fear*, pp.293, 190; Ministry of Health, *Report on the Influenza Pandemic*, p.267; Alfred Crosby, *America's Forgotten Pandemic* (Cambridge, 2003), p.218; Richard Collier, *The Plague of the Spanish Lady* (London, 1974), pp.82–3.
27. *Irish Opinion*, 8 March 1919, p.631; for reports on the prevalence of the disease among the military see the *Connacht Tribune*, 22 June 1918; *Derry People and Donegal News*, 9 November 1918; *Irish Times*, 12 February 1919; *Derry Journal*, 26 June 1918; *King's County Chronicle*, 11 July 1918.
28. *Mayo News*, 16 November 1918; *Connacht Tribune*, 7 December 1918; E. Margaret Crawford, 'Typhus in Nineteenth-Century Ireland', in Elizabeth Malcolm and Greta Jones (eds), *Medicine, Disease and the State in Ireland, 1650–1940* (Cork, 1999), pp.124–5.
29. Jeanine Cogan and Gregory Herek, 'Stigma' (http://www.thebody.com/content/art14039.html (Accessed 14 June 2008)).
30. Deborah Lupton, *Medicine as Culture: Illness, Disease and the Body in Western Societies* (London, 1994), p.71; Thomas Wrigley Grimshaw, *Report on the Smallpox Epidemic, 1871–73, as Observed in Cork Street Fever Hospital* (Dublin, 1873), p.15.
31. 'Report Upon the Recent Epidemic Fever in Ireland', *Dublin Quarterly Journal of Medical Science*, 8 (1849), pp.317–8; Ministry of Health, *Report on the Pandemic*, pp.70, 80–2, xiv.
32. Ministry of Health, *Report on the Pandemic*, pp.77–85.
33. Cogan and Herek, 'Stigma'; T.P.C. Kirkpatrick, *The Control of Consumption* (Dublin, 1903), p.10.
34. *Limerick Chronicle*, 18 March 1919; *Connacht Tribune*, 8 March 1919; *Belfast Telegraph*, 22 November 1918.
35. The Kathleen Lynn Diaries, Volume I, p.27; *Freeman's Journal*, 26 October 1918, 5 November 1918; *Cork Examiner*, 22 October 1918; CSO RP 1919/9553; see also RIC Reports CO 904/108, p.712; CO 904/107, pp.280, 739; *Wicklow People*, 26 October 1918.
36. *Wicklow People*, 2 November 1918, 26 October 1918, 19 October 1918; *Cork Examiner*, 12 November 1918; Piaras Béaslaí Papers, Ms 33, 972 (14).
37. *Freeman's Journal*, 4 November 1918; *Mayo News*, 2 November 1918; *Church of Ireland Gazette*, 22 November 1918, p.778; *Irish Rosary*, 22, 11 (November 1918), p.865; *Wicklow People*, 9 November 1918; *Cork Examiner*, 12 November 1918; GPB 1918/6895.
38. *Meath Chronicle*, 2 November 1918; *Belfast Telegraph*, 26 October 1918; Robert Darnton, *The Kiss of Lamourette: Reflections in Cultural History* (London, 1990), p.336; Neil J. Smelser, *Theory of Collective Behavior* (London, 1962), p.141.
39. *Freeman's Journal*, 28 October 1918, 28 February 1919, 5 November 1918; *Medical Press and Circular*, 157, 21 (1918), p.379; Ralph H. Turner, 'Collective Behavior', in Robert E.L. Faris (ed.), *Handbook of Modern Sociology* (Chicago, IL, 1964), p.402.

40. *Cork Examiner*, 12 November 1918; *Mayo News*, 4 December 1918; McHugh, 'The Famine in Irish Oral Tradition', p.44.
41. Margaret Humphreys, 'No Safe Place: Disease and Panic in American History', *American Literary History*, 14, 4 (2002), pp.848–9.
42. GPB 1918/6894; *Freeman's Journal*, 10 March 1919, 8 March 1919.
43. Peacocke, 'Influenza', pp.395–6; *Cork Examiner*, 2 July 1918, 25–6 June 1918, 9 October 1918; *Irish Times*, 2 July 1918.
44. Humphreys, 'No Safe Place', p.849; John Moore, 'Influenza from a Clinical Standpoint', *The Practitioner*, 102, 1 (January 1919), p.29; GPB 1918/6894; Captain John Speares, 'Influenza', *Transactions of the Royal Academy of Medicine in Ireland*, 37 (1919), p.406; Peacocke, 'Influenza', pp.393–5; GPB 1918/6970; Murphy, 'The Tower of Hunger', p.278.
45. *The Lancet*, 4 January 1919, p.4.
46. *Freeman's Journal*, 25 October 1918, 28 October 1918; Guy Beiner, 'Out in the Cold and Back: New-Found Interest in the Great Flu', *Cultural and Social History*, 3, 4 (2006), p.502; Peacocke, 'Influenza', pp.394–5; *The Lancet*, 4 January 1919, p.4; William M. Crofton, 'The Influenza Epidemic', *Studies*, 7, 28 (1919), p.661.
47. S.J. Connolly, 'The "Blessed Turf": Cholera and Popular Panic in Ireland, June 1832', *Irish Historical Studies*, 23, 91 (1983); Robert J. Graves, 'On the Progress of Asiatic Cholera', *Dublin Journal of Medical Science*, 7 (1849), p.32.
48. Patrick J. Henry, *Sligo: Medical Care in the Past 1800–1965* (Manorhamilton, 1995), p.83; 'Report on the Epidemic Fever in Ireland', *Dublin Quarterly Journal of Medical Science*, 7 (1849), p.377; Connolly, 'The "Blessed Turf"'; *Copies of the Correspondence between the Local Government Board and its Inspector with Regard to the Present Epidemic of Smallpox at Athenry* [Cmd. 422], H.C. 1875, lx, pp.12, 15.
49. Henry, *Sligo: Medical Care in the Past*, p.83; 'Report on the Epidemic Fever in Ireland', *Dublin Quarterly Journal of Medical Science*, 7 (1849), p.377; Connolly, 'The "Blessed Turf"'; *Copies of the Correspondence between the Local Government Board and its Inspector with Regard to the Present Epidemic of Smallpox at Athenry*, pp.12, 15, 32; *Irish Builder*, 17, 374, (15 July 1875), p.193; Crawford, 'Typhus in Nineteenth-Century Ireland', pp.124–5.
50. William Wilde, *Irish Popular Superstitions* (Dublin, 1979), pp.120, 122; Kevin Danaher, 'The Healing Art', *Biatas*, 20, 7 (October 1966), p.313; Joseph Robins, *The Miasma: Epidemic and Panic in Nineteenth Century Ireland* (Dublin, 1995), p.9; Theodore Zeldin, *An Intimate History of Humanity* (London, 1998), p.173.
51. *Connacht Tribune*, 2 November 1918, 8 March 1919; GPB 1918/ 6895; *Irish Times*, 1 November 1918.
52. David Shuttleton, 'A Culture of Disfigurement: Imagining Smallpox in the Long Eighteenth Century', in George Sebastian Rousseau, Miranda Gill, David Haycock, and Malte Herwig (eds), *Framing and Imagining Disease in Cultural History* (New York, 2003), pp.80–1; Jane Weiss, '"This Pestilence Which Walketh in Darkness": Reconceptualizing the 1832 New York Cholera Epidemic', in Rousseau et al., *Framing and Imagining Disease in Cultural History*, p.98.
53. 'Report upon the Recent Epidemic Fever in Ireland', *Dublin Quarterly Journal of Medical Science*, 8 (1849), pp.270–2; *Abstract Return of Reps. to Coms. of Poor Laws in Ireland, Relative to Appearance and Spread of Cholera, and Correspondence* [Cmd. 109], H.C. 1854, lvii, p.18; *Irish Times*, 9 January 1890.
54. Robert J. Graves, 'On the Progress of Asiatic Cholera', *Dublin Quarterly Journal of Medical Science*, 7 (1849), p.35; *Irish Times*, 25 January 1892; Martin S. Pernick, 'Contagion and Culture', *American Literary History*, 14, 4 (2002), p.860.
55. Sir William P. MacArthur, 'Medical History of the Famine', in R. Dudley Edwards and T. Desmond Williams (eds), *The Great Famine* (New York, 1957), p.291.

CHAPTER FIVE: MEDICAL RESPONSE TO THE OUTBREAK

1. D.W. Macnamara, 'Memories of 1918 and "the 'Flu"', *Journal of the Irish Medical Association*, 35, 208 (1954), p.308.
2. Allen M. Brandt and Martha Gardner, 'The Golden Age of Medicine?', in Roger Cooter and John Pickstone (eds), *Medicine in the Twentieth Century* (Amsterdam, 2000), p.21; C.J. Campbell and J.A. Fairer, 'Clinical Observations on the 1918 "Influenza" Epidemic', *The Practitioner*, 102, 6 (1919), p.295.

3. Laurence M. Geary, '"The Late Disastrous Epidemic": Medical Relief and the Great Famine', in Chris Morash and Richard Hayes (eds), *'Fearful Realities': New Perspectives on the Famine* (Dublin, 1996), p.50; The Kathleen Lynn Diaries, Volume 1, p.27; *Derry Journal*, 23 October 1918.

4. *Tipperary Star*, 14 December 1918; *Connacht Tribune*, 23 June 1918; *Meath Chronicle*, 16 November 1918; *Ulster Guardian*, 23 November 1918.

5. Guy Beiner, 'Out in the Cold and Back: New-Found Interest in the Great Flu', *Cultural and Social History*, 3, 4 (2006), p.497; Niall Johnson, *Britain and the 1918–19 Influenza Pandemic: A Dark Epilogue* (London, 2006), p.146; Sandra M. Tomkins, 'The Failure of Expertise: Public Health Policy in Britain during the 1918–19 Influenza Epidemic', *Social History of Medicine*, 5, 3 (1992), p.435.

6. *Tipperary Star*, 26 October 1918; *Fermanagh Times*, 19 December 1918.

7. *Medical Press*, 157, 20 (13 November 1918), p.359.

8. Geoffrey W. Rice and Edwina Palmer, 'Pandemic Influenza in Japan, 1918–19: Mortality Patterns and Official Responses', *Journal of Japanese Studies*, 19, 2 (1993), p.391; Kevin McCracken and Peter Curson, 'Flu Downunder. A Demographic and Geographic Analysis of the 1919 Epidemic in Sydney, Australia', in Howard Phillips and David Killingray (eds), *The Spanish Influenza Pandemic of 1918–19: New Perspectives* (London, 2003), p.115; Johnson, *Britain and the 1918–19 Influenza Pandemic*, p.119; Anne Hardy, *Health and Medicine in Great Britain since 1860* (Hampshire, 2001), p.75; Nancy K. Bristow, '"You Can't do Anything for Influenza". Doctors, Nurses and the Power of Gender during the Influenza Pandemic in the United States', in Phillips and Killingray (eds), *The Spanish Influenza Pandemic of 1918–19*, p.3; *Irish Times*, 8 November 1918; *Sligo Champion*, 22 February 1919.

9. John Cowell, *'A Noontide Blazing': Brigid Lyons Thornton – Rebel, Soldier, Doctor* (Dublin, 2005), p.145.

10. Jeremiah Murphy, *When Youth was Mine: A Memoir of Kerry 1902–1925* (Dublin, 1998), p.114; BMH WS/385, p.4; BMH WS/398, p.19; BMH WS/568, p.27.

11. Macnamara, 'Memories of 1918', pp.305, 308.

12. BMH WS/1764.

13. *Meath Chronicle*, 16 November 1918, 23 November 1918; *Tipperary Star*, 26 October 1918 and 23 November 1918; *Mayo News*, 16 November 1919, 9 November 1918; *Fermanagh Times*, 19 December 1918; Cork Poor Law Union Board of Guardians Minute Books, BG 69 A 150, pp.160, 87–88.

14. *Annual Report of the Local Government Board for Ireland 1918–19* [Cmd. 578], H.C. 1920, xxi, p.28; Ruth Barrington, *Health, Medicine and Politics in Ireland 1900–1970* (Dublin, 1987), p.8.

15. BMH WS/ 357, part 2, p.9; The Kathleen Lynn Diaries, Volume I, pp.13–17, 26–7.

16. *Connacht Tribune*, 12 April 1919; CSO RP 1919/175.

17. *Cork Examiner*, 8 November 1918.

18. *Medical Press and Circular*, 157, 8 (19 February 1919), p.144; *Meath Chronicle*, 16 November 1918; R.F. Tobin, 'Present State of the Irish Poor Law Medical Service', *Dublin Journal of Medical Science*, 116, 384, Third Series (1903), p.466; *The Lancet*, 7 September 1918, p.324; Minute Books of Rathdrum Union, PLUR/WR/136, pp.438–9.

19. *Tipperary Star*, 23 November 1918. For the deaths of doctors from influenza and pneumonia in 1918–19, see for instance: *Mayo News*, 30 November 1918; *Limerick Chronicle*, 7 November 1918; *Wicklow People*, 22 February 1919; *The Kerryman*, 16 November 1918, 7 December 1918; *Tuam Herald*, 16 November 1918; *Derry Journal*, 29 November 1918; T. Hennessy, 'Ireland and a Ministry of Health', *Transactions of the Royal Academy of Medicine in Ireland*, 37 (1919), p.467.

20. *Meath Chronicle*, 9 November 1918; *The Kerryman*, 26 April 1919; Minute Books of Rathdrum Union, PLUR/WR/136, p.440; *Down Recorder*, 28 December 1918; Cork Poor Law Union Board of Guardian Minute Books, BG 96 A 149, p.496.

21. GPB 1918/7278; Cork Poor Law Union Board of Guardians Minute Books, BG 69 A 150, p.88; *Meath Chronicle*, 26 October 1918; *Irish Times*, 8 and 12 November 1918.

22. Minute Books of Rathdrum Union, PLUR/WR/136, p.438. See also Minutes of Gort Rural District Council Meetings, GO1/10/15, p.182; *Sligo Champion*, 10 May 1919.

23. *Irish Times*, 3 March 1919, 22 February 1919; *Donegal Vindicator*, 24 January 1919; GPB

1918/7063; *Meath Chronicle*, 16 November 1918; Rathdrum Union Minute Book 1919, PLUR/WR/137, pp.213–4; L.A. Clarkson and E. Margaret Crawford, *Feast and Famine: Food and Nutrition in Ireland 1500–1920* (Oxford, 2001), pp.195–6, 234, 280; Ruairí Ó hEithir, 'Folk Medical Beliefs and Practices in the Aran Islands, Co. Galway' (MA thesis, University College Dublin, 1983), pp.141–2.

24. *British Medical Journal*, 28 December 1918, p.718; 20 July 1918, p.51; 14 December 1918, p.665; Eugenia Tognotti, 'Scientific Triumphalism and Learning from Facts: Bacteriology and the "Spanish Flu" Challenge of 1918', *Social History of Medicine*, 16, 1 (2003), p.101.

25. Passage cited in the *Meath Chronicle*, 2 November 1918; see also *The Irish Times*: 'influenza…is an acute specific fever' (*Irish Times*, 22 October 1918).

26. Tognotti, 'Scientific Triumphalism', p.100; John Moore, 'Influenza from a Clinical Standpoint', *The Practitioner*, 102, 1 (1919), p.30; George Peacocke, 'Influenza', *Transactions of the Royal Academy of Medicine in Ireland*, 37 (1919), pp.394–5; *The Lancet*, 22 March 1919, p.481; *The Kerryman*, 16 November 1918.

27. Moore, 'Influenza from a Clinical Standpoint', pp.30–1; Macnamara, 'Memories of 1918', p.305; J.H. Walters, 'Influenza 1918: the Contemporary Perspective', *Bulletin of the New York Academy of Medicine*, 54, 9 (October 1978), pp.856, 861; *The Lancet*, 4 January 1919, pp.5–6.

28. John Speares, 'Influenza', *Transactions of the Royal Academy of Medicine in Ireland*, 37 (1919), p.399; *The Lancet*, 2 November 1918, p.602; Speares, 'Influenza', p.399; Moore, 'Influenza from a Clinical Standpoint', p.31; *Meath Chronicle*, 2 November 1918; *British Medical Journal*, 27 February 1918, p.82; 23 November 1918, pp.566–7; 30 November 1918, p.603; Sir James Mackenzie, 'The Cardiac Complications of Influenza', *The Practitioner*, 102, 1 (January 1919), p.20; Moore, 'Influenza from a Clinical Standpoint', pp.31–2.

29. *Down Recorder*, 2 November 1918; *Cork Examiner*, 13 November 1918, 19 November 1918; Cork Poor Law Union Board of Guardians Minute Books, BG 69 A 150, p.247; Speares, 'Influenza', p.406.

30. *Irish Times*, 30 October 1918; *Down Recorder*, 2 November 1918; *Cork Examiner*, 19 November 1918; Cork Poor Law Union Board of Guardians Minute Books, BG 69 A 150, p.247; Speares, 'Influenza', p.406; *Cork Examiner*, 13 November 1918; 'Royal Academy of Medicine in Ireland', *The Lancet*, 28 December 1918, p.884; *The Lancet*, 5 April 1919, p.563; D. Ann Herring, '"There Were Young People and Old People and Babies Dying Every Week": The 1918–1919 Influenza Pandemic at Norway House', *Ethnohistory*, 41, 1 (1994), p.81; *The Lancet*, 28 December 1918, p.873. For a sample of the outbreaks of typhoid which occurred in Ireland in the same period as the epidemic, see the following: *The Kerryman*, 9 November 1918; Minutes of Gort Rural District Council Meetings, GO1/10/15, pp.124, 136; Minutes of Shillelagh Rural District Council, WLAA/RDCS/M/18, p.121.

31. *Irish Times*, 22 October 1918; 'Practical Notes', *The Practitioner*, 102, 6 (1919), p.101; Moore, 'Influenza from a Clinical Standpoint', p.33; Speares, 'Influenza', p.398. See also Peacocke, 'Influenza', p.395 and *Medical Press and Circular*, 157, 2 (July 1918), p.20; *Meath Chronicle*, 12 April 1919.

32. Terence Ranger, 'A Historian's Foreword', in Phillips and Killingray (eds), *The Spanish Influenza Pandemic of 1918–19*, p.xx ; Speares, 'Influenza', p.407.

33. *Connacht Tribune*, 17 April 1919; *Fermanagh Times*, 24 December 1918; Shillelagh Board of Guardians Minutes 1918, PLUS/WR/76, p.439; *British Medical Journal*, 26 October 1918, p.465; GPB 1918/8338; *Ulster Guardian*, 13 July 1918; *Down Recorder*, 2 November 1918; *Annual Report of the Local Government Board for Ireland 1918–19*, p.39.

34. Clifden Poor Law Minutes 18 September 1918–26 November 1919, pp.176–7; peritonitis is an inflammation of the peritoneum, the serous membrane which lines part of the abdominal cavity and viscera.

35. Rathdrum Union Minute Books 1919, PLUR/WR/137, pp.213–4.

36. 'Medical Miscellany', *Dublin Journal of Medical Science*, 89, 220 (April 1890), pp.364–5; The Kathleen Lynn Diaries, Volume I, p.29; *Connacht Tribune*, 26 April 1919.

37. Niall MacFhionnghaile, *Dr McGinley and His Times: Donegal 1900–1950* (Letterkenny, 1985), p.110.

38. *The Lancet*, 4 January 1919, p.5.

39. *Connacht Tribune*, 26 April 1919.

40. *Connacht Tribune*, 21 May 1919, 26 April 1919; MacFhionnghaile, *Dr McGinley and His Times*, p.110; Milford Union Board of Guardians Minutes BG 119/1/86, p.34.

41. Macnamara, 'Memories of 1918', pp.306–7.
42. *British Medical Journal*, 2, 6205 (1979), pp.1632–3.
43. Peacocke, 'Influenza', p.396.
44. Moore, 'Influenza from a Clinical Standpoint', p.29.
45. Geoffrey W. Rice and Edwina Palmer, 'A Japanese Physician's Response to Pandemic Influenza: Ijirō Gomibuchi and the "Spanish Flu" in Yaita-Chō, 1918–1919', *Bulletin of the History of Medicine*, 66, 4 (1992), p.569.
46. Isaac Starr, 'Influenza in 1918: Recollections of the Epidemic in Philadelphia', *Annals of Internal Medicine*, 85, 4 (1976), p.517.
47. Bristow, '"You Can't do Anything for Influenza"', p.59.
48. Annie M.P. Smithson, *Myself and Others: An Autobiography* (Dublin, 1944), p.239; Bristow, '"You Can't do Anything for Influenza"', p.59.
49. BMH WS/385, p.4; BMH WS/398, p.19.
50. Bristow, '"You Can't do Anything for Influenza"', pp.63, 69.
51. Starr, 'Influenza in 1918', p.518; Smithson, *Myself and Others*, p.239; Patrick N. Meenan, 'Epidemic Influenza', *Irish Journal of Medical Science*, 386, Sixth Series (1958), pp.51–2.
52. Bristow, '"You Can't do Anything for Influenza"', pp.62–3; Tim Brady, 'The Great Flu Epidemic' (http://www.alumni.umn.edu/printview/581094c9-0994-4369-befa-6f849eadfccb.html (Accessed 9 September 2008)); Beiner, 'Out in the Cold and Back', p.504.
53. Caitriona Clear, *Social Change and Everyday Life in Ireland* (Manchester, 2007), p.92.
54. Ministry of Health, *Report on the Pandemic of Influenza* (London, 1920), p.93.
55. Elizabeth J. Davies, 'The Influenza Epidemic and How We Tried to Control It', *Public Health Nurse*, 11, 1 (1919), p.47; K. David Patterson, 'The Influenza Epidemic of 1918–19 in the Gold Coast', *Journal of African Studies*, 24, 4 (1983), p.488; Ministry of Health, *Report on the Pandemic*, p.xviii.

CHAPTER SIX: RESPONSIBILITY AND ACCOUNTABILITY DURING THE EPIDEMIC

1. *Irish Times*, 26 February 1919.
2. Richard Collier, *The Plague of the Spanish Lady* (London, 1974), pp.92, 89.
3. *Cork Examiner*, 13 November 1918; *Church of Ireland Gazette*, 8 November 1918, p.747; Niall Johnson, *Britain and the 1918–19 Influenza Pandemic: A Dark Epilogue* (London, 2006), p.133.
4. Johnson, *Britain and the 1918–19 Influenza Pandemic*, p.137.
5. *Forty-seventh Annual Report of the Local Government Board for Ireland* [Cmd. 578], H.C. 1920, xxi, pp.39–40.
6. *Irish Times*, 26 February 1919; CSO RP 1919/7278; Dorothy Porter, *Health, Civilisation and the State* (London, 1999), p.136.
7. *Medical Press and Circular*, 5 March 1919, p.177; *Irish Times*, 30 October 1918.
8. *Irish Times*, 5 November 1918; *Catholic Bulletin*, 9, 3 (March 1919), p.105.
9. Folder 6, Dr Lynn's papers, 106/59 (Allen Library); *Derry People and Donegal News*, 9 November 1918; *Mayo News*, 14 December 1918.
10. *Freeman's Journal*, 24 October 1918; *Wicklow People*, 19 October 1918; *Down Recorder*, 22 March 1919; *Medical Press and Circular*, 5 March 1919, p.177.
11. Johnson, *Britain and the 1918–19 Influenza Pandemic*, p.141; Mary E. Daly, *The Buffer State: The Historical Roots of the Department of the Environment* (Dublin, 1997), p.27; Ruth Barrington, *Health, Medicine and Politics in Ireland 1900–1970* (Dublin, 1987), pp.19, 73; Sir Henry Robinson, *Memories: Wise and Otherwise* (London, 1923), pp.283–4.
12. Sandra M. Tomkins, 'The Failure of Expertise: Public Health Policy in Britain during the 1918–19 Influenza Epidemic', *Social History of Medicine*, 5, 3 (1992), p.445.
13. *Sligo Champion*, 5 April 1919; *Irish Times*, 9 January 1919; *Down Recorder*, 1 March 1919; Niall MacFhionnghaile, *Dr McGinley and His Times: Donegal 1900–1950* (Letterkenny, 1985), p.18; Letterkenny Poor Law Union Minute Book, BG/109/1/75, p.83.
14. *Fermanagh Times*, 27 March 1919.
15. Galway Poor Law Union Minutes 1919 No 1, p.268.
16. Wilfred Witte, 'The Plague that Was Not Allowed to Happen', in Howard Phillips and David Killingray (eds), *The Spanish Influenza Pandemic of 1918–19: New Perspectives* (London, 2003), p.57; Porter, *Health, Civilisation and the State*, p.198; Tomkins, 'The Failure of Expertise'.

17. Eugenia Tognotti, 'Scientific Triumphalism and Learning from Facts: Bacteriology and the "Spanish Flu" Challenge of 1918', *Social History of Medicine*, 16, 1 (2003), p.102; Martha Hildreth, 'The Influenza Epidemic of 1918–1919 in France', *Social History of Medicine*, 4, 2 (1991), p.285; *Irish Times*, 28 February 1919, 5 November 1918, 26 February 1919; François Delaporte, *Disease and Civilisation* (London, 1986), p.63; *Freeman's Journal*, 28 October 1918; *Cork Examiner*, 29 October 1918; *Ulster Guardian*, 2 November 1918.

18. *Irish Times*, 26 February 1919; Jacinta Prunty, *Dublin Slums: A Study in Urban Geography* (Dublin, 1998), p.156; *The Kerryman*, 12 October 1918.

19. *Wicklow People*, 9 November 1918; *Irish Times*, 30 October 1918; *Mayo News*, 9 November 1918.

20. Inishowen Board of Guardians Minute Books, BG/97/1/58, pp.363, 434, 452; BG/97/1/59, pp.54, 144; *Roscommon Herald*, 3 August 1918, 2 November 1918; *Meath Chronicle*, 21 December 1918; Castletown Board of Guardians Minute Books, BG 59 A 87, p.167. See also *Tuam Herald*, 22 March 1919; *Fermanagh Times*, 23 January 1919.

21. *Cork Examiner*, 8 and 11 November 1918; *Tipperary Star*, 16 November 1918.

22. *Cork Examiner*, 8 November 1918; *Connacht Tribune*, 23 November 1918; *Mayo News*, 1 March 1919.

23. *Derry Journal*, 6 November 1918; *The People* (Wexford), 20 November 1918.

24. *Church of Ireland Gazette*, 14 February 1919, p.100.

25. *Fermanagh Times*, 6 March 1919; *Irish Times*, 9 November 1918, 22 October 1918.

26. Daly, *The Buffer State*, p.44; *Down Recorder*, 1 March 1919.

27. Barrington, *Health, Medicine and Politics*, pp.81–8.

28. *Report of the Irish Public Health Council on the Public Health and Medical Services in Ireland* [Cmd. 761], H.C. 1920, xvii, pp.1077–80.

29. *Irish Times*, 20 and 27 February 1919.

30. *Irish Times*, 3 March 1919; GPB 1918/7063; *Society of St Vincent de Paul. Report of the Council for the Year 1918* (Dublin, 1919), p.20; *Derry Journal*, 20 November 1918.

31. *Freeman's Journal*, 31 October 1918; St Ultan's Hospital: 'First Minute Book', 7 November 1918.

32. *Freeman's Journal*, 9 November 1918. For this link between philanthropy and morality, see also *Freeman's Journal*, 24 February 1919; *Society of St Vincent de Paul. Reports of the Council of Ireland 1918*, pp.28, 31–2, 49–50, 60–2; *Society of St Vincent de Paul. Reports of the Council of Ireland 1919* (Dublin, 1920), pp.25–6, 29, 55.

33. Micheal O'Suilleabhain, *Where Mountainy Men Have Sown* (Tralee, 1965), p.48; Robert D. Putnam, *Bowling Alone* (New York, 2000), p.35.

34. *Freeman's Journal*, 5 November 1918; Lil Conlon, *Cumann na mBan and the Women of Ireland* (Kilkenny, 1969), p.70; even their first-aid training was undertaken on the basis that it could potentially aid the Volunteers (Aideen Sheehan, 'Cumann na mBan: Policies and Activities', in David Fitzpatrick (ed.), *Revolution? Ireland 1917–1923* (Dublin, 1990), p.96).

35. *Wicklow People*, 16 November 1918; *Cork Examiner*, 12 November 1918; *Meath Chronicle*, 25 January 1919; James P. Murray, *Galway: A Medico-Social History* (Galway, 1996), p.139.

36. *Freeman's Journal*, 11 November 1918; *Irish Times*, 8 November 1918; *The People* (Wexford), 2 November 1918; GPB 1918/7063.

37. Turtle Bunbury and James Fennell, *Vanishing Ireland* (Dublin, 2006), p.140. See also: *Cork Examiner*, 18 November 1918; 11 November 1918; *Sligo Champion*, 23 November 1918; *Wicklow People*, 26 October 1918; GPB 1918/7063.

38. Richard L. Simpson, 'The Sociology of the Community: Current Status and Prospects', in Howard Bell and Colin Newby (eds), *The Sociology of Community* (London, 1974), p.324; *Freeman's Journal*, 5 November 1918, 12 November 1918, 16 November 1918; *Cork Examiner*, 14 November 1918; CSO RP 1919/175; *Connacht Tribune*, 12 April 1919.

39. *Kilkenny People*, 9 November 1918; *Cork Examiner*, 20 November 1918; Pierre Bourdieu, *In Other Words: Essays towards a Reflexive Sociology* (Oxford, 1990), pp.128–9.

40. Jeremiah Murphy, *When Youth Was Mine: A Memoir of Kerry 1902–1925* (Dublin, 1998), p.114; MacFhionnghaile, *Dr McGinley and His Times*, p.110; CO 904/164, p.1129; *Down Recorder*, 29 March 1919.

41. Putnam, *Bowling Alone*, pp.20–1, 134; Bunbury and Fennell, *Vanishing Ireland*, p.100.

42. Allen H. Barton, *Communities in Disaster: A Sociological Analysis of Collective Stress Situations* (London, 1969), pp.209–10, 263.

43. Ibid., pp.241, 269–70.

44. Johnson, *Britain and the Influenza Pandemic of 1918–19*, p.123; Crosby, *America's Forgotten Pandemic*, p.249; Martin Bootsma and Neil Ferguson, 'The Effect of Public Health Measures on the 1918 Influenza Pandemic in US Cities', *Proceedings of the National Academy of Sciences of the United States of America*, 104, 18 (2007), pp.7591–2.
45. Virginia Crossman, *Local Government in Nineteenth Century Ireland* (Belfast, 1994), p.93.
46. Barrington, *Health, Medicine and Politics in Ireland*, p.86.
47. Rajnarayan Chandavarkar, 'Plague Panic and Epidemic Politics in India, 1896–1914', in Terence Ranger and Paul Slack (eds), *Epidemics and Ideas* (Cambridge, 1992), p.211.
48. Sandra Tomkins, 'Colonial Administration in British Africa during the Influenza Pandemic of 1918–19', *Canadian Journal of African Studies*, 28, 1 (1994), pp.69, 64; K. David Patterson, 'The Influenza Epidemic of 1918–19 in the Gold Coast', *Journal of African History*, 24, 4 (1983), p.493; Mridula Ramanna, 'Coping with the Influenza Pandemic: The Bombay Experience', in Phillips and Killingray (eds), *The Spanish Influenza Pandemic of 1918–19*, pp.87–90.
49. *Freeman's Journal*, 3 March 1919; *Cork Examiner*, 8 November 1918; *Medical Press and Circular*, 159, 7 (13 August 1919), p.121.
50. Tomkins, 'Failure of Expertise', p.435; Bootsma and Ferguson, 'The Effect of Public Health Measures on the 1918 Influenza Pandemic in US Cities', p.7588; Witte, 'The Plague that was not Allowed to Happen', p.51.
51. Barrington, *Health, Medicine and Politics*, p.11; 'Reports at Proceedings at 10 sittings of 1st Dáil', DE 4/1/1; The Kathleen Lynn Diaries, Volume 1, p.33.

CHAPTER SEVEN: NAMING AND UNDERSTANDING THE GREAT FLU

1. *Cork Examiner*, 16 July 1918.
2. *Connacht Tribune*, 12 April 1919; *Freeman's Journal*, 2 July 1918.
3. *Freeman's Journal*, 8 October 1918; *Tuam Herald*, 29 June 1918; BMH WS/1093, pp.25–6; BMH WS/1076, pp.2–3; BMH WS/398, p.19; BMH WS/1731, pp.3–4; The term 'discourse' is used here in the sense of 'language in action' (Margaret Healy, 'Discourses of the plague in early modern London' (http://www.history.ac.uk/cmh/epiheal.html (Accessed 25 June 2008)); *Irish Rosary*, 22, 11 (1918), p.865; *The Kerryman*, 16 November 1918; Deborah Lupton, *The Imperative of Health* (London, 1997), p.65; *Cork Examiner*, 14 November 1918; *Irish Times*, 24 February 1919; *Tipperary Star*, 2 November 1918.
4. GPB 1918/8338.
5. J.M. Synge, *The Aran Islands* (London, 1992), p.16; Pierre Bourdieu, 'Cultural Power', in Lyn Spillman (ed.), *Cultural Sociology* (Oxford, 2002), p.72.
6. Neil J. Smelser, *Theory of Collective Behavior* (London, 1962), p.159
7. Niall Johnson, *Britain and the 1918–19 Influenza Pandemic: A Dark Epilogue* (London, 2006), p.157.
8. BMH WS/336, p.8; BMH WS/838, p.81; BMH WS/1068, p.34; Lucy Taksa, 'The Masked Disease: Oral History, Memory and the Influenza Pandemic 1918–19', in Kate Darian-Smith and Paula Hamilton (eds), *Memory and History in Twentieth-Century Australia* (Oxford, 1994), p.83; *Irish Times*, 1 January 1890, 4 January 1892, 7 January 1892.
9. *Freeman's Journal*, 22 June 1918, 4 July 1918, 24 October 1918; GPB 1918/8338; *Donegal Vindicator*, 28 June 1918. In the southwest, one choice was 'the prevailing mysterious distemper' (*The Kerryman*, 9 November 1918); *Cork Examiner*, 12 November 1918; *Tipperary Star*, 26 October 1918. The *Tipperary Star* eventually adopted uncertainly 'an fliu', 9 November 1918); *Meath Chronicle*, 2 November 1918.
10. *The Kerryman*, 12 October 1918; *Irish Times*, 4 January 1890, 10 March 1919; *Freeman's Journal*, 2 July 1918, 17 November 1918; Henry Dixon Papers, Ms 35,262/1 (29); *Cork Examiner*, 24 June 1918; 28 October 1918; *The Kerryman*, 2 November 1918.
11. Johnson, *Britain and The 1918–19 Influenza Pandemic*, p.159; Beatriz Echeverri, 'Spanish Influenza Seen from Spain', in Howard Phillips and David Killingray (eds), *The Spanish Influenza Pandemic of 1918–19: New Perspectives* (London, 2003), p.177; the *Sligo Champion* described it at one point as a 'very dangerous type of foreign influenza' (26 October 1918). For associations made between the flu and the Great War, see for instance *Freeman's Journal*, 24 June 1918; *Irish Opinion*, 8 March 1919, p.631; *Sligo Champion*, 29 June 1918; John H. Walters, 'Influenza 1918: The Contemporary Perspective', *Bulletin of the New York Academy of Medicine*, 54, 9 (1978), p.857; *Tipperary Star*, 16 November 1918.

12. *Freeman's Journal*, 5 November 1918; Stephen Kern, *The Culture of Time and Space, 1880–1918* (London, 2003), p.228; *Connacht Tribune*, 21 December 1918; Oliver Coogan, *Politics and War in Meath 1919–23* (Dublin, 1983), pp.83–4; Jeremiah Murphy, *When Youth Was Mine: A Memoir of Kerry 1902–1925* (Dublin, 1998), p.114; Micheál MacCárthaigh, *A Tipperary Parish: A History of Knockavilla-Donaskeigh* (Midleton, 1986), p.276; Brian Behan, *Mother of All the Behans: The Story of Kathleen Behan as Told to Brian Behan* (Essex, 1984), p.43; BMH WS/1741, p.35; BMH WS/1764, p.14; BMH WS/1076, pp.2–3; BMH WS/1093, pp.25–6.

13. Howard Phillips and David Killingray, 'Introduction', in Phillips and Killingray (eds), *The Spanish Influenza Pandemic of 1918–19*, p.13; BMH WS/398, p.9; BMH WS/385, p.4; BMH WS/1566, p.3; *Minute Book of the Dublin Trades' Council*, 4 November 1918, Ms 12,780 A; *Supplement to the Tipperary Star*, 18 January 1919; *Tipperary Star*, 26 October 1918; Cathal Póirtéir, *Famine Echoes* (Dublin, 1995), p.100.

14. BMH WS/336; BMH WS/1770, part VI, p.825; Macnamara, 'Memories of 1918 and "the Flu"', p.305; BMH WS/838, p.82; Ministry of Health, *Report on the Pandemic*, pp.69, 73.

15. Macnamara, 'Memories of 1918 and "the Flu"', p.304; Ministry of Health, *Report on the Pandemic*, p.67; D. Ann Herring and Lisa Sattenspiel, 'Death in Winter: Spanish Flu in the Canadian Subarctic', in Phillips and Killingray (eds), *The Spanish Influenza Pandemic of 1918–19*, p.161.

16. Macnamara, 'Memories of 1918 and "the Flu"', pp.305, 308; BMH WS/852, p.2.

17. BMH WS/702, p.41; BMH WS/1595, pp.15–17; BMH WS/838, pp.63, 70–2; Niall MacFhionnghaile, *Dr McGinley and His Times: Donegal 1900–1950* (Letterkenny, 1985), p.18.

18. BMH WS/939, p.96.

19. *The Kerryman*, 28 December 1918; *Tipperary Star*, 9 November 1918.

20. Cathal Póirtéir, *Glórtha ón Ghorta* (Dublin, 1996), p.125; *Abstract Return of Reps. to Coms. of Poor Laws in Ireland, Relative to Appearance and Spread of Cholera, and Correspondence* [Cmd. 109], H.C. 1854, lvii, p.28; *Irish Times*, 12 January 1892; Brigitte Nerlich and Patrick Wallis, 'Disease Metaphors in New Epidemics: The UK Media Framing of the 2003 SARS Epidemic', *Social Science and Medicine*, 60, 11 (2005), p.2633.

21. F.O.C. Meenan, *St.Vincent's Hospital, 1934–1994* (Dublin, 1995), p.93; Johnson, *Britain and the 1918–19 Influenza Pandemic*, p.154; *The Kerryman*, 23 November 1918.

22. *King's County Chronicle*, 11 July 1918.

23. *Western News*, 29 June 1918; *Irish Times*, 22 February 1919; *Cork Examiner*, 26 October 1918; Andrew Wear, 'Puritan Perceptions of Illness in Seventeenth Century England', in Roy Porter (ed.), *Patients and Practitioners: Lay Perceptions of Medicine in Pre-Industrial Society* (Cambridge, 2002), p.83; Lupton, *The Imperative of Health*, p.23.

24. Jay Winter for instance is unconvinced of the connection between the flu and the war, while John Barry and Carol Byerly contend that the pandemic is in fact inextricable from the conflict (Beiner, 'Out in the Cold and Back', p.502); Eugenia Tognotti, 'Scientific Triumphalism and Learning from Facts: Bacteriology and the "Spanish Flu" Challenge of 1918', *Social History of Medicine*, 16, 1 (2003), p.101; Herring and Sattenspiel, 'Death in Winter', p.161; Patrick Zylberman, 'A Holocaust within a Holocaust. The Influenza Epidemic in France', in Phillips and Killingray (eds), *The Spanish Influenza Pandemic of 1918–19*, p.199; 'Book Reviews', *International Journal of African Historical Studies*, 24, 2 (1991), p.471; *Donegal Vindicator*, 28 June 1918.

25. *Fermanagh Times*, 30 May 1918; Murphy, *When Youth Was Mine*, p.114; *Connacht Tribune*, 23 June 1918; *The Kerryman*, 16 November 1918; *Roscommon Herald*, 29 June 1918; *The People* (Wexford), 16 November 1918; *Derry Journal*, 24 June 1918; *King's County Chronicle*, 4 July 1918; Roger Cooter, 'Of War and Epidemics: Unnatural Couplings, Problematic Conceptions', *Social History of Medicine*, 16, 2 (2003), p.289.

26. *Connacht Tribune*, 13 July 1918; *Roscommon Herald*, 26 October 1918.

27. BMH WS/1595, pp.15–17; Kathleen Lynn, 'Report on Influenza Epidemic, March, 1919', *Ard-Fheis (Extraordinary) Sinn Féin, 8th April 1919 Reports*, p.104.

28. *The Kerryman*, 21 December 1918; Lupton, *The Imperative of Health*, p.20.

29. Rhodesia is the former name of a large territory in central southern Africa, divided into Northern Rhodesia (now Zambia) and Southern Rhodesia (now Zimbabwe); Terence Ranger, 'The Influenza Pandemic in Southern Rhodesia: A Crisis of Comprehension', in David Arnold (ed.), *Imperial Medicine and Indigenous Societies* (Manchester, 1988), p.180.

30. David Arnold, 'Introduction', in Arnold (ed.), *Imperial Medicine and Indigenous Societies*, p.7.
31. Charles Rosenberg, *Explaining Epidemics and Other Studies in the History of Medicine* (Cambridge, 1992), p.282; Patrick J. Henry, *Sligo: Medical Care in the Past 1800–1965* (Manorhamilton, 1995), p.83; S. J. Connolly, 'The "Blessed Turf": Cholera and Popular Panic in Ireland, June 1832', *Irish Historical Studies*, 23, 91 (1983); James S. Donnelly, Jr, 'The Marian Shrine of Knock: The First Decade', *Éire-Ireland*, 28, 2 (1993).
32. *Wicklow People*, 9 November 1918.
33. *Sligo Champion*, 15 March 1919, 1 February 1919; *Mayo News*, 9 November 1918, 19 October 1918.
34. Wear, 'Puritan Perceptions of Illness in Seventeenth Century England', pp.75–6; Richard J. Evans, *Death in Hamburg: Society and Politics in the Cholera Years, 1830–1910* (Oxford, 1987), p.359; GPB 1918/6894; *Derry People and Donegal News*, 23 November 1918; *Mayo News*, 30 November 1918, 21 December 1918.
35. *Mayo News*, 16 November 1918, 30 November 1918; Wear, 'Puritan Perceptions of Illness in Seventeenth Century England', p.60.
36. *Freeman's Journal*, 30 October 1918. In parts of America too, people wore holy medals to 'ward off the evil of this terrible disease' (Kelley Colihan, 'Witness to 1918 flu: "Death was there all the time"' (http://edition.cnn.com/2005/HEALTH/conditions/10/07/1918.flu.witness/index.html (Accessed 9 September 2008)). For more background on the protective powers of the Sacred Heart badge, see *The People* (Wexford), 30 October 1918; Laurence M. Geary, 'Prince Hohenlohe, Signor Pastorini and Miraculous Healing in Early Nineteenth Century Ireland', in Greta Jones and Elizabeth Malcolm (eds), *Medicine, Disease and the State in Ireland, 1650–1940* (Cork, 1999), pp.48–9.
37. Mary E. Fissell, *Patients, Power and the Poor in Eighteenth-Century Bristol* (Cambridge, 1991), p.198; Wear, 'Puritan Perceptions of Illness in Seventeenth Century England', p.57.
38. *The Kerryman*, 2 November 1918.
39. *Wicklow People*, 9 November 1918.
40. *Meath Chronicle*, 5 March 1919.
41. Connolly, 'The "Blessed Turf": Cholera and Popular Panic in Ireland, June 1832', pp.225, 222; *Irish Times*, 6 January 1892, January 1890.
42. *Sligo Champion*, 9 November 1918, 30 November 1918; Henry Dixon Papers, Ms 35,262/1 (26); *Irish Times*, 9 November 1918; *Connacht Tribune*, 2 November 1918.
43. *Cork Examiner*, 4 July 1918; see also *Meath Chronicle*, 9 November 1918; *Tipperary Star*, 9 November 1918; Lynn, 'Report on Influenza Epidemic. March 1919'; *Freeman's Journal*, 30 October 1918.
44. Margaret Pelling, Virginia Berridge, Mark Harrison, and Paul Weindling, 'The Era of Public Health, 1848 to 1918', in Charles Webster (ed.), *Caring for Health: History and Diversity* (Buckingham, 2001) p.102.
45. *Irish Times*, 14 January 1919; *Freeman's Journal*, 1 July 1918, 15 November 1918, 21 February 1919, 22 February 1919; *Wicklow People*, 16 November 1918; *Sligo Champion*, 7 December 1918.
46. *Irish Times*, 28 February 1919.
47. *Freeman's Journal*, 1 November 1918, 12 February 1919; *Wicklow People*, 21 December 1918, 8 March 1919, 2 November 1918; *Connacht Tribune*, 7 December 1918; *Belfast Telegraph*, 6 November 1918; Katherine Ott, *Fevered Lives: Tuberculosis in American Culture since 1870* (London, 1996) p.49.
48. Nancy Tomes, 'Epidemic Entertainments: Disease and Popular Culture in Early Twentieth-Century America', *American Literary History*, 14, 4 (2002).
49. Jay Winter, *Sites of Memory, Sites of Mourning* (Cambridge, 1998), pp.5, 7, 9, 178, 223–4; *Roscommon Herald*, 30 November 1918; *The People* (Wexford), 16 November 1918.
50. *King's County Chronicle*, 24 October 1918; *Kilkenny People*, 9 November 1918; *Tipperary Star*, 19 October 1918, 23 November 1918.
51. Stephen Kern, *The Culture of Time and Space, 1880–1918* (Cambridge, 2003), pp.23, 36; Barry Schwartz, 'Memory as a Cultural System: Abraham Lincoln in World War II', *American Sociological Review*, 61, 5 (1996), pp.910, 921.
52. Niall Ó Cíosáin, 'Famine Memory and the Popular Presentation of Scarcity', in Ian McBride (ed.), *History and Memory in Modern Ireland* (Cambridge, 2001), p.117; *Derry People and Donegal News*, 9 November 1918; *Connacht Tribune*, 22 March 1919; Ministry of Health, *Report on the Pandemic*, p.182.

53. Schwartz, 'Memory as a Cultural System', pp.921, 912; Taksa, 'The Masked Disease', p.84; Paul Fussell, *The Great War and Modern Memory* (Oxford, 1975).
54. *Freeman's Journal*, 24 October 1918; *Wicklow People*, 26 October 1918, 2 November 1918; *Sligo Champion*, 1 February 1919; *Irish Times*, 10 July 1918.
55. *Sligo Champion*, 2 November 1918; *Wicklow People*, 9 November 1918; *Cork Examiner*, 19 November 1918; *Derry People and Donegal News*, 26 October 1918; *Irish Times*, 5 November 1918; Ministry of Health, *Report on the Pandemic*, pp.vi, 40; *The People* (Wexford), 2 November 1918.
56. Shillelagh Board of Guardian Minutes 1918, PLUS/WR/76, p.439; *Tuam Herald*, 22 March 1919; Ministry of Health, *Report on the Pandemic*, pp.99–100.
57. *The People* (Wexford), 23 October 1918; Moore, 'Influenza from a Clinical Standpoint', *The Practitioner*, 102, 1 (1919), p.29. For other comments on the epidemic which employed memory images and analogies, see the following: *Down Recorder*, 22 February 1919, 30 November 1918; *Belfast Telegraph*, 21 November 1918; *Sligo Champion*, 1 February 1919.
58. *Roscommon Herald*, 19 February 1919; Lynn, 'Report on Influenza Epidemic', p.104.
59. Kern, *The Culture of Time and Space*, p.87; *Limerick Chronicle*, 4 February 1919; *Mayo News*, 4 January 1919, 28 December 1918; *Tipperary Star*, 26 October 1918.
60. *Freeman's Journal*, 28 October 1918; *King's County Chronicle*, 28 November 1918.
61. Winter, *Sites of Memory, Sites of Mourning*, p.224; *Roscommon Herald*, 21 December 1918; *Tipperary Star*, 16 November 1918, 14 December 1918; 23 November 1918, *Sligo Champion*, 25 January 1919, 1 March 1919; *Mayo News*: 19 October 1918, 9 November 1918, 16 November 1918, 30 November 1918, 14 December 1918, 25 January 1919; *Meath Chronicle*, 9 November 1918; *Freeman's Journal*, 9 November 1918; *King's County Chronicle*, 21 November 1918; *Westmeath Examiner*, 24 August 1918; *Donegal Vindicator*, 21 March 1919.
62. Sherwin B. Nuland, 'Medical History for the General Reader', in Frank Huisman and John Harley Warner (eds), *Locating Medical History* (London, 2004), p.455; *Cork Examiner*, 23 October 1918; Jacques Le Goff, 'Mentalities: A History of Ambiguities', in Jacques Le Goff and Pierre Nora (eds), *Constructing the Past: Essays in Historical Methodology* (London, 1985), p.170; Deborah Brunton, 'Introduction', in Deborah Brunton (ed.), *Medicine Transformed: Health, Disease and Society in Europe, 1800–1930* (London, 2004), p.xvii; Phillips and Killingray, 'Introduction', pp.9–10.
63. Wear, 'Puritan Perceptions of Illness in Seventeenth Century England', p.78; Ranger, 'The Influenza Epidemic in Southern Rhodesia', p.180.
64. *Kilkenny People*, 2 November 1918; Taksa, 'The Masked Disease', p.83; *The People* (Wexford), 16 November 1918, 8 January 1919; *Sligo Champion*, 22 February 1919; *Derry Journal*, 23 October 1918; *Irish Times*, 8 November 1918; 'abnormal' was used by various sources such as the Minute Book of Rathdrum Union, PLUR/WR/136, p.438, *The Kerryman* (2 November 1918), and the *Derry People and Donegal News* (23 November 1918).

CHAPTER EIGHT: 'THE PLAGUE WILL LONG BE REMEMBERED'?

1. 'Witness to 1918 flu' (http://edition.cnn.com/2005/HEALTH/conditions/10/07/1918.flu. witness/index.html (Accessed 9 July 2010)); Niall MacFhionnghaile, *Dr McGinley and His Times: Donegal 1900–1950* (Letterkenny, 1985), p.110; D. Ann Herring and Lisa Sattenspiel, 'Death in Winter: Spanish Flu in the Canadian Subarctic', in Howard Phillips and David Killingray (eds), *The Spanish Influenza Pandemic of 1918–19: New Perspectives* (London, 2003), p.159.
2. 'Influenza of 1918 (Spanish Flu) and the US Navy' (http://www.history.navy.mil/library/on-line/influenza_main.htm (Accessed 6 August 2010)); Christopher Langford, 'The Age Pattern of Mortality in the 1918–19 Influenza Pandemic: An Attempted Explanation Based on Data for England and Wales', *Medical History*, 46, 1 (2002), p.19.
3. William McNeill, 'The Flu of Flus', *New York Review of Books*, 47, 2 (2000), p.29; Gina Kolata, *Flu: The Story of the Great Influenza Pandemic of 1918 and the Search for the Virus that Caused it* (London, 1999), p.199.
4. Kolata, *Flu*, p.17; John Oxford, R. Lambkin, A. Sefton, R. Daniels, A. Elliot, R. Brown, and D. Gill, 'A Hypothesis: The Conjunction of Soldiers, Gas, Pigs, Ducks, Geese and Horses in Northern France during the Great War Provided the Conditions for the Emergence of the "Spanish" Influenza Pandemic of 1918–1919', *Vaccine*, 23, 7 (2005), p.942; Niall Johnson, 'The

Overshadowed Killer: Influenza in Britain in 1918–19', in Phillips and Killingray (eds), *The Spanish Influenza Pandemic of 1918–19*, p.154.

5. Terence Ranger, 'The Influenza Pandemic in Southern Rhodesia: A Crisis of Comprehension', in David Arnold (ed.), *Imperial Medicine in Indigenous Societies* (Manchester, 1988), p.175; Terence Ranger, 'A Historian's Foreword', in Phillips and Killingray (eds), *The Spanish Influenza Pandemic of 1918–19:* p.xx; K. David Patterson, 'The Influenza Epidemic of 1918–19 in the Gold Coast', *Journal of African History*, 24, 4 (1983), p.502; Colin Brown, 'The Influenza Pandemic of 1918 in Indonesia', in Norman G. Owen (ed.), *Death and Disease in Southeast Asia: Explorations in Social, Medical and Demographic History* (Oxford, 1987), p.253.

6. Howard Schuman and Jacqueline Scott, 'Generations and Social Memories', *American Sociological Review*, 54, 3 (1989), p.373; *Tipperary Star*, 16 November 1918.

7. *King's County Chronicle*, 21 November 1918; Jay Winter and Emmanuel Sivan, 'Setting the Framework', in Jay Winter and Emmanuel Sivan (eds), *War and Remembrance in the Twentieth Century* (New York, 1999), p.12; *Down Recorder*, 29 March 1919.

8. Kevin Danaher, 'The Plague!', *Biatas*, 18, 9 (December 1964), p.544; Annie M.P. Smithson, *Myself and Others: An Autobiography* (Dublin, 1944), p.238; Darrell Figgis, *Recollections of the Irish War* (London, 1927), pp.237–9.

9. David Middleton and Derek Edwards, *Collective Remembering* (London, 1990), p.3; BMH WS/398, p.9; BMH WS/385, p.4; BMH WS/1566, p.3; Edward O'Malley, *Memories of a Mayoman* (Dublin, 1981), p.19; Kenneth Griffith and Timothy E. O'Grady (eds), *Curious Journey: An Oral History of Ireland's Unfinished Revolution* (London, 1982), p.120; BMH WS/1741, p.35; BMH WS/1764, p.14; BMH WS/1076, p.23; BMH WS/1093, pp.25–6; Brian Behan, *Mother of All the Behans: The Story of Kathleen Behan as Told to Brian Behan* (Dublin, 1984), p.43; Frank Shouldice and George Geraghty, 'The Break-Out from Usk Jail in Wales by Four "German Plot" Prisoners', in Florence O'Donoghue (ed.), *Sworn to be Free: The Complete Book of IRA Jailbreaks 1918–1921* (Tralee, 1971), p.31.

10. Niall Ó Cíosáin, 'Famine Memory and the Popular Representation of Scarcity', in Ian McBride (ed.), *History and Memory in Modern Ireland* (Cambridge, 2001), p.101.

11. Behan, *Mother of all the Behans*, p.43; David Hogan, *The Four Glorious Years* (London, 1971), p.47; Fionán Lynch, 'Recollections of Jail Riots and Hungerstrikes: Grim Times in Mountjoy, Dundalk and Belfast Jails', in Florence O'Donoghue (ed.), *Sworn to be Free: The Complete Book of IRA Jailbreaks 1918–1921* (Tralee, 1971), p.68; BMH WS/1595, p.15.

12. Bill Kelly, 'Escape of de Valera, McGarry and Milroy ("German Plot" Prisoners) from Lincoln Jail', in O'Donoghue (ed.), *Sworn to be Free*, p.45; Seán Moylan, *Seán Moylan in His Own Words: His Memoir of the Irish War of Independence* (Aubane Historical Society, 2004), p.39; Micheál MacCárthaigh, *A Tipperary Parish: A History of Knockavilla-Donaskeigh* (Midleton, Cork, 1996), p.276.

13. BMH WS/1195, p.8; BMH WS/385, p.4; BMH WS/896, p.11; BMH WS/955, p.10; BMH WS/1731, p.3; BMH WS/398, p.19; BMH WS/852, p.2.

14. Behan, *Mother of all the Behans*, p.43; BMH WS/1595, p.15; BMH WS/398, p.19; Peter Somerville-Large, *Irish Voices: Fifty Years of Irish Life, 1916–1966* (London, 1966), p.20; D.W. Macnamara, 'Memories of 1918 and "the 'Flu"', *Journal of the Irish Medical Association*, 35, 208 (1954), p.306; BMH WS/1093, p.25.

15. Howard Phillips and David Killingray, 'Introduction', in Phillips and Killingray (eds), *The Spanish Influenza Pandemic of 1918–19*, p.11; Alfred Crosby, *America's Forgotten Pandemic* (Cambridge, 2003), p.320; BMH WS/1322, p.36. See also Jeremiah Murphy, *When Youth Was Mine: A Memoir of Kerry, 1902–1925* (Dublin, 1998), p.114; BMH WS/1595, pp.15–17; Figgis, *Recollections of the Irish War*, p.237; BMH WS/290, p.43; Hogan, *The Four Glorious Years*, p.47.

16. Liam Deasy, *Towards Ireland Free* (Cork, 1992), p.43. See also Michael Brennan, *The War in Clare, 1911–1921: Personal Memoirs of the War of Independence* (Dublin, 1980), pp.35–7; Lil Conlon, *Cumann na mBan and the Women of Ireland* (Kilkenny, 1969), p.70; Donie Murphy, 'The Men of the South' in the War of Independence (Cork, 1991), p.53.

17. Florence O'Donoghue, *Tomás MacCurtain* (Tralee, 1958), p.143. See also J. Anthony Gaughan, *Austin Stack: Portrait of a Separatist* (Naas, 1977), p.88; John Cowell, 'A Noontide Blazing': Brigid Lyons Thornton – Rebel, Soldier, Doctor (Dublin, 2005), pp.145–7; Jim Maher, *Harry Boland* (Cork, 1998), p.70.

18. Michael J. Rafter, *The Quiet County: Towards a History of the Laois Brigade IRA and*

Revolutionary Activity in the County 1913–23 (Portlaoise, 1995), p.42; see also Jim Maher, *The Flying Column – West Kilkenny 1916–21* (Dublin, 1987), p.9; Oliver Coogan, *Politics and War in Meath, 1913–23* (Dublin, 1983), pp.83–4; Michael Farry, *Sligo 1914–21: A Chronicle of Conflict* (Trim, 1992), p.150.

19. BMH WS/1741, p.35; BMH WS/852, p.2; BMH WS/702, p.41; John H. Walters, 'Influenza 1918: The Contemporary Perspective', *Bulletin of the New York Academy of Medicine*, 54, 9 (1978), p.861.

20. Smithson, *Myself and Others*, p.239; BMH WS/336, pp.8–9; BMH WS/838, pp.63, 70–72, 81, 82; BMH WS/290, pp.43–4; BMH WS/1313, pp.3–4.

21. BMH WS/938, p.1; BMH WS/1545, p.2. For statements tying the epidemic to the end of 1918, see: BMH WS/1131, pp.2, 8; BMH WS/290, pp.43–4; BMH WS/955, p.10; BMH WS/1137, p.3; BMH WS/1566, p.3; BMH WS/568, p.27. BMH WS/1283, pp.17, 7; BMH WS/1692, pp.4–5.

22. Hogan, *The Four Glorious Years*, p.47; Moylan, *Seán Moylan: In His Own Words*, p.39; BMH WS/1093, p.25.

23. Murphy, *When Youth Was Mine*, p.114. An article in *The Lancet* described how phlebitis 'of one or other leg, with typical painful swelling of the whole limb' was encountered in a small number of cases (*The Lancet*, 4 January 1919, p.6); see also Edward O'Malley, *Memories of a Mayoman* (Dublin, 1981), p.19.

24. Micheál Ó Muircheartaigh, *From Dún Síon to Croke Park* (Dublin, 2005), p.62; 'An Irishman's Diary', *Irish Times*, 11 November 2003.

25. Davis Coakley, *Baggot Street: A Short History of the Royal City of Dublin Hospital* (Dublin, 1995), p.55; Peter Gatenby, *Dublin's Meath Hospital* (Dublin, 1996), p.95; David Mitchell, *A 'Peculiar' Place: The Adelaide Hospital, Dublin, 1939–1989* (Dublin, 1989), p.154.

26. James P. Murray, *Galway: A Medico-Social History* (Galway, 1996), p.139. Wicklow suffered some of the highest influenza mortality rates in both years of the epidemic, 1918 and 1919 (*Fifty-fifth Detailed Annual Report of the Registrar-General for Ireland* [Cmd. 450], H.C. 1919, p.xvia; *Fifty-sixth Detailed Annual Report of the Registrar-General for Ireland* [Cmd. 997], H.C. 1920, xi, p.xvii); MacCárthaigh, *A Tipperary Parish*, p.276; James Kelleher, *Memories of Macroom* (Blarney, 1995), p.27; John Kavanagh, 'The Influenza Epidemic of 1918 in Wicklow Town and District', *Wicklow Historical Society Journal*, 1, 3 (July 1990), p.36; David E. Allen and Gabrielle Hatfield, *Medicinal Plants in Folk Tradition: An Ethnobotany of Britain and Ireland* (Cambridge, 2004), p.328. Sincere thanks to Dr Susan Kelly for bringing this reference to my attention.

27. The mortality rate of Spanish flu was thought to be approximately 2 per cent, and with more than 20,000 deaths in Ireland, this would suggest that possibly up to one million people were infected by the virus (Crosby, *America's Forgotten Pandemic*, p.321); Michael Hopkinson, *Green Against Green: The Irish Civil War* (Dublin, 1988), p.273; Ruth Barrington, *Health, Medicine and Politics* (Dublin, 1987), p.74; Pete Davies, *Catching Cold*, p.86; *Weekend Review, Irish Times*, 29 March 2008; *Weekend, Irish Times*, 21 August 1999; *Magazine, Irish Times*, 12 November 2005; 'Influenza: Preparing for the Flu', *UCD Today*, March 2007, p.7. The epidemic is absent from most surveys which cover twentieth-century Ireland such as John A. Murphy's *Ireland in the Twentieth Century* (Dublin, 1975); Dermot Keogh's *Twentieth Century Ireland: Nation and State* (Dublin, 1994) and *Nineteenth Century Ireland: The Search for Stability* (Dublin, 1990); Charles Townshend, *Ireland in the Twentieth Century* (New York, 1998); F.S.L. Lyons, *Ireland Since the Famine* (London, 1985); Roy Foster, *Modern Ireland 1600–1972* (London, 1988); J.J. Lee, *Ireland, 1912–1985: Politics and Society* (Cambridge, 1989). Two of the exceptions are Diarmaid Ferriter's *The Transformation of Ireland* (London, 2004), p.185, and Caitriona Clear, *Social Change and Everyday Life in Ireland, 1850–1922* (Manchester, 2007), p.98, although even here the references to the epidemic are brief.

28. Patrick Hutton, 'Recent Scholarship on Memory and History', *The History Teacher*, 33, 4 (2000), p.536; Seán Farrell Moran, 'History, Memory and Education: Teaching the Irish Story', in Lawrence W. McBride (ed.), *Reading Irish Histories* (Dublin, 2003), pp.212–14; Ferriter, *The Transformation of Ireland*, p.21.

29. Greta Jones, *'Captain of All These Men of Death'. The History of Tuberculosis in Nineteenth and Twentieth Century Ireland* (New York, 2001), p.2; *Fifty-sixth Detailed Annual Report of the Registrar-General for Ireland*, p.xii; GPB 1918/6895 (Box 7); *Dublin Journal of Medical Science*, 116, 380 (1903), p.148; Bruce M. Ross, *Remembering the Past: Descriptions of Autobiographical Memory* (New York, 1991), p.163.

30. Claire O'Connell, 'The Virus that Waged its Own War', *Weekend Review, Irish Times*, 29 March 2008; Peter Burke, 'History as Social Memory', in Thomas Butler (ed.), *Memory: History, Culture and the Mind* (Oxford, 1989), p.110; David Lowenthal, 'The Timeless Past: Some Anglo-American Historical Preconceptions', *Journal of American History*, 75, 4 (1989), p.1263; Susan A. Crane, 'Writing the Individual Back into Collective Memory', *American Historical Review*, 102, 5 (1997), p.1384; Noa Gedi and Yigal Elam, 'Collective Memory: What Is It?', *History and Memory*, 8, 1 (1996), p.42.

31. D. George Boyce, '"No Lack of Ghosts": Memory, Commemoration, and the State in Ireland', in Ian McBride (ed.), *History and Memory in Modern Ireland* (Cambridge, 2001), p.255; see also Patrick Hutton, *History as an Art of Memory* (Hanover, VT, 1993), p.105; *Parliamentary Debates. House of Commons. Volume 110* (London, 1919), pp.1462, 1585.

32. CO 904/164, p.908; CO 904/164, p.871; CO 904/164, pp.904–5; *New Ireland*, 7, 19 (5 March 1919), pp.299–301, in Pierce McCann Papers 2, Ms 26,772 (6); Christopher Morash, 'Making Memories: The Literature of the Irish Famine', in Patrick O'Sullivan (ed.), *The Meaning of the Famine* (London, 2000), p.43.

33. Eugenia Tognotti, 'Scientific Triumphalism and Learning from Facts: Bacteriology and the "Spanish Flu" Challenge of 1918', *Social History of Medicine*, 16, 1 (2003), p.110.

34. Wulf Kansteiner, 'Finding Meaning in Memory: A Methodological Critique of Collective Memory Studies', *History and Theory*, 41, 2 (2002), pp.188–9; Iwona Irwin-Zarecka, *Frames of Remembrance: The Dynamics of Collective Memory* (New Jersey, 1994), pp.57, 55.

35. BMH WS/1137, p.1; BMH WS/1650, p.1; BMH WS/955, p.1; BMH WS/1313, p.1.

36. Gedi and Elam, 'Collective Memory: What is it?', p.47; Macnamara, 'Memories of 1918', pp.308, 305.

37. Murphy, *When Youth Was Mine*, p.114; Hogan, *The Four Glorious Years*, p.47; BMH WS/336, p.9; Turtle Bunbury and David Fennell, *Vanishing Ireland* (Dublin, 2006), p.114; MacCárthaigh, *A Tipperary Parish*, p.276.

38. *Cork County Eagle and Munster Advertiser*, 16 November 1918 and 21 December 1918; Carmel Quinlan, 'A Punishment from God: The Famine in the Centenary Folklore Questionnaire', *Irish Review*, 19 (1996), p.84.

39. *Tipperary Star*, 23 November 1918.

40. Gearóid Ó Crualaoich, 'The "Merry Wake"', in James S. Donnelly, Jr. and Kerby S. Miller (eds), *Irish Popular Culture, 1650–1850* (Dublin, 1998), p.195; *Fifty-fifth Detailed Annual Report of the Registrar-General for Ireland*, p.xvia; *Fifty-sixth Detailed Annual Report of the Registrar-General for Ireland*, p.xvii; Phillips and Killingray, 'Introduction', p.24; Howard Schuman and Jacqueline Scott, 'Generations and Social Memories', *American Sociological Review*, 54, 3 (1989), pp.371, 377; Jeffrey K. Olick, 'Collective Memory: The Two Cultures', *Sociological Theory*, 17, 3 (1999), p.339.

41. Natalie Zemon Davis and Randolph Starn, 'Introduction', *Representations*, 26 (1989), p.4; David Fentress and Charles Wickham, *Social Memory* (Oxford, 1992), p.88; Morash, 'Making Memories', p.50.

42. Hutton, *History as an Art of Memory*, p.7; Fentress and Wickham, *Social Memory*, p.127.

43. *Mayo News*, 14 and 21 December 1918; *Limerick Chronicle*, 6 March 1919; *Cork Examiner*, 28 October 1918; *Irish Times*, 26 February 1919; Jay Winter, *Sites of Memory, Sites of Mourning: The Great War in European Cultural History* (Cambridge, 1995); Keith Jeffery, 'The Great War in Modern Irish Memory', in T.G. Fraser and Keith Jeffery (eds), *Men, Women and War: Irish Historical Studies XVIII* (Dublin, 1993), pp.136–57.

44. Macnamara, 'Memories of 1918', p.304; Middleton and Edwards, *Collective Remembering*, p.3.

45. CO 904/164, p.698; Quinlan, 'A Punishment from God', p.85; Ranger, 'A Historian's Foreword', p.xxi; Beiner, 'Out in the Cold and Back', p.504.

46. Macnamara, 'Memories of 1918', p.304; Taksa, 'The Masked Disease', pp.81, 85; Patrick Logan, *Making the Cure* (Dublin, 1972), p.27; *Kilkenny People*, 2 November 1918.

47. Christopher Morash, 'Famine/Holocaust: Fragmented Bodies', *Éire-Ireland*, 32, 1 (1997), p.137; Morash, 'Making Memories', pp.41–3.

48. Guy Beiner, *Remembering the Year of the French: Irish Folk History and Social Memory* (London, 2007), p.14; Olick, 'Collective Memory: The Two Cultures', p.345; Schuman and Scott, 'Generations and Social Memories', p.362.

49. Beverly Gage, '"Business as Usual": The 1920 Wall Street Explosion and the Politics of Forgetting' (http://www.newschool.edu/gf/historymatters/papers/BeverlyGage.pdf (Accessed 24 June 2008)); Winter and Sivan, 'Setting the Framework', p.16.

CHAPTER NINE: CONSEQUENCES

1. Howard Phillips and David Killingray, 'Introduction', in Howard Phillips and David Killingray (eds), *The Spanish Influenza Epidemic of 1918–19: New Perspectives* (London, 2003), pp.18, 20.
2. *Forty-seventh Annual Report of the Local Government Board for Ireland* [Cmd. 578], H.C. 1920, xxi, p.36; Sir William J. Thompson, 'Mortality from Influenza in Ireland', *Dublin Journal of Medical Science*, 4, Fourth Series (1920), p.186.
3. Ministry of Health, *Report on the Pandemic of Influenza, 1918–19* (London, 1920), p.238. In the Ministry's report, it was noted that 'nephritis was constant in the fatal cases', the 'common lesion being that which gives the swollen blood-oozing kidney' (pp.81, 83); *Fifty-sixth Detailed Annual Report of the Registrar-General for Ireland* [Cmd.997], H.C. 1920, xi, pp.xiv–xv.
4. Ministry of Health, *Report on the Pandemic*, pp.88–9; *Fifty-sixth Detailed Annual Report of the Registrar-General for Ireland*, pp.xiv–xv.
5. *Fifty-sixth Detailed Annual Report of the Registrar-General for Ireland*, p.xii; L.P. Curtis, Jr, 'Ireland in 1914', in W.E. Vaughan (ed.), *A New History of Ireland, Volume VI: Ireland under the Union, II 1870–1921* (Oxford, 1996), p.146.
6. Phillips and Killingray, 'Introduction', p.9; I.D. Mills, 'The 1918–1919 Influenza Pandemic: The Indian Experience', *The Indian Economic and Social History Review*, 23, 1 (1986), p.36.
7. CO 904/164, p.1053; The Kathleen Lynn Diaries, Volume I, p.46; Ruairí Ó hEithir, 'Folk Medical Beliefs and Practices in the Aran Islands, Co. Galway' (MA thesis, University College Dublin, 1983), p.106.
8. *Forty-first Report of the General Prisons Board, Ireland, 1918–1919* [Cmd. 687], H.C. 1920, xxiii, p.58; William Murphy, 'The Tower of Hunger: Political Imprisonment in Ireland, 1910–1921' (PhD thesis, University College Dublin, 2006).
9. Murphy, 'The Tower of Hunger', pp.258–80.
10. *Irish Catholic*, 23 November 1918; Davis Coakley, *Baggot Street: A Short History of the Royal City of Dublin Hospital* (Dublin, 1995), p.55.
11. *Freeman's Journal*, 9 November 1918; *Society of St Vincent de Paul Ireland. Report of the Council of Ireland for the Year 1918* (Dublin, 1919), p.11; *Connacht Tribune*, 7 June 1919.
12. Diarmaid Ferriter, *The Transformation of Ireland* (London, 2004), p.6; Anne Hardy, *Health and Medicine in Great Britain since 1860* (Hampshire, 2001), p.76.
13. *Cork Examiner*, 26 October 1918; *Irish Times*, 5 November 1918, 22 February 1919; *Wicklow People*, 9 November 1918; *Irish Rosary*, 22, 11 (November 1918), p.865; *Galway Observer*, 24 August 1918; *Irish Independent*, 2 November 1918; *Derry People and Donegal News*, 23 November 1918; *Irish Catholic*, 2 November 1918, p.1; *Freeman's Journal*, 30 October 1918.
14. Gary Owens, 'Social History', in Laurence M. Geary and Margaret Kelleher (eds), *Nineteenth-Century Ireland: A Guide to Recent Research* (Dublin, 2005), p.34; Deborah Lupton, *Medicine as Culture: Illness, Disease and the Body in Western Societies* (London, 1994), p.44; Joanna Bourke, *Fear: A Cultural History* (London, 2005), p.3; Linda Bryder, '"Lessons" of the 1918 Influenza Epidemic in Auckland', *The New Zealand Journal of History*, 16, 2 (1982), pp.119, 98; *Wicklow People*, 19 October 1918, 9 November 1918, 14 December 1918, 20 July 1918; *Derry People and Donegal News*, 23 November 1918.
15. Mike Crang, 'Time: Space', in Paul Cloke and Ron Johnston (eds), *Spaces of Geographical Thought* (London, 2005), p.200; Doreen Massey, *For Space* (London, 2005), p.62; Stuart Elden, *Mapping the Present: Heidegger, Foucault, and the Project of a Spatial History* (London, 2001), p.3.
16. Deborah Lupton, *The Imperative of Health: Public Health and the Regulated Body* (London, 1997), pp.16, 19; Thomas Wrigley Grimshaw, *Report on the Smallpox Epidemic, 1871–73, as Observed in Cork Street Fever Hospital* (Dublin, 1873), pp.6–7.
17. Cathal Póirtéir, *Famine Echoes* (Dublin, 1995), pp.102–4; Cathal Póirtéir, *Glórtha ón Ghorta* (Dublin, 1996), p.128.
18. Niall Ó Cíosáin, 'Famine Memory and the Popular Representation of Scarcity', in Ian McBride (ed.), *History and Memory in Modern Ireland* (Cambridge, 2001), p.117; Póirtéir, *Famine Echoes*, pp.106, 113–4.
19. Elden, *Mapping the Present*, p.128; Póirtéir, *Glórtha ón Ghorta*, pp.125–6, 142; Roger J. McHugh, 'The Famine in Irish Oral Tradition', in R. Dudley Edwards and T. Desmond Williams (eds), *The Great Famine* (New York, 1957), p.418.
20. David Armstrong, *Political Anatomy of the Body: Medical Knowledge in Britain in the Twentieth Century* (Cambridge, 1983), p.11.

21. Andy Merrifield, 'Henri Lefebvre: A Socialist in Space', in Mike Crang and Nigel Thrift (eds), *Thinking Space* (London, 2000), p.174; Michael Dear, 'Postmodern Bloodlines', in Georges Benko and Ulf Strohmayer (eds), *Space and Social Theory* (Oxford: Blackwell, 1997), p.51; Arild Holt-Jensen, *Geography. History and Concepts* (London, 2006), p.83; *The People* (Wexford), 2 November 1918. The 'enactment' of space denotes the importance of 'physical gestures and movements' in its production (Merrifield, 'Henri Lefebvre', p.177). See also Massey, *For Space*, p.61: Massey asserts that 'if time unfolds as change, then space unfolds as interaction'.

22. John Agnew, 'Space: Place', in Paul Cloke and Ron Johnston (eds), *Spaces of Geographical Thought* (London, 2005), p.81.

23. Thompson, 'Mortality from Influenza in Ireland', p.174.

24. S.J. Connolly, 'The "Blessed Turf": Cholera and Popular Panic in Ireland, June 1832', *Irish Historical Studies*, 23, 91 (1983); Joseph Robins, *The Miasma: Epidemic and Panic in Nineteenth-Century Ireland* (Dublin, 1995), pp.92–3; Robins, *The Miasma*, p.76; Theodore Zeldin, 'Personal History and the History of the Emotions', *Journal of Social History*, 15, 3 (1982), p.345; *Tuam Herald*, 29 June 1918.

25. Terence Ranger, 'A Historian's Foreword', in Phillips and Killingray (eds), *The Spanish Influenza Pandemic of 1918–19*, p.xxi; Phillips and Killingray, 'Introduction', p.11; *Connacht Tribune*, 23 November 1918; at Ferns Petty Sessions for instance, four children whose parents died during the 'influenza plague', and at Enniscorthy Petty Sessions, eight children whose father, a labourer, died from the same cause, were ordered to be sent to industrial schools (*Irish Times*, 8 January 1919); *Fifty-seventh Report of the Inspector Appointed to Visit the Reformatory and Industrial Schools of Ireland* [Cmd. 571], H.C. 1920, xxv, pp.14–15; *Freeman's Journal*, 4 November 1918.

CONCLUSION: A 'TALE OF DISASTER'?

1. GPB 1918/ 7063; *Cork Examiner*, 15 November 1918.

2. *Sixty-second Annual Report of the Board of Superintendence of the Dublin Hospitals with Appendices. For the year 1919–1920* [Cmd. 1260], H.C. 1921, xiii, p.862; for instance, there is no mention of it in the Baggot St Hospital Minute book, 1910–1928 (BR/2006/98), with scant reference to the epidemic in the Galway Hospital collection covering this period (Galway Hospital Archives Collection (GH1/10, GH1/11)).

3. *Irish Times*, 22 October 1918; *Mayo News*, 9 November 1918 – for example in Claremorris Union, one doctor attended to 800 cases; Margaret Pearl Treacy, '"Invisible"' Nursing', in Gerard M. Fealey (ed.), *Care to Remember: Nursing and Midwifery in Ireland* (Cork, 2005), p.42.

4. Allen H. Barton, *Communities in Disaster: A Sociological Analysis of Collective Stress Situations* (London, 1969), p.54; N.P.A.S. Johnson and Juergen Mueller, 'Updating the Accounts: Global Mortality of the 1918–1920 "Spanish" Influenza Pandemic', *Bulletin of the History of Medicine*, 76, 1 (2002), p.113; it was noted at the time that 'things have not been nearly so bad with us here in Ireland' as abroad (*Meath Chronicle*, 2 November 1918); Geoffrey W. Rice and Edwina Palmer, 'Pandemic Influenza in Japan 1918–19: Mortality Patterns and Official Responses', *Journal of Japanese Studies*, 29, 2 (1993), p.400; Joseph Robins, *The Miasma: Epidemic and Panic in Nineteenth-Century Ireland* (Dublin, 1995), pp.53–5.

5. John McGahern, *Memoir* (London, 2005), p.32; Diarmaid Ferriter, *The Transformation of Ireland* (London, 2004), pp.12–13.

6. Barton, *Communities in Disaster*, p.20.

7. Niall Johnson, 'Scottish Flu: The Scottish Experience of 'Spanish Flu', *Scottish Historical Review*, 83, 2 (2004); K. David Patterson and Gerald F. Pyle, 'The Geography and Mortality of the 1918 Influenza Pandemic', *Bulletin of the History of Medicine*, 44, 1 (1991), p.20; Sandra Tomkins, 'The Influenza Epidemic of 1918–19 in Western Samoa', *Journal of Pacific History*, 27, 2 (1992), p.181.

8. *Derry People and Donegal News*, 9 November 1918; *Irish Times*, 5 March 1919; Ministry of Health, *Report on the Pandemic of Influenza, 1918–19* (London, 1920), pp.275, 220, 237, 339.

9. Christopher Murray, Alan D. Lopez, Brian Chin, Dennis Feehan, Kenneth H. Hill, 'Estimation of Potential Global Pandemic Influenza Mortality on the Basis of Vital Registry Data from the 1918–20 Pandemic: A Quantitative Analysis', *The Lancet*, 368, 9554 (23 December 2006), pp.2211–18.

10. Ministry of Health, *Report on the Pandemic,* pp.259, 267, 275, 338, 208.
11. See for instance Matthew Heaton and Toyin Falola, 'Global Explanations versus Local Inter-pretations: The Historiography of the Influenza Pandemic of 1918–19 in Africa', *History in Africa,* 33 (2006).
12. Patterson and Pyle, 'The Geography and Mortality of the 1918 Influenza Pandemic', p.10; Robert Brown, 'The Great War and the Great Flu Pandemic of 1918', *Wellcome History,* Issue 24 (October 2003), p.6.
13. Esyllt W. Jones, '"Co-operation in all Human Endeavour": Quarantine and Immigrant Disease Vectors in the 1918–1919 Influenza Pandemic in Winnipeg', *Canadian Bulletin of Medical History,* 22, 1 (2005); Catherine Rollet, 'The "Other War" II: Setbacks in Public Health', in Jay Winter and Jean-Louis Robert (eds), *Capital Cities at War* (Cambridge, 1997); Ministry of Health, *Report on the Pandemic,* pp.275, 214, 254.
14. Ministry of Health, *Report on the Pandemic,* pp.237, 242, 208, 259, 337; Alfred Crosby, *America's Forgotten Pandemic* (Cambridge, 2003), p.46; Diane Puklin, 'Paris', in Fred van Hartesveldt (ed.), *The 1918–19 Pandemic of Influenza: The Urban Impact in the Western World* (New York, 1992), pp.80–1; Ministry of Health, *Report on the Pandemic,* p.xxii.
15. N.P.A.S. Johnson, 'The Overshadowed Killer: Influenza in Britain in 1918–19', in Phillips and Killingray (eds), *The Spanish Influenza Pandemic of 1918–19,* p.154; Wilfried Witte, 'The Plague that was Not Allowed to Happen. German Medicine and theInfluenza Epidemic of 1918–19 in Baden', in Phillips and Killingray (eds), *The Spanish Influenza Pandemic of 1918–19,* pp.52, 56; Beatriz Echeverri, 'Spanish Influenza Seen from Spain', in Phillips and Killingray (eds), *The Spanish Influenza Pandemic of 1918–19,* p.179; *The Lancet,* 23 November 1918, p.699; *The Medical Press and Circular,* 8 January 1919, pp.24–5; Moore, 'Influenza from a Clinical Standpoint', *The Practitioner,* 102, 1 (1919), p.33.
16. Eugenia Tognotti, 'Scientific Triumphalism and Learning from Facts: Bacteriology and the "Spanish Flu" Challenge of 1918', *Social History of Medicine,* 16, 1 (2003), p.110; Guy Beiner, 'Out in the Cold and Back: New-Found Interest in the Great Flu', *Cultural and Social History,* 3, 4 (2006), p.503; Witte, 'The Plague that was Not Allowed to Happen', p.57; *Connacht Tribune,* 22 March 1919, p.7; Inishowen Rural District Council Minutes, 11 March 1918–11 May 1920, p.165; T. Hennessy, 'Ireland and a Ministry of Health', *Transactions of the Royal Academy of Medicine in Ireland,* 37 (1919), p.463.
17. Tognotti, 'Scientific Triumphalism', p.99; Niall Johnson, *Britain and the 1918–19 Influenza Pandemic: A Dark Epilogue* (London, 2006), pp.157–160. For references to the 'popular epithet' of 'Spanish Influenza', see the following: Rice and Palmer, 'Pandemic Influenza in Japan, 1918–19', p.390; Mills, 'The Influenza Pandemic of 1918–1919: The Indian Experience', p.390; Christopher Langford, 'The Age Pattern of Mortality in the 1918–19 Influenza Pandemic: An Attempted Explanation Based on Data for England and Wales', *Medical History,* 46, 1 (2002), p.5; Patterson and Pyle, 'The Geography and Mortality of the 1918 Influenza Epidemic', p.7.
18. Richard Collier, *The Plague of the Spanish Lady* (London, 1974), pp.82–3; Emmanuel Le Roy Ladurie, *The Mind and Method of the Historian,* translated by Siân and Ben Reynolds (Brighton, 1981), p.29; Johnson, *Britain and the 1918–19 Influenza Pandemic,* p.160.
19. Drew Gilpin Faust, *This Republic of Suffering: Death and the American Civil War* (New York, 2008), pp.259–60.
20. Rice and Palmer, 'Pandemic Influenza in Japan', p.419; J.S. Oxford, R. Lambkin, A. Sefton, R. Daniels, A. Elliot, R. Brown, and D. Gill, 'A Hypothesis: The Conjunction of Soldiers, Gas, Pigs, Ducks, Geese and Horses in Northern France during the Great War Provided the Conditions for the Emergence of the "Spanish" Influenza Pandemic of 1918–1919', *Vaccine,* 23, 7 (2005), p.940; Gina Kolata, *Flu: The Story of the Great Influenza Pandemic of 1918 and the Search for the Virus that Caused it* (London, 1999), p.8; Pete Davis, *Catching Cold: 1918's Forgotten Tragedy and the Scientific Hunt for the Virus that Caused it* (London, 1999).
21. Kathleen Lynn letter, p.1 (Folder 6, Kathleen Lynn Papers, 106/59, Allen Library).

Select Bibliography

PRIMARY SOURCES

Newspapers and Periodicals
Belfast Telegraph
British Medical Journal
Catholic Bulletin
Church of Ireland Gazette
Connacht Tribune
Cork County Eagle and Munster Advertiser
Cork Examiner
Derry Journal
Derry People and Donegal News
Donegal Vindicator
Down Recorder
Farmer's Gazette
Fermanagh Times
Freeman's Journal
Galway Observer
Irish Builder
Irish Catholic
Irish Citizen
Irish Opinion: The Voice of Labour
Ireland's Own
Irish Rosary
Irish Times
The Kerryman
King's County Chronicle (Offaly)
Labour Leader
The Lancet
Leitrim Observer
Limerick Chronicle
Mayo News
Meath Chronicle
Medical Press and Circular

The People (Wexford)
The Practitioner
Roscommon Herald
Sligo Champion
Tuam Herald
Tipperary Star
Ulster Guardian
Westmeath Examiner and Longford and Meath Reporter
Western News
Wicklow People

CONTEMPORARY PRINTED MATERIAL

Cameron, Sir Charles, 'The Smallpox Epidemic in Dublin, 1903', *Dublin Journal of Medical Science*, 116, 381, Third Series (1903); continued in vol. 116, no. 382 (1903).

Cameron, Sir C.A., *Report upon the State of Public Health in the City of Dublin for the Year 1917* (Dublin, 1918).

Cameron, Sir C.A., *Report upon the State of Public Health in the City of Dublin for the Year 1918* (Dublin, 1919).

Cameron, Sir C.A., *Report upon the State of Public Health in the City of Dublin for the Year 1919* (Dublin, 1920).

Crofton, William M., 'The Influenza Epidemic', *Studies*, 7, 28 (1919).

Figgis, Darrell, *A Second Chronicle of Jails* (Dublin, 1919).

Grimshaw, Thomas Wrigley, *Report on the Smallpox Epidemic, 1871–73, As Observed in Cork Street Fever Hospital* (Dublin, 1873) (P 870 (9), National Library of Ireland).

Hedderman, B.N., *Glimpses of My Life in Aran: Some Experiences of a District Nurse in these Remote Islands, off the West Coast of Ireland* (Bristol, 1917).

Hennessy, T., 'Ireland and a Ministry of Health', *Transactions of the Royal Academy of Medicine in Ireland*, 37 (1919).

Kirkpatrick, T.P.C., *Pulmonary Phthisis* (Dublin, 1898).

Lynn, Kathleen, 'Report on Influenza Epidemic', in *Árd-Fheis (Extraordinary) Sinn Féin, 8th April, 1919, Reports* (ILB 300 P5, National Library of Ireland).

Ministry of Health, *Report on the Pandemic of Influenza, 1918–19* (London, 1920).

Peacocke, George, 'Influenza', *Transactions of the Royal Academy of Medicine in Ireland*, 37 (1919).

'Report upon the Recent Epidemic Fever in Ireland', *Dublin Quarterly Journal of Medical Science*, 7 and 8 (1849).

Robinson, Sir Henry, *Memories: Wise and Otherwise* (London, 1923).

Speares, John, 'Influenza', *Transactions of the Royal Academy of Medicine in Ireland*, 37 (1919).

Thompson, Sir William J., 'Mortality from Influenza in Ireland', *Journal of the Statistical and Social Inquiry Society of Ireland*, 14 (1920), and *Dublin Journal of Medical Science*, 4, Fourth Series (1920).

Tobin, R.F., 'Present State of the Irish Poor Law Medical Service', *Dublin Journal of Medical Science*, 116, 384 (1903).

British Parliamentary Papers

Abstract Return of Reps. to Coms. of Poor Laws in Ireland, Relative to Appearance and Spread of Cholera, and Correspondence [Cmd.109], H.C. 1854, lvii.

Annual Report of the Commissioners of Education in Ireland. For the Year 1919 [Cmd. 884], H.C. 1920, xv.

Appendix of the Department Committee Appointed by the Local Government Board for Ireland to Inquire into the Housing Conditions of the Working Classes in the City of Dublin [Cmd. 7317], H.C. 1914, xix.

Belfast Prison Inquiry. Report by the Right Honourable Mr Justice Dodd of the Proceedings at the Inquiry Directed by the Special Commission (Belfast Prison) Act, 1918 [Cmd. 83], H.C. 1919, xxvii.

Copies of the Correspondence between the Local Government Board and its Inspector with Regard to the Present Epidemic of Smallpox at Athenry; And of Correspondence between the Local Government Board and any Poor Law Unions with Regard to the Same Outbreak of Smallpox [Cmd. 422], H.C. 1875, lx.

Counties of Donegal and Sligo (Report from Local Government Board's Inspectors) [Cmd. 141], H.C. 1883–4, lix.

Eighteenth Annual Report of the Local Government Board for Ireland (1890) [Cmd. 6094], H.C. 1890, xxxiv.

Eighty-fifth Report of the Commissioners of National Education in Ireland, School Year, 1918–19 [Cmd. 1048], H.C. 1920, xv.

Fifty-fifth Detailed Annual Report of the Registrar-General for Ireland [Cmd. 450], H.C. 1919, x.

Fifty-fourth Detailed Annual Report of the Registrar-General for Ireland [Cd. 9123], H.C. 1918, vi.

Fifty-seventh Annual Report of the Registrar-General for Ireland [Cmd. 1532], H.C. 1921, viii–ix.

Fifty-seventh Report of the Inspector Appointed to Visit the Reformatory and Industrial Schools of Ireland [Cmd. 571], H.C. 1920, xxv.

Fifty-sixth Detailed Annual Report of the Registrar-General for Ireland Containing a General Abstract of the Numbers of Marriages, Births, and Deaths Registered in Ireland during the Year 1919 [Cmd. 997], H.C. 1920, xi.

Forty-first Report of the General Prisons Board, Ireland, 1918–19, with an Appendix [Cmd. 687], H.C. 1920, xxiii.

Forty-seventh Annual Report of the Local Government Board for Ireland [Cmd. 578], H.C. 1920, xxi.

Report of the Commissioners of Health, Ireland, on the Epidemics of 1846 to 1850 [Cmd. 1562], H.C. 1852–3, xli.

Report on Influenza Epidemic of 1889–90 by Dr Parsons; with Introduction by Medical Officer of Local Government Board [Cmd. 6387], H.C. 1890–91, xxxiv.

Sixtieth Annual Report of the Board of Superintendence of the Dublin Hospitals, with Appendices for the Year 1917–18 [Cmd. 31], H.C. 1919, xiii (part 1).

Sixty-eighth Annual Report of the Inspectors of Lunatics Ireland, Being for the Year ending 31st December, 1918 [Cmd. 579], H.C. 1920, xxi.

Sixty-first Annual Report of the Board of Superintendence of the Dublin Hospitals, with Appendices for the Year 1918–19 [Cmd. 480], H.C. 1919, xiii (part 1).

Sixty-second Annual Report of the Board of Superintendence of the Dublin Hospitals, with Appendices for the Year 1919–1920 [Cmd. 1260], H.C. 1920, xiii.

Sixty-seventh Annual report of the Inspectors of Lunatics (Ireland) [Cmd. 32], H.C. 1919, xxv.

Third Report of Her Majesty's Commissioners for Inquiring into the Housing Conditions of the Working Classes – Ireland [Cmd. 4547], H.C. 1884–5, xxxi.

Twenty-Ninth Annual Report of the Registrar-General (Ireland) [C. 7255], H.C. 1893–4, xxi.

National Library of Ireland

Henry Dixon Papers (Ms 35,262/1).

Irish Labour Party and Trade Union Congress. Annual Reports (1918, 1919) (Ir 33188 i 2).

Irish Transport and General Workers' Union Annual Reports (1918, 1919, 1920) (I 3318 i 4).

Minute Book of the Dublin Trades' Council (Ms 12,780 A).

Piaras Béaslaí Papers (Ms 33,972).

Pierce McCann Papers (Ms 26,772).

Richmond District Asylum, Dublin, *Annual Report of the Medical Superintendent to the Joint Committee of Management for the Years 1918 and 1919* (Dublin, 1921).

Society of St Vincent de Paul, Ireland. Report of the Council of Ireland for the Year 1918 (Dublin, 1919) (Ir 361 S4).

Society of St Vincent de Paul, Ireland. Report of the Council of Ireland for the Year 1919 (Dublin, 1920) (Ir 361 S4).

National Archives of Ireland, Bishop Street

Balrothery Union Minute Books. Microfilm: MFGS 49 BG 40 A 143; MFGS BG 40 A 144.

Bureau of Military History, Witness Statements.
General Prisons Board Files 1918–1919.
Miontuairiscí na Dála, DE/4/1/1; DE/4/13/10; DE/2/471; DE/2/508; DE/2/519.
Rathdown Union Minute Books (BG 137 A 152).
Ninetieth Annual Report of the Protestant Orphan Society for the Period Ending 31st January, 1919 (1045/1/90).
Ninety-First Annual Report of the Protestant Orphan Society for the Period Ending 31st January, 1920 (1045/1/1/91).
Ninety-Second Annual Report of the Protestant Orphan Society for the Period Ending 31st January, 1921, 1045/1/1/92.
Registered Papers of the Chief Secretary's Office for 1918 and 1919 (CSO RP/1918, CSO RP/1919).
South Dublin Poor Law Union Minute Books (BG 79/A80–A82).

Allen Library, Edmund Rice House, North Richmond Street, Dublin
Folder 6, Dr Lynn's papers (106/59).

University College, Dublin
Directorate of Military Intelligence, Postal Censorship, CO 904/164.
RIC Reports CO 904/107, CO 904/108.
Parliamentary Debates: House of Commons, Volumes 110, 112, 113, 115, 117, 121 (London, 1919).

Royal College of Physicians of Ireland, Kildare Street
St Ultan's Hospital: 'First Minute Book' (A (iv) Strong Box).
The Kathleen Lynn Diaries, Volume I.

Cork City and County Archives:
Castletown Board of Guardians Minute Book 11 July 1918–13 November 1919 (BG 59 A 87).
Cork Poor Law Union Board of Guardians Minute Book 4 April 1918–26 September 1918 (BG 69 A 149), and 3 October 1918–3 April 1919 (BG 69 A 150).
Dunmanway Poor Law Union Board of Guardians Minute Book 1918–1919 (BG 83 A 107).

Donegal County Council Archives
Ballyshannon Union Board of Guardians Minutes (BG/38/1/84).
Inishowen Board of Guardians Minute Books 11 February 1918–6 January 1918 (BG/97/1/58); 13 January 1919–10 November 1919 (BG/97/1/59).
Letterkenny Poor Law Union Board of Guardians Minutes 1 June 1918–3 January 1919 (BG/109/1/74); 10 January 1919–25 July 1919 (BG/109/1/75).

Milford Union Board of Guardians Minutes 21 December 1918–18 October 1919 (BG 119/1/86).

Galway County Council Archives

Clifden Poor Law Minutes (16 July 1917–11 September 1918, and 18 September 1918–26 November 1919).
Galway Poor Law Union Minutes 1918 No. 1, and 1919 No. 1.
Galway Rural District Council Collection, 1904–1925 (GOI/9/3).
Minutes of Board of Guardians Meetings Gort (GOI/12/100).
Minutes of Gort Rural District Council Meetings (GO1/10/15).
Galway Hospital Archives Collection (GH1/10, GH1/11).

Wicklow County Archives

Minute Books of Rathdrum Board of Guardians (PLUR/WR/136; PLUR/WR/137).
Minute Book of Rathdrum Rural District Council (WLAA/RDCR/ M/18).
Minute Books of Shillelagh Board of Guardians (PLUS/WR/76).
Minute Book of Shillelagh Rural District Council (WLAA/RDCS/ M/18).

BOOKS, ARTICLES AND OTHER PUBLISHED MATERIAL

Afkami, Amir, 'The 1918 Influenza Pandemic in Iran', *Bulletin of the History of Medicine*, 76, 22 (2003).
Agnew, John, 'Space: Place', in Paul Cloke and Ron Johnston (eds), *Spaces of Geographical Thought* (London, 2005).
Allen, David E. and Gabrielle Hatfield, *Medicinal Plants in Folk Tradition: An Ethnobotany of Britain and Ireland* (Cambridge, 2004).
Arensburg, Conrad H. *The Irish Countryman* (Gloucester, MA, 1959).
Armstrong, David, *Political Anatomy of the Body: Medical Knowledge in Britain in the Twentieth Century* (Cambridge, 1983).
Arnold, David, 'Introduction', in David Arnold (ed.), *Imperial Medicine and Indigenous Societies* (Manchester, 1988).
Barrington, Ruth, *Health, Medicine and Politics in Ireland 1900–1970* (Dublin, 1987).
Barry, John M. *The Great Influenza* (New York, 2005).
Barton, Allen H. *Communities in Disaster: A Sociological Analysis of Collective Stress Situations* (London, 1969).
Béaslaí, Piaras, 'Twenty Got Away in the Big Daylight Escape from Mountjoy Jail', in Florence O'Donoghue (ed.), *Sworn to be Free: The Complete Book of IRA Jailbreaks, 1918–1921* (Tralee, 1971).
Behan, Brian, *Mother of all the Behans: The Story of Kathleen Behan as Told to Brian Behan* (Essex, 1984).
Beiner, Guy, 'Out in the Cold and Back: New-Found Interest in the Great Flu', *Cultural and Social History*, 3, 4 (2006).

Beveridge, W.I.B. *Influenza* (London, 1977).

Bootsma, Martin and Neil Ferguson, 'The Effect of Public Health Measures on the 1918 Influenza Pandemic in US Cities', *Proceedings of the National Academy of Sciences of the United States of America*, 104, 18 (2007).

Bourdieu, Pierre, *In Other Words: Essays towards a Reflexive Sociology* (Oxford, 1990).

Bourdieu, Pierre, 'Cultural Power', in Lyn Spillman (ed.), *Cultural Sociology* (Oxford, 2002).

Bourke, Joanna, *Dismembering the Male: Men's Bodies, Britain and the Great War* (London, 1996).

Bourke, Joanna, *Fear: A Cultural History* (London, 2005).

Boyce, D. George, '"No Lack of Ghosts": Memory, Commemoration, and the State in Ireland', in Ian McBride (ed.), *History and Memory in Modern Ireland* (Cambridge, 2001).

Brady, Tim, 'The Great Flu Epidemic' (http://www.alumni.umn.edu/printview/581094c9-0994-4369-befa-6f849eadfccb.html (Accessed 9 September 2008)).

Brandt, Allen M. and Martha Gardner, 'The Golden Age of Medicine?', in Roger Cooter and John Pickstone (eds), *Medicine in the Twentieth Century* (Amsterdam, 2000).

Breathnach, Ciara, *The Congested Districts Board of Ireland, 1891–1923* (Dublin, 2005).

Brennan, Michael, *The War in Clare, 1911–1921: Personal Memoirs of the War of Independence* (Dublin, 1980).

Bric, Deaglan, 'Pierce McCan, MP (1882–1919), Part II', *Tipperary Historical Journal* (1989).

Bristow, Nancy K., '"You Can't Do Anything for Influenza". Doctors, Nurses and the Power of Gender during the Influenza Pandemic in the United States', in Howard Phillips and David Killingray (eds), *The Spanish Influenza Pandemic of 1918–19: New Perspectives* (London, 2003).

Brown, Colin, 'The Influenza Pandemic of 1918 in Indonesia', in Norman G. Owen (ed.), *Death and Disease in Southeast Asia: Explorations in Social, Medical and Demographic History* (Oxford, 1987).

Brown, Robert J. 'The Great War and the Great Flu Pandemic of 1918', *Wellcome History*, 24 (October 2003).

Brown, Robert J. 'Revising Spanish Flu', *Wellcome Science*, 1 (October 2005).

Brunton, Deborah, 'Introduction', in Deborah Brunton (ed.), *Medicine Transformed: Health, Disease and Society in Europe, 1800–1930* (London, 2004).

Bryder, Linda, '"Lessons" of the 1918 Influenza Epidemic in Auckland', *The New Zealand Journal of History*, 16, 2 (1982).

Bunbury, Turtle and James Fennell, *Vanishing Ireland* (Dublin, 2006).

Burke, Peter, 'History as Social Memory', in Thomas Butler (ed.), *Memory: History, Culture and the Mind* (Oxford, 1989).

Callan, Patrick, 'Recruiting for the British Army in Ireland during the First World War', *The Irish Sword*, 17 (1987).

Chandavarkar, Rajnarayan, 'Plague Panic and Epidemic Politics in India, 1896–1914', in Terence Ranger and Paul Slack (eds), *Epidemics and Ideas: Essays on the Historical Perception of Pestilence* (Cambridge, 1992).

Chowell, Gerardo, L.M.A. Bettencourt, N. Johnson, W.J. Alonso, and C. Viboud, 'The 1918–1919 influenza Pandemic in England and Wales: Spatial Patterns in Transmissibility and Mortality Impact', *Proceedings of the Royal Society B*, 275 (2008).

Clarkson, L.A. and E. Margaret Crawford, *Feast and Famine: Food and Nutrition in Ireland 1500–1920* (Oxford, 2001).

Clear, Caitriona, *Social Change and Everyday Life in Ireland* (Manchester, 2007).

Cliff, A.D., P. Haggett, and J.K. Ord, *Spatial Aspects of Influenza Epidemics* (London, 1986).

Cliff, A.D., P. Haggett, J.K. Ord and G.R. Versey, *Spatial Diffusion: An Historical Geography of Epidemics in an Island Community* (Cambridge, 1981).

Cliff, Andrew D., Matthew Smallman-Raynor, and Niall Johnson, 'The Spatial Anatomy of an Epidemic: Influenza in London and the County Boroughs of England and Wales, 1918–1919', *Transactions of the Institute of British Geographers*, 27, 4 (2002).

Coakley, Davis, *Baggot Street: A Short History of the Royal City of Dublin Hospital* (Dublin, 1995).

Cogan, Jeanine and Gregory Herek, 'Stigma' (http://www.thebody. com/content/art14039.html (14 June 2008)).

Cohen, Marilyn and Joan Vincent, 'Anthropological and Sociological Studies', in Laurence M. Geary and Margaret Kelleher (eds), *Nineteenth Century Ireland: A Guide to Recent Research* (Dublin, 2005).

Colihan, Kelley, 'Witness to 1918 Flu: "Death was there all the Time"' (http://edition.cnn.com/2005/HEALTH/conditions/10/07/1918.flu.witness/index.html (9 Sept. 2008)).

Collier, Richard, *The Plague of the Spanish Lady* (London, 1974).

Confino, Alan, 'Collective Memory and Cultural History: Problems of Method', in Robert M. Burns (ed.), *Historiography: Critical Concepts in Historical Studies. Volume IV: Culture* (New York, 2006).

Conlon, Lil, *Cumann na mBan and the Women of Ireland* (Kilkenny, 1969).

Connolly, S.J., 'The "Blessed Turf": Cholera and Popular Panic in Ireland, June 1832', *Irish Historical Studies*, 23, 91 (1983).

Coogan, Oliver, *Politics and War in Meath, 1913–1923* (Dublin, 1983).

Cooter, Roger, 'Of War and Epidemics: Unnatural Couplings, Problematic Conceptions', *Social History of Medicine*, 16, 2 (2003).

Cowell, John, *'A Noontide Blazing': Brigid Lyons Thornton – Rebel, Soldier, Doctor* (Dublin, 2005).

Crang, Mike, 'Time: Space', in Paul Cloke and Ron Johnston (eds), *Spaces of Geographical Thought* (London, 2005).

Crane, Susan A., 'Writing the Individual Back into Collective Memory', *American Historical Review*, 102, 5 (1997).

Crawford, E. Margaret, 'Typhus in Nineteenth-Century Ireland', in Elizabeth Malcolm and Greta Jones (eds), *Medicine, Disease and the State in Ireland, 1650–1940* (Cork, 1999).

Crosby, Alfred, *America's Forgotten Pandemic* (Cambridge, 2003).

Crossman, Virginia, *Local Government in Nineteenth Century Ireland* (Belfast, 1994).

Curtis, Jr, L.P. 'Ireland in 1914', in W.E. Vaughan (ed.), *A New History of Ireland, Vol. VI: Ireland under the Union, II 1870–1921* (Oxford, 1996).

Daly, Mary E. *The Buffer State: The Historical Roots of the Department of the Environment* (Dublin, 1997).

Danaher, Kevin, 'The Plague!', *Biatas*, 18, 9 (1964).

Danaher, Kevin, 'The Healing Art', *Biatas*, 20, 7 (1966).

Darnton, Robert, *The Kiss of Lamourette: Reflections in Cultural History* (London, 1990).

Davies, Pete, *Catching Cold: 1918's Forgotten Tragedy and the Scientific hunt for the Virus that Caused It* (London, 1999).

Dear, Michael, 'Postmodern Bloodlines', in Georges Benko and Ulf Strohmayer (eds), *Space and Social Theory* (Oxford: Blackwell, 1997).

Deasy, Liam, *Towards Ireland Free* (Cork, 1992).

Delaporte, François, *Disease and Civilisation* (London, 1986).

Devitt, Terry, 'Study uncovers a lethal secret of the 1918 influenza virus' (http://www.news.wisc.edu/13360.html (Accessed 27 April 2007)).

Dolan, Anne, *Commemorating the Irish Civil War: History and Memory, 1923–2000* (Cambridge, 2003).

Donnelly, Jr, James S. 'The Marian Shrine of Knock: The First Decade', *Éire-Ireland*, 28, 2 (1993).

Dowell, Scott F. and Joseph S. Bresee, 'Pandemic Lessons from Iceland', *Proceedings of the National Academy of Sciences*, 105, 4 (2008).

Earner-Byrne, Lindsey, '"In Respect of Motherhood": Maternity Policy and Provision in Dublin City, 1922 to 1956' (PhD thesis, University College, Dublin, 2001).

Echenberg, Myron, '"The dog that did not bark". Memory and the 1918 Influenza Epidemic in Senegal', in Howard Phillips and David Killingray (eds), *The Spanish Influenza Pandemic of 1918–19: New Perspectives* (London, 2003).

Echeverri, Beatriz, 'Spanish Influenza Seen from Spain', in Howard Phillips and David Killingray (eds), *The Spanish Influenza Pandemic of 1918–19: New Perspectives* (London, 2003).

Elden, Stuart, *Mapping the Present: Heidegger, Foucault and the Project of a Spatial History* (London, 2001).

Elias, Norbert and J.L. Scotson, 'Cohesion, Conflict and Community Character', in Colin Bell (ed.), *The Sociology of Community* (London, 1974).

Evans, Richard J. *Death in Hamburg: Society and Politics in the Cholera Years, 1830–1910* (Oxford, 1987).

Farrell Moran, Seán, 'History, Memory and Education: Teaching the Irish Story', in Lawrence W. McBride (ed.), *Reading Irish Histories* (Dublin, 2003).

Farry, Michael, *Sligo 1914–1921: A Chronicle of Conflict* (Trim, 1992).

Fentress, David and Charles Wickham, *Social Memory* (Oxford, 1992).

Ferriter, Diarmaid, 'Local Government, Public Health and Welfare in Twentieth-Century Ireland', in Mary E. Daly (ed.), *County and Town: One Hundred Years of Local Government in Ireland* (Dublin, 2001).

Ferriter, Diarmaid, *The Transformation of Ireland* (London, 2004).

Figgis, Darrell, *Recollections of the Irish War* (London, 1927).

Fissell, Mary E. *Patients, Power and the Poor in Eighteenth-Century Bristol* (Cambridge, 1991).

Fissell, Mary E. 'Making Meaning from the Margins: The New Cultural History of Medicine', in Frank Huisman and John Harley Warner (eds), *Locating Medical History* (London, 2004).

Fitzpatrick, David, 'Militarism in Ireland, 1900–1922', in Keith Jeffery and Thomas Bartlett (eds), *A Military History of Ireland* (Cambridge, 1996).

Foucault, Michel, *Madness and Civilisation* (London, 1993).

Froggatt, Peter, 'The Response of the Medical Profession to the Great Famine', in E. Margaret Crawford (ed.), *Famine: The Irish Experience* (Edinburgh, 1989).

Fussell, Paul, *The Great War and Modern Memory* (Oxford, 1975).

Gage, Beverly, '"Business as Usual": The 1920 Wall Street Explosion and the Politics of Forgetting' (http://www.newschool.edu/nssr/historymatters/papers/BeverlyGage.pdf (Accessed 24 June 2008)).

Gale Jr, Michael and Yueh-Ming Loo, 'Fatal Immunity and the 1918 Virus', *Nature*, 445, 7125 (2007).

Galvin, John, 'Spanish Flu Pandemic: 1918' (http://www.popularme chanics.com/science/worst_case_scenarios/4219884.html?page=1&series=31 (Accessed 9 September 2008)).

Gatenby, Peter, *Dublin's Meath Hospital* (Dublin, 1996).

Gaughan, J. Anthony, *Austin Stack: Portrait of a Separatist* (Naas, 1971).

Geary, Laurence M. '"The Late Disastrous Epidemic": Medical Relief and the Great Famine', in Chris Morash and Richard Hayes (eds), *'Fearful Realities': New Perspectives on the Famine* (Dublin, 1996).

Geary, Laurence M. 'Prince Hohenlohe, Signor Pastorini and Miraculous Healing in Early Nineteenth-Century Ireland', in Greta Jones and Elizabeth Malcolm (eds), *Medicine, Disease and the State in Ireland, 1650–1940* (Cork, 1999).

Gedi, Noa and Yigal Elam, 'Collective Memory: What is it?', *History and Memory*, 8, 1 (1996).

Geraghty, George and Frank Shouldice, 'The Break-Out from Usk Jail in Wales by Four "German Plot" Prisoners', in Florence O'Donoghue (ed.), *Sworn* to be Free: The Complete Book of IRA Jailbreaks 1918–1921 (Tralee, 1971).

Gottfredsson, Magnus, 'Lessons from the Past: Familial Aggregation Analysis of Fatal Pandemic Influenza (Spanish Flu) in Iceland in 1918', Proceedings of the National Academy of Sciences, 105, 4 (2008).

Griffith, Kenneth and Timothy E. O'Grady (eds), Curious Journey: An Oral History of Ireland's Unfinished Revolution (London, 1982).

Hardy, Anne, Health and Medicine in Great Britain since 1860 (Hampshire, 2001).

Hart, Peter, The IRA and its Enemies (Oxford, 1998).

Hassan, John, The Seaside, Health and the Environment in England and Wales since 1800 (Aldershot, 2003).

Healy, Margaret, 'Discourses of the plague in early modern London', (http://www.history.ac.uk/cmh/epiheal.html (Accessed 25 June 2008)).

Heaton, Matthew and Toyin Falola, 'Global Explanations Versus Local Interpretations: The Historiography of the Influenza Pandemic of 1918–19 in Africa', History in Africa, 33 (2006).

Henley, Cornelia, 'The Toxic Second Period of the 1918–1919 Influenza Panepidemic in Hungary', The Medical Journal of Australia, 1, 18 (1975).

Henry, Patrick J. Sligo: Medical Care in the Past 1800–1965 (Manorhamilton, 1995).

Herring, D. Ann, '"There Were Young People and Old People and Babies Dying Every Week": The 1918–1919 Influenza Pandemic at Norway House', Ethnohistory, 41, 1 (1994).

Herring, D. Ann and Lisa Sattenspiel, 'Death in Winter: Spanish Flu in the Canadian Subarctic', in Howard Phillips and David Killingray (eds), The Spanish Influenza Pandemic of 1918–19: New Perspectives (London, 2003).

Hildreth, Martha L., 'The Influenza Epidemic of 1918–1919 in France: Contemporary Concepts of Aetiology, Therapy, and Prevention', Social History of Medicine, 4, 2 (1991).

Hogan, David, The Four Glorious Years (London, 1971).

Holt-Jensen, Arild, Geography. History and Concepts (London, 2006).

Hopkinson, Michael, The War of Independence (Dublin, 2002).

Humphreys, Margaret, 'No Safe Place: Disease and Panic in American History', American Literary History, 14, 4 (2002).

Hutton, Patrick, History as an Art of Memory (Hanover, VT, 1993).

Hutton, Patrick, 'Recent Scholarship on Memory and History', The History Teacher, 33, 4 (2000).

Irwin-Zarecka, Iwona, Frames of Remembrance: The Dynamics of Collective Memory (New Jersey, 1994).

Jeffery, Keith, Ireland and the Great War (Cambridge, 2000).

Jeffery, Keith, 'The Great War in Modern Irish Memory', in T.G. Fraser and Keith Jeffery (eds), Men, Women and War: Irish Historical Studies XVIII (Dublin, 1993).

Johnson, Niall, *Britain and the 1918–19 Influenza Pandemic: A Dark Epilogue* (New York, 2006).

Johnson, Niall, 'Scottish Flu: The Scottish Experience of "Spanish Flu"', *Scottish Historical Review*, 83, 2 (2004).

Johnson, N.P.A.S. 'The Overshadowed Killer. Influenza in Britain in 1918–19', in Howard Phillips and David Killingray (eds), *The Spanish Influenza Pandemic of 1918–19: New Perspectives* (London, 2003).

Jones, Esyllt W. '"Co-Operation in All Human Endeavour": Quarantine and Immigrant Disease Vectors in the 1918–1919 Influenza Pandemic in Winnipeg', *Canadian Bulletin of Medical History*, 29, 1 (2005).

Jones, Greta, *'Captain of All these Men of Death': The History of Tuberculosis in Nineteenth and Twentieth Century Ireland* (New York, 2001).

Kansteiner, Wulf, 'Finding Meaning in Memory: A Methodological Critique of Collective Memory Studies', *History and Theory*, 41, 2 (2002).

Katz, Robert S. 'Influenza 1918–1919: A Further Study in Mortality', *Bulletin of the History of Medicine*, 51, 4 (1977).

Kavanagh, John, 'The Influenza Epidemic of 1918 in Wicklow Town and District', *Wicklow Historical Society Journal*, 1, 3 (1990).

Kelleher, James, *Memories of Macroom* (Blarney, 1995).

Kelly, Bill, 'Escape of de Valera, McGarry and Milroy ("German Plot" Prisoners) from Lincoln Jail', in Florence O'Donoghue (ed.), *Sworn to be Free: The Complete Book of IRA Jailbreaks 1918–1921* (Tralee, 1971).

Kern, Stephen, *The Culture of Time and Space, 1880–1918* (London, 2003).

Killingray, David, 'The Influenza Pandemic of 1918–1919 in the British Caribbean', *Social History of Medicine*, 7, 1 (1994).

Kipling, Rudyard, *The Irish Guards in the Great War: The First Battalion* (Kent, 1997).

Kipling, Rudyard, *The Irish Guards in the Great War: The Second Battalion* (Kent, 1997).

Kolata, Gina, *Flu: The Story of the Great Influenza Pandemic of 1918 and the Search for the Virus that Caused it* (London, 1999).

Langford, Christopher, 'The Age Pattern of Mortality in the 1918–19 Influenza Pandemic: An Attempted Explanation Based on Data for England and Wales', *Medical History*, 46, 1 (2002).

Le Goff, Jacques, 'Mentalities: A History of Ambiguities', in Jacques Le Goff and Pierre Nora (eds), *Constructing the Past: Essays in Historical Methodology* (London, 1985).

Le Roy Ladurie, Emmanuel, *The Mind and Method of the Historian*, transl. Siân and Ben Reynolds (Brighton, 1981).

Lichteim, George, *Europe in the Twentieth Century* (London, 1972).

Loeb, Lori, 'Beating the Flu: Orthodox and Commercial Responses to Influenza in Britain, 1889–1919', *Social History of Medicine*, 18, 2 (2005).

Lowenthal, David, 'The Timeless Past: Some Anglo-American Historical Preconceptions', *Journal of American History*, 75, 4 (1989).

Lucas, Colin, 'Introduction', in Jacques Le Goff and Pierre Nora (eds), *Constructing the Past: Essays in Historical Methodology* (Cambridge, 1985).

Lupton, Deborah, *Medicine as Culture: Illness, Disease and the Body in Western Societies* (London, 1994).

Lupton, Deborah, *The Imperative of Health: Public Health and the Regulated Body* (London, 1997).

Lynch, Fionan, 'Recollections of Jail Riots and Hungerstrikes – Grim Times in Mountjoy, Dundalk and Belfast Jails', in Florence O'Donoghue (ed.), *Sworn to be Free: The Complete Book of IRA Jailbreaks 1918–1921* (Tralee, 1971).

MacArthur, Sir William P., 'Medical History of the Famine', in R. Dudley Edwards and T. Desmond Williams (eds), *The Great Famine* (New York, 1957).

MacCárthaigh, Micheál, *A Tipperary Parish: A History of Knockavilla-Donaskeigh* (Midleton, 1986).

MacFhionnghaile, Niall, *Dr McGinley and His Times: Donegal 1900–1950* (Letterkenny, 1985).

Macnamara, D.W., 'Memories of 1918 and "the 'Flu"', *Journal of the Irish Medical Association*, 35, 208 (1954).

McCracken, Kevin and Peter Curson, 'Flu Downunder. A Demographic and Geographic Analysis of the 1919 Epidemic in Sydney, Australia', in Howard Phillips and David Killingray (eds), *The Spanish Influenza Pandemic of 1918–19: New Perspectives* (London, 2003).

McCreery, David, 'Guatemala City', in Fred R. van Hartesveldt (ed.), *The 1918–19 Pandemic of Influenza: The Urban Impact in the Western World* (New York, 1992).

McHugh, Roger J., 'The Famine in Irish Oral Tradition', in R. Dudley Edwards and T. Desmond Williams (eds), *The Great Famine* (New York, 1957).

McNeill, William, 'The Flu of Flus', *The New York Review of Books*, 47, 2 (2000).

McQueen, Humphrey, '"Spanish 'Flu" – 1919: Political, Medical and Social Aspects', *The Medical Journal of Australia*, 1, 18 (1975).

McQueen, Humphrey, 'The "Spanish" Influenza Pandemic in Australia, 1912–19', in Jill Roe (ed.), *Social Policy in Australia* (Melbourne, 1976).

Maher, Jim, *The Flying Column – West Kilkenny 1916–1921* (Dublin, 1987).

Maher, Jim, *Harry Boland* (Cork, 1998).

Mamelund, Svenn Erik, 'A Socially Neutral Disease? Individual Social Class, Household Wealth and Mortality from Spanish Influenza in Two Socially Contrasting Parishes in Kristiania in 1918–19', *Social Science and Medicine*, 62, 4 (2006).

Marnane, Denis G. *'A Lamp Kindled': The Sisters of Mercy and Tipperary Town* (Tipperary, 2000).

Massey, Doreen, *For Space* (London, 2005).

Meenan, Patrick N. 'Epidemic Influenza', *The Irish Journal of Medical Science*, 386, Sixth Series (1958).

Merrifield, Andy, 'Henri Lefebvre: A Socialist in Space', in Mike Crang and Nigel Thrift (eds), *Thinking Space* (London, 2000).

Middleton, David and Derek Edwards, *Collective Remembering* (London, 1990).

Mills, I.D. 'The 1918–1919 Influenza Pandemic: The Indian Experience', *The Indian Economic and Social History Review*, 23, 1 (1986).

Mitchell, David, *A 'Peculiar' Place: The Adelaide Hospital, Dublin, 1839–1989* (Dublin, 1989).

Morash, Chris, 'Famine/Holocaust: Fragmented Bodies', *Éire-Ireland*, 32, 1 (1997).

Morash, Chris, 'Making Memories: The Literature of the Irish Famine', in Patrick O'Sullivan (ed.), *The Meaning of the Famine* (London, 2000).

Moylan, Seán, *Seán Moylan in His Own Words: His Memoir of the Irish War of Independence* (Aubane Historical Society, 2004).

Mueller, Juergen and Niall P.A.S. Johnson, 'Updating the Accounts: Global Mortality of the 1918–1920 "Spanish" Influenza Pandemic', *Bulletin of the History of Medicine*, 76, 1 (2002).

Murray, Christopher, Alan Lopez, Brian Chin, Dennis Feehan and Kenneth H. Hill, 'Estimation of Potential Global Pandemic Influenza Mortality on the Basis of Vital Registry from the 1918–20 Pandemic: a Quantitative Analysis', *The Lancet*, 368, 9554 (2006).

Murphy, Daniel J. (ed.), *Lady Gregory's Journals. Volume One* (Buckingham, 1978).

Murphy, Donie, *'The Men of the South' in the War of Independence* (Cork, 1991).

Murphy, Jeremiah, *When Youth Was Mine: A Memoir of Kerry 1902–1925* (Dublin, 1998).

Murray, James P. *Galway: A Medico-Social History* (Galway, 1996).

Nerlich, Brigitte, and Patrick Wallis, 'Disease Metaphors in New Epidemics: The UK Media Framing of the 2003 SARS Epidemic', *Social Science and Medicine*, 60, 11 (2005).

Nuland, Sherwin B. 'Medical History for the General Reader', in Frank Huisman and John Harley Warner (eds), *Locating Medical History* (London, 2004).

Ó Cíosáin, Niall, 'Famine Memory and the Popular Representation of Scarcity', in Ian McBride (ed.), *History and Memory in Modern Ireland* (Cambridge, 2001).

Ó Crualaoich, Gearóid, 'The "Merry Wake"', in James S. Donnelly and Kerby A. Miller (eds), *Irish Popular Culture, 1650–1850* (Dublin, 1998).

O'Donoghue, Florence, *Tomás MacCurtain* (Tralee, 1958).

Ó hEithir, Ruairí, 'Folk Medical Beliefs and Practices in the Aran Islands, Co. Galway' (MA thesis, University College, Dublin, 1983).

Ohadike, Don C. 'Diffusion and Physiological Responses to the Influenza Pandemic of 1918–19 in Nigeria', *Social Science and Medicine*, 32, 12 (1991).

Olick, Jeffrey K. 'Collective Memory: The Two Cultures', *Sociological Theory*, 17, 3 (1999).

Olson, Donald R., Lone Simonsen, Paul J. Edelson and Stephen S. Morse, 'Epidemiological Evidence of an Early Wave of the 1918 Influenza Pandemic in New York City', *Proceedings of the National Academy of Sciences of the United States of America*, 102, 31 (2005).

O'Malley, Edward, *Memories of a Mayoman* (Dublin, 1981).

O'Muircheartaigh, Micheál, *From Dún Síon to Croke Park* (Dublin, 2005).

O'Suilleabhain, Michael, *Where Mountainy Men have Sown* (Tralee, 1965).

O'Suilleabhain, Sean, *A Handbook of Irish Folklore* (Wexford, 1942).

Ott, Katherine, *Fevered Lives: Tuberculosis in American Culture since 1870* (London, 1996).

Oxford, J. S., A. Sefton, R. Jackson, N.P.A.S. Johnson and R.S. Daniels, 'Who's that Lady?', *Nature Medicine*, 5, 12 (1999).

Oxford, J.S., 'Influenza A Pandemics of the 20th Century with Special Reference to 1918: Virology, Pathology and Epidemiology', *Reviews in Medical Virology*, 10, 2 (2000).

Oxford, J.S. 'The So-Called Great Spanish Influenza Pandemic May Have Originated in France in 1916', *Philosophical Transactions of the Royal Society of London B*, 356, 1416 (2001).

Oxford, John, 'A Virologist's Foreword', in Howard Phillips and David Killingray (eds), *The Spanish Influenza Pandemic of 1918–19: New Perspectives* (London, 2003).

Oxford, J.S., R. Lambkin, A. Sefton, R. Daniels, A. Elliot, R. Brown and D. Gill, 'A Hypothesis: The Conjunction of Soldiers, Gas, Pigs, Ducks, Geese and Horses in Northern France during the Great War Provided the Conditions for the Emergence of the "Spanish" Influenza Pandemic of 1918–1919', *Vaccine*, 23, 7 (2005).

Patterson, K. David, 'The Influenza Epidemic of 1918–19 in the Gold Coast', *Journal of African History*, 24, 4 (1983).

Patterson, K. David and Gerald F. Pyle, 'The Diffusion of Influenza in Sub-Saharan Africa during the 1918–1919 Pandemic', *Social Science and Medicine*, 17, 17 (1983).

Patterson, K. David and Gerald F. Pyle, 'The Geography and Mortality of the 1918 Influenza Epidemic', *Bulletin of the History of Medicine*, 65, 1 (1991).

Patterson, S.W. 'The Pathology of Influenza in France', http://www. vlib.us/ medical/mja/htm (Accessed 26 June 2010).

Pelling, Margaret, Virginia Berridge, Mark Harrison and Paul Weindling, 'The Era of Public Health, 1848 to1918', in Charles Webster (ed.), *Caring for Health: History and Diversity* (Buckingham, 2001).

Pernick, Martin S. 'Contagion and Culture', *American Literary History*, 14, 4 (2002).

Phillips, Howard, and David Killingray, 'Introduction', in Howard Phillips and David Killingray (eds), *The Spanish Influenza Pandemic of 1918: New Perspectives* (London, 2003).

Póirtéir, Cathal, *Famine Echoes* (Dublin, 1995).

Póirtéir, Cathal, *Glórtha ón Ghorta* (Dublin, 1996).

Porter, Dorothy, *Health, Civilisation and the State* (London, 1999).

Porter, Roy, 'The Patient's View: Doing Medical History from Below', *Theory and History*, 14, 2 (1989).

Porter, Roy, 'Disease and the Historian', in Peter Burke (ed.), *History and Historians in the Twentieth Century* (Oxford, 1992).

Prunty, Jacinta, *Dublin Slums: A Study in Urban Geography* (Dublin, 1998).

Putnam, Robert D. *Bowling Alone* (New York, 2000).

Puklin, Diane A.V. 'Paris', in Fred R. van Hartesveldt (ed.), *The 1918–19 Pandemic of Influenza: The Urban Impact in the Western World* (New York, 1992).

Pyle, Hilary, *Cesca's Diary* (Dublin, 2005).

Quinlan, Carmel, 'A Punishment from God: The Famine in the Centenary Folklore Questionnaire', *Irish Review*, 19, 1 (1996).

Rafter, Michael J. *The Quiet County: Towards a History of the Laois Brigade IRA and Revolutionary Activity in the County 1913–1923* (Portlaoise, 1995).

Ramanna, Mridula, 'Coping with the Influenza Pandemic. The Bombay Experience', in Howard Phillips and David Killingray (eds), *The Spanish Influenza Pandemic of 1918: New Perspectives* (London, 2003).

Ranger, Terence, 'The Influenza Pandemic in Southern Rhodesia: A Crisis of Comprehension', in David Arnold (ed.), *Imperial Medicine in Indigenous Societies* (Manchester, 1988).

Ranger, Terence, 'A Historian's Foreword', in Howard Phillips and David Killingray (eds), *The Spanish Influenza Pandemic of 1918: New Perspectives* (London, 2003).

Reid, Alice, 'The Effects of the 1918–1919 Influenza Pandemic on Infant and Child Health in Derbyshire', *Medical History*, 69, 1 (2005).

Reid, Ann H., Jeffrey Taubenberger and Thomas G. Fanning, 'The 1918 Spanish Influenza: Integrating History and Biology', *Microbes and Infection*, 3, 1 (2001).

Rice, Geoffrey W. 'Japan and New Zealand in the 1918 influenza Pandemic', in Howard Phillips and David Killingray (eds), *The Spanish Influenza Pandemic of 1918–19: New Perspectives* (London, 2003).

Rice, Geoffrey W. and Edwina Palmer, 'A Japanese Physician's Response to Pandemic Influenza: Ijirō Gomibuchi and the "Spanish Flu" in Yaita-Chō, 1918–1919', *Bulletin of the History of Medicine*, 66, 4 (1992).

Rice, Geoffrey W. and Edwina Palmer, 'Pandemic Influenza in Japan, 1918–19: Mortality Patterns and Official Responses', *Journal of Japanese Studies*, 19, 2 (1993).

Richard, S.A., N. Sugaya, L. Simonsen, M.A. Miller and C. Viboud, 'A Comparative Study of the 1918–1920 Influenza Pandemic in Japan, USA and UK', *Epidemiology and Infection*, 137, 8 (2009).

Roberts, Penny and William G. Naphy, 'Introduction', in Penny Roberts and William G. Naphy (eds), *Fear in Early Modern Society* (Manchester, 1997).

Robins, Joseph, *The Miasma: Epidemic and Panic in Nineteenth-Century Ireland* (Dublin, 1995).

Robinson, Sir Henry, *Memories: Wise and Otherwise* (London, 1923).

Rollet, Catherine, 'The "Other War" II: Setbacks in Public Health', in Jay Winter and Jean-Louis Robert (eds), *Capital Cities at War* (Cambridge, 1997).

Rosenberg, Charles E. *Explaining Epidemics and Other Studies in the History of Medicine* (Cambridge, 1992).

Ross, Bruce M. *Remembering the Past: Descriptions of Autobiographical Memory* (New York, 1991).

Rudin, Harry R. *Armistice 1918* (New Haven, 1967).

Schuman, Howard and Jacqueline Scott, 'Generations and Social Memories', *American Sociological Review,* 54, 3 (1989).

Schwartz, Barry, 'Memory as a Cultural System: Abraham Lincoln in World War II', *American Sociological Review*, 61, 5 (1996).

Sheehan, Aideen, 'Cumann na mBan: Policies and Activities', in David Fitzpatrick (ed.), *Revolution? Ireland 1917–1923* (Dublin, 1990).

Shils, Edward, *Center and Periphery: Essays in Macrosociology* (Chicago, IL, 1975).

Simpson, Richard L., 'The Sociology of the Community: Current Status and Prospects', in Howard Bell and Colin Newby (eds), *The Sociology of Community* (London, 1974).

Shuttleton, David, 'A Culture of Disfigurement: Imagining Smallpox in the Long Eighteenth Century', in George Sebastian Rousseau, Miranda Gill, David Haycock and Malte Herwig (eds), *Framing and Imagining Disease in Cultural History* (New York, 2003).

Sivan, Emmanuel, 'Private Pain and Public Remembrance in Israel', in Jay Winter and Emmanuel Sivan (eds), *War and Remembrance in the Twentieth Century* (New York, 1999).

Smelser, Neil J. *Theory of Collective Behavior* (London, 1962).

Smith, F.B. 'The Russian Influenza in the United Kingdom', *Social History of Medicine*, 8, 1 (1995).

Smithson, Annie M.P. *Myself and Others: An Autobiography* (Dublin, 1944).

Somerville-Large, Peter, *Cappaghglass* (London, 1985).

Somerville-Large, Peter, *Irish Voices: Fifty Years of Irish Life, 1916–1966* (London, 1999).

Stack, Austin, 'Journal of the Big Belfast Jail Riot', in Florence O'Donoghue (ed.), *Sworn to be Free: The Complete Book of IRA Jailbreaks 1918–1921* (Tralee, 1971).

Starn, Randolph and Natalie Zemon Davis, 'Introduction', *Representations*, 26 (1989).

Starr, Isaac, 'Influenza in 1918: Recollections of the Epidemic in Philadelphia', *Annals of Internal Medicine*, 85, 4 (1976).

Starr, Paul, *The Social Transformation of American Medicine* (New York, 1982).

Stearns, Peter N. and Carol Z. Stearns, 'Emotionology: Clarifying the History of Emotions and Emotional Standards', *The American Historical Review*, 90, 4 (1985).

Stout, Matthew, 'Historical Geography', in Laurence M. Geary and Margaret Kelleher (eds), *Nineteenth-Century Ireland: A Guide to Recent Research* (Dublin, 2005).

Synge, J.M. *The Aran Islands* (London, 1992).

Taksa, Lucy, 'The Masked Disease: Oral History, Memory and the Influenza Pandemic 1918–19', in Kate Darian-Smith and Paula Hamilton (eds), *Memory and History in Twentieth-Century Australia* (Oxford, 1994).

Taubenberger, Jeffrey K. and David M. Morens, 'The Pathology of Influenza Virus Infections', *Annual Review of Pathology Mechanisms of Disease*, 3, 1 (2008).

Thoits, Peggy A. 'The Sociology of Emotion', *Annual Review of Sociology*, 15 (1989).

Tognotti, Eugenia, 'Scientific Triumphalism and Learning from Facts: Bacteriology and the "Spanish Flu" Challenge of 1918', *Social History of Medicine*, 16, 1 (2003).

Tomes, Nancy, 'Epidemic Entertainments: Disease and Popular Culture in Early Twentieth-Century America', *American Literary History*, 14, 4 (2002).

Tomkins, Sandra, 'The Influenza Epidemic of 1918–19 in Western Samoa', *Journal of Pacific History*, 27, 2 (1992).

Tomkins, Sandra M. 'The Failure of Expertise: Public Health Policy in Britain during the 1918–19 Influenza Epidemic', *Social History of Medicine*, 5, 3 (1992).

Tomkins, Sandra M. 'Colonial Administration in British Africa during the Influenza Epidemic of 1918–19', *Canadian Journal of African Studies*, 28, 1 (1994).

Townshend, Charles, *Ireland: The 20th Century* (London, 1999).

Treacy, Margaret Pearl, '"Invisible" Nursing', in Gerard M. Fealey (ed.), *Care to Remember: Nursing and Midwifery in Ireland* (Cork, 2005).

Tumpey, Terence M. 'Characterization of the Reconstructed 1918 Spanish Influenza Pandemic Virus', *Science*, 310, 5745 (7 October 2005).

Turner, Ralph H. 'Collective Behavior', in Robert E.L. Faris (ed.), *Handbook of Modern Sociology* (Chicago, IL, 1964).

Von Bubnoff, Andreas, 'The 1918 Flu Virus is Resurrected', *Nature*, 437, 7060 (2005).

Walters, John H. 'Influenza 1918: The Contemporary Perspective', *Bulletin of the New York Academy of Medicine*, 54, 9 (1978).

Wear, Andrew, 'Puritan Perceptions of Illness in Seventeenth Century England', in Roy Porter (ed.), *Patients and Practitioners: Lay Perceptions of Medicine in Pre-Industrial Society* (Cambridge, 2002).

Weiss, Jane, '"This Pestilence Which Walketh in Darkness": Reconceptualizing the 1832 New York Cholera Epidemic', in George Sebastian Rousseau, Miranda Gill, David Haycock and Malte Herwig (eds), *Framing and Imagining Disease in Cultural History* (New York, 2003).

Wilde, William, *Irish Popular Superstitions* (Dublin, 1979).

Winter, Jay, *The Great War and the British People* (London, 1986).

Winter, Jay, *Sites of Memory, Sites of Mourning: The Great War in European Cultural History* (Cambridge, 1995).

Winter, Jay and Emmanuel Sivan, 'Setting the framework', in Jay Winter and Emmanuel Sivan (eds), *War and Remembrance in the Twentieth Century* (New York, 1999).

Witte, Wilfried, 'The Plague that was not Allowed to Happen. German Medicine and the Influenza Epidemic of 1918–19 in Baden', in Howard Phillips and David Killingray (eds), *The Spanish Influenza Pandemic of 1918–19: New Perspectives* (London, 2003).

Zeldin, Theodore, 'Personal History and the History of the Emotions', *Journal of Social History*, 15, 3 (1982).

Zeldin, Theodore, *An Intimate History of Humanity* (London, 1998).

Zylberman, Patrick, 'A Holocaust in a Holocaust. The Great War and the 1918 Influenza Epidemic in France', in Howard Phillips and David Killingray (eds), *The Spanish Influenza Pandemic of 1918–19: New Perspectives* (London, 2003).

Index

Abbey Theatre, 63, 153
academic studies of pandemic, 6
Achill Island, 52, 71
advertising and commercial opportunism, 129–31
Africa, 2, 14, 37, 68, 117, 126, 135, 138, 167
age factors
    in 1892 outbreak, 30fig, 32
    in typical flu outbreaks, 5, 32, 33
    young adults as chief victims, viii, 5, 6, 9, 29–32,
        33, 80, 95, 135, 149–50, 160–1, 166
agriculture and farming, 42, 53–4, 114–15
alcohol, viii, 54–5, 73, 92, 149, 168
anthrax, 85
Aran Islands, 19, 64, 90, 107, 119, 155
Ariés, Phillippe, 157
Arklow (Co. Wicklow), 93, 128–9
Armagh, County, 19
Arranmore, island of, 43, 90, 113
Ashe, Thomas, 57
Asia, 14, 138
Athlone, 2, 20
Athy (Co. Kildare), 24
Australia, 13, 52, 87
autopsy evidence, 4, 77, 94, 133

Babington, Seamus, 122, 125, 140
Ballinasloe (Co. Galway), 15, 17, 19, 25, 71, 75, 160
Ballyhaunis (Co. Mayo), 89, 134
Bardon, George, 145
Barrington, Ruth, 8, 118, 146
Barry, John, 2, 6
Barry, Tadhg, 56–7, 69
Barton, Allen, 115
Barton, Robert, 59–60
Béaslaí, Piaras, 70, 78
Beaumont, Máirín, 99
Behan, Kathleen, 140, 141
Beiner, Guy, 11, 64
Belfast, 15, 25, 27, 45, 53, 107–8, 132, 151, 167
Belfast Prison, 70–1, 78–9, 80, 83
    attitude of authorities to outbreak, 38, 55, 56,
    58–9,
        155
    illness of political prisoners, 7–8, 38, 55–6, 58–9,
    81,
        123, 127, 140, 141–2, 143, 147, 155
Berlin, 16, 34
birth rate, 154
blame, 12, 67, 75, 82, 121, 124–5, 126, 169
Blythe, Ernest, 123
bodies, dead
    fear of, 62–3, 69, 72–3, 79, 96, 126

    unburied war dead theory, 125–6
body, human
    body-spirit links, 128
    emotions/imagination and, 83–4
Boland, Harry, 58, 142
Bootsma, Martin, 116
borstal system, 38–9, 163
Bourdieu, Pierre, 48, 120
Bourke, Joanna, 25, 75
Boyce, D. George, 147
Brady, Jimmy, 137
Bray (Co. Wicklow), 50, 52, 78, 105, 108, 112–13
Brennan, Michael, 7–8
Brennan, Robert, 140
Bristow, Nancy, 87, 98, 99, 100
Britain, 6, 15, 16, 25, 26, 87, 138, 147–8, 156
    military camps, 6, 13
    mortality rates in, 3, 117, 148
    responses to pandemic, 86–7, 100, 103, 106,
    109,
        117–18, 148, 168
    see also political prisoners
Brown, Colin, 138
Brown, Robert, 5–6, 25
Brugha, Cathal, 34, 58
Brugha, Mrs Caitlín, 34–5
Brunton, Deborah, 135
Bryder, Linda, 157
Budapest, 52
Buncrana (Co. Donegal), 111
Bureau of Military History Archive, 34, 121, 138,
    148
Burgess, Bill, 33, 65, 149
businesses, viii, 47, 53, 69, 73–4, 156, 160, 165

Cahill, Patrick, 114
Cameron, Sir Charles, 51, 74, 78, 79, 133
Canada, 2, 9, 15, 25, 27–8, 52, 122, 124, 137, 166,
    167
Carlow, County, 24, 47, 66, 113
Carney, Winifred, 56
Castlebar (Co. Mayo), 52, 53, 65
Catholic Church, 52–3, 164–5
causality
    fear and, 83–4
    Great War and, 3, 6, 11, 13, 124–6, 135, 141–2,
        169
    medical science and, 85, 92–3, 101
    miasma theory, 125–6, 168
    popular attitudes/explanations, 11, 124–6
    religious interpretations, 126–8, 135, 136, 157,
        169